THE SOCIAL COGNITIVE NEUROSCIENCE OF LEADING ORGANIZATIONAL CHANGE

In a very understandable, practical and accessible manner, this book applies recent groundbreaking findings from behavioral neuroscience to the most complex and vexing challenges in organizations today. In particular, it addresses managing large-scale organizational changes, such as mergers and acquisitions, providing lessons and tactics that can be usefully applied in many different settings. In addition to discussing successful practices, it also identifies the reasons why most past comprehensive, long-term change projects have failed and unmasks the counterproductive effects of the typical evolutionary or emotion-based attempts to change group and individual behavior, using neuroscience as its principal tool.

Robert A. Snyder holds a Ph.D. in Organizational Psychology from the University of Maryland and is Professor of Management in the Haile/U.S. Bank College of Business at Northern Kentucky University. Over the last 40 years, he has consulted on performance improvement and learning effectiveness issues with over 100 private and public sector organizations.

"Large-scale change is a frequent reality in contemporary organizations. Such change is typically complex and stressful for participants, rarely fully achieves its goals, and all too often can be evaluated as a failure. That track record has led to many books that purport to provide THE ANSWER to successful organizational change, but most are only rehashes of simple ideas intermixed with a few 'war stories' from the authors. Rob Snyder has written a very different book. In a style that engages the reader, Dr. Snyder presents an excellent summary of recent research in social cognitive neuroscience and carefully describes the implications and application of these findings to how organizational change efforts should be led and managed. This innovative approach challenges many widely-held beliefs about human motivation and behavior and builds a solid case for following the change principles that are offered. It is a valuable book for the newcomer and veteran, the academic and practitioner, and the change agent and general manager."
—James L. Farr, Ph.D., Professor Emeritus of Industrial-Organizational Psychology, Pennsylvania State University. President, Society for Industrial and Organizational Psychology, 1996–1997.

"TiER1's approach to changing the performance of people sets them apart from the competition and it shows in their results. This books explains why."
—Christy Godden, Vice President, Learning and Development, Macy's.

"In this excellent book, Rob Snyder summarizes and explains the fast-developing research field of Social Cognitive Neuroscience and applies its findings to the many challenges of leading large-scale organizational changes. I think much of current management theory will have to be revised because of this new thinking coming from neuroscience. I recommend that both practicing managers and academics read this book as an introduction to many very new ideas. It uses straightforward language and clear examples to help readers understand some very non-intuitive results."
—Joe Seltzer, Professor of Management, LaSalle University. President, OBTS: Teaching Society for Management Educators.

"This guide is a treasure-trove of information that's easily accessible to anyone facing the challenges of managing change. Unlike so many other books on the subject, it focuses primarily on the underpinnings of what the behavioral sciences and most recently, neuroscience, have taught us about how people experience, react to and ultimately deal with change. Most of all, it establishes a comprehensive, contemporary and defensible standard in how to manage the changes so common among organizations today. It debunks some old myths that have been around for a long time and provides great new insights that are counter-intuitive. **No matter what you think you know about managing change, this book has something to teach you.**"
—Charles S. Raben, Ph.D., Founder, Raben Consulting.

THE SOCIAL COGNITIVE NEUROSCIENCE OF LEADING ORGANIZATIONAL CHANGE

TiER1 Performance Solutions' Guide for Managers and Consultants

Robert A. Snyder, Ph.D.

Routledge
Taylor & Francis Group

NEW YORK AND LONDON

First published 2016
by Routledge
711 Third Avenue, New York, NY 10017

and by Routledge
27 Church Road, Hove, East Sussex BN3 2FA

Routledge is an imprint of the Taylor & Francis Group, an informa business

Library of Congress Cataloging in Publication Data
Names: Snyder, Robert A., author.
Title: The social cognitive neuroscience of leading organizational change:
TiER1 performance solutions' guide for managers and consultants /
Robert A. Snyder.
Description: New York, NY : Routledge, 2016. Identifiers: LCCN
2015034334| ISBN 9781138859852 (hardback : alk. paper) |
ISBN 9781138859869 (pbk. : alk. paper) | ISBN 9781315707785 (ebk)
Subjects: LCSH: Organizational change—Management. | Organizational
behavior. | Cognitive neuroscience. | Psychology, Industrial.
Classification: LCC HD58.8 .S645 2016 | DDC 658.4/06—dc23
LC record available at http://lccn.loc.gov/2015034334

ISBN: 978-1-138-85985-2 (hbk)
ISBN: 978-1-138-85986-9 (pbk)
ISBN: 978-1-315-70778-5 (ebk)

Typeset in Bembo
by Keystroke, Station Road, Codsall, Wolverhampton

Chuck Raben, Jim Morris: Great colleagues, greater friends

CONTENTS

FOREWORD

I recently had a conversation with the founder of a software company that had grown from nothing to over $50 million in revenue in the matter of a few years. He shared with me that he regularly told his management team that they should get used to change. "A year from now," he would say to them, "your title, your co-workers, your reports, your boss, and even the chair you sit in will be different. Get used to it." That's the nature of a high growth company.

Change is becoming the norm—not just for those on the high-growth track, but for *every* organization. To compete, companies are bringing in new employees, creating new products, forming new business units, introducing new processes, implementing new systems, and identifying new positions faster than ever before. The market demands it, but this often leaves people trying to catch their breath as one new initiative after another washes over them like waves hitting the beach.

In TiER1's early days, we leveraged classic change methodologies to help businesses roll out initiatives and adjust to their new normal. But we were struck by the fact that these methodologies emphasized a push of information from a central group to thousands of employees, often with little regard for what these thousands of individuals were going through personally.

Frankly, this bothered us. After all, any organizational shift that needs to happen—whether it impacts 40 employees or 40,000—starts with *people* making a change. So we brought Rob Snyder in to help us design a program that would approach change from the perspective of the individuals affected. For the previous two years, Rob had been immersing himself in the burgeoning work being done in the neuroscience of change. He helped us design a new methodology, one that provided our clients with the true underlying, brain-based causes of work behavior and created change leadership best practices based on rock-solid applied science. Out of that work, this book was born.

At TiER1, everything we do is focused on helping organizations maximize performance through their people, and we've found that a key part of that mission is helping those people realize their true potential. To build and maintain highly effective cultures, leaders have to understand why individual team members do what they do (or don't do)—why they respond to leadership; why they change or resist doing so; why they engage in the organization and its work. The science of human behavior gives us these insights.

This book is meant to be practical, sharing the latest in neuroscience in a way that can be immediately applied to managing day-to-day work. It is both a book about change and a book about leadership. I've long held that the primary function of leadership is to influence change. If there is no need for change, there is little need for leadership. Understanding the neuroscience of change leadership will make you better at both.

It's also a blueprint for people who want to be better consultants. Over the years I've talked with countless executives—many of them CIOs and CHROs—who expressed an interest in making their teams better "internal consultants" to the business. Whether you strive to make a business better from inside the organization or outside of it, this book provides a clear path to the knowledge and skills you need.

Change is inevitable—it's the only way we'll grow personally and professionally. As leaders we influence change, so it makes sense that a better understanding of how and why people function would enable us to influence our people to reach their highest potential. I'm confident you'll find this book as insightful, reflective, useful, and thought-provoking as I have. In doing so, I hope you'll realize your own potential to impact change.

Greg Harmeyer
CEO and Co-Founder, TiER1 Performance Solutions

PROLOGUE

Brain science's transformation of management isn't just about another new technique or model. It's about shifting our paradigm to incorporate the hard data of science and fundamentally changing the way we think about business. When we do, we're able to gain access to an integrated set of management practices that really do deliver on the promise of superior performance.

—Charles S. Jacobs (2009, p. 3)

Social Cognitive Neuroscience Provides the Foundation for Many Assertions in This Guide

With roots in various subdisciplines of psychology and other behavioral sciences, "social cognitive neuroscience" (short-handed to "SCN" or "neuroscience" in all the other sections of this Guide) explores why we act and react the ways that we do—in *any* set of circumstances—primarily but not exclusively through the technologies that have been developed in the more general, more traditional fields of neuroscience such as neuromedicine, neurosurgery and neuropsychology (Lieberman, 2010). Social cognitive neuroscientists try to answer the same questions that social or cognitive or organizational psychologists have been studying and trying to answer for decades. The primary differences between the two approaches are: 1) how the focal questions are framed or asked and, much more importantly, 2) **the methods and tools that are typically used to seek answers** (e.g., a wide variety of brain activity recording technologies for social cognitive neuroscientists vs. observation of behavior, interviews, surveys, searches of archival information and studies in which two or more subsets of people are treated differently in a systematic way followed by the careful recording of their subsequent behaviors (that is, laboratory or field experiments)—by the other group of researchers. Both

FIGURE 0.1
Diffusion Tensor Image of
Corpus Callosum

Source: Whitford, Kubicki &
Shenton, 2011

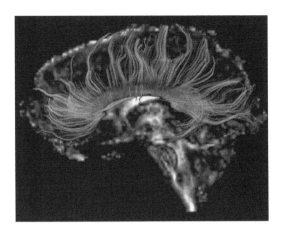

of these approaches (i.e., both ways of framing questions, both sets of methods and tools) are needed if we expect to maximize our understanding of human behavior and organizational effectiveness).

There have been many recent, rapid and extraordinary innovations in mobile, dynamic brain-activity-recording technology used by social cognitive neuroscientists such as the continued refinement of functional magnetic resonance imaging and quantitative encephalography as well as the development of newer technologies like magnetoencephalography, diffusion tensor imaging, transcranial magnetic stimulation and several others. Metaphorically, these improvements in neuroscientific tools can be compared to the invention of the microscope in biology. Scientists can now "see" things that most would have been unable to imagine. **With these improved technologies, it has become possible to record and time-map intricate patterns of brain activity, in real and precise time, against people's life experiences in everything from shopping to competing in a sport to potential use of lethal force by police officers.**

FIGURE 0.2
Consumer Research
with Eye Tracking Glasses
from SensoMotoric
Instruments (SMI) and a
Brain-Activity Recording
Neuroheadset from Emotiv

Photo courtesy SMI

In marketing research for example, experts no longer have to rely solely on consumers' notoriously error-prone and unreliable self-proclaimed reasons why they chose one product rather than another. Figure 0.2 shows a visual-activity recording device (glasses) developed by SensoMotoric Instruments that records *directly* what shoppers attend to (or fail to attend to) in promotional displays, on product labels, etc. and neuroheadgear developed by Emotiv that records the relative amount of interest the brain's visual recording system is showing in response to the simultaneous combination of inputs that the glasses are tracking. In fact, it is now possible for technology to determine that a person has made a decision prior to that person's conscious recognition of the fact (Soon, He, Bode & Haynes, 2013).

SCN research has confirmed the validity of many previously held beliefs about behavior in the workplace. For example, it has demonstrated—albeit more definitively—that interviewers make tentative—but difficult to overturn—employment decisions very, very shortly after each interview has begun (Waytz & Mason, 2013). **However, SCN studies have demonstrated that many widely accepted ideas in social and organizational psychology (and many common business practices) are just *completely wrong*!**

For example, from the time of the Vietnam War, we've been treating soldiers suffering from posttraumatic stress disorder (PTSD) primarily by "desensitization." That is, therapists would have PTSD sufferers go over and over and over their traumatic experiences so that eventually they would become less traumatic, in much the same way as a child is less afraid during the tenth parental reading of a scary book than during the first reading. Highly rigorous neuroscience research has now shown us that that is the worst thing that could be done to these brave people. Rumination increases terror, it doesn't dissuade it (Cooney, Joorman, Eugene, Dennis & Gotlib, 2010; Doidge, 2007; Nolen-Hoeksema, Wisco & Lyubomirsky, 2008). We now know that the thing we need to do is just the opposite: We need to get these war fighters thinking of anything *but* what happened to them in battle. That is the shortest road to recovery.

With a big smile that I hope demonstrates an admission of unbridled hyperbole, I have often told my clients that SCN research demonstrates that 75 percent of what I learned in graduate school was flawed if not completely inaccurate. (Granted, I went to graduate school back in the day *well before* back in the day. Nonetheless . . .) The inflated percentage aside, the claim is basically true. For example, I learned that if you want to change John's behavior, the very first thing you have to do is convince John that the way he is currently behaving is wrong or ineffective or, at the very least, far from as good as it could be. We now know that when we take that approach, John's brain will probably secrete noxious neurochemicals that can dramatically decrease the likelihood that he will comply with the change we expect in his behavior (Carey, Mansell & Tai, 2014; Pulakos, Hanson, Arad & Moye, Forthcoming).

Another prescription I had to unlearn: When there is serious bad news to be delivered to employees, you should: 1) get as many of those employees as possible into one big room, 2) have the highest level executive available work from a carefully crafted script, 3) present all the detailed information that is known at that point in time on 4) the premise that it's best if as many people as possible hear *all* of the news at the *same* time, 5) follow up that meeting by sending out a hard copy of the executive's speech and, finally, 6) stand around in little groups saying "that went as well as we could expect" and "Thank God we're done with that!" Of course, thanks to SCN research we now know that such a meeting is likely to be very unproductive, if not counterproductive, because when people hear extremely bad news, or even expect to, hormones may be secreted in their brains that literally make it impossible for them to comprehend most of what is being said or presented to them (Goleman & Boyatzis, 2008; Rock, 2009a, 2009b).

FIGURE 0.3 When People Hear Extremely Bad News, Or Even Expect To, Fear-Response-Arousing Hormones Can Be Secreted In Their Brains that Literally Make It Impossible For Them to Comprehend Most of What Is Being Said Or Presented To Them

Here are *only a very few* of the many additional organization- and management-related, counterintuitive findings that have been uncovered by recent SCN research. I have provided (in bold and in brackets) a few samples of specific functions or duties of management where these findings might be relevant; I could have inserted **Leading Change** in every one:

- When a person says "maybe" in response to a request for assistance, other people are likely to hear "yes" (i.e., they record it in their brains and remember it as assent; Sharot, 2011)[1] **[Negotiation; conflict resolution]**
- In high-stimulation, frenetically paced jobs (e.g., traders on the floor of a stock exchange), neurochemical changes in people's brains can cause their decision-making to become extremely reckless, without their conscious awareness of the change (Bennett, 2012)[2] **[Decision-making; stress management; negotiation]**
- People are more likely to admit to fear and dishonesty than they are to admit to being envious (Angier, 2009) **[Performance management; management of equity perceptions]**
- Managers can become more influential and perceived as better leaders by speaking less (Rock, 2006)[3] **[Leadership; performance management]**
- People who need to become better listeners can greatly reduce the likelihood that they will interrupt another person if they take notes while that other person is speaking (Van Hecke, Callahan, Kolar & Paller, 2010) **[Performance management; listening skills]**
- If you are trained in the exact location where you will perform the trained-for task on the job, you will remember more of the training and your performance will be higher after training (Medina, 2008)[4] **[Training; embedded agents (war fighters)]**
- Talking aloud to one's self can cause a nearly instantaneous reduction in anxiety and facilitate creativity (Lieberman, 2010) **[Stress management; innovation]**
- People are more likely to come up with creative solutions to a problem when they are forced to not think about it (i.e., the problem; Van Hecke et al., 2010)[5] **[Problem-solving innovation; decision making]**
- If you repeat part of a sentence that another person has just spoken, that person is much more likely to believe that the two of you are in agreement on whatever topic is being discussed (Vedantam, 2010)[6] **[Negotiation; interviewing; sales]**
- A single, not-so-recent memory is very likely to include erroneously things that happened at different times (Medina, 2008) **[Leadership; performance management]**
- Trainees are more engaged in training and perform better on the job when they believe that their trainer is prestigious (Howard, 2006) **[Training; communication]**
- Contrary to what has been taught in business schools for decades, under certain circumstances, hunches and emotion can improve decision-making (Waytz & Mason, 2013) **[Strategy; decision-making]**

- Even though a belief statement can be blatantly false, the more often people hear that statement, the more likely they are to come to believe it (Wang & Aamodt, 2008)[7] **[Communication; attitude change; sales]**
- While on the job, the brain activity patterns of long-time assembly line workers are very similar to the brain activity patterns of hospital patients who are comatose (Rock, 2006). **[Training; safety]**

This isn't science fiction. It's neuroscience nonfiction. And, findings such as these have important implications for whether people resist or embrace change and for how, and under what conditions, people learn best—that is, how people acquire, retain, retrieve and apply knowledge most effectively and efficiently (which is, of course, a very crucial component of large-scale change effectiveness). I believe deeply that people will be in a much better position to lead/manage major organizational change efforts when they are aware of these sorts of human "quirks." This belief is widely held and far from extreme. In fact, many experts believe that applied SCN research is rapidly changing the very foundations of *the entire fields of* psychology, psychiatry and counseling among others (Farah, 2014; Levitin, Gazzanega, Saxe & Wang, 2009). Additional experts have argued that SCN research findings **should change much of the existing prescriptive paradigm for managing others** (and ourselves) in work organizations (Altman, 2011; Anchors, 2011; Becker & Cropanzano, 2010, 2011; Becker, Cropanzano & Sanfey, 2011; Rock & Schwartz, 2007; Rominiecki, 2009; Waytz & Mason, 2013).

There Are Some Very Smart People Out There Who Believe Equally Strongly that SCN Research Isn't Nearly What It's Cracked Up to Be

In 1993, Frances Rauscher and two of her colleagues had published a 464-word *letter* to the Editors of *Nature* (Rauscher, Shaw & Ky, 1993). In it, they described a weakly designed (my opinion—but one shared in print by many others) study involving 36 college students who were found to have a "temporary" (i.e., lasting for a few minutes) increase in spatial reasoning test scores after listening to a Mozart sonata for ten minutes. Shortly thereafter, this little study was described in the press as scientific research vetted by the prestigious journal, *Nature*; the results were labeled the "Mozart Effect"; Rauscher ended up on the NBC Evening News with Tom Brokaw; and Rauscher began receiving death threats for her (non-existent) condemnation of rock music (Weinberger, 2011). Most incredibly, the Mozart Effect had an impact on public policy. Five years after the original study, *The New York Times* (Goode, 1999) reported: "In Florida, a new law requires toddlers in state-run schools to listen to classical music everyday" and "Gov. Zell Miller of Georgia is so convinced [of the Mozart Effect] that he is providing CDs to every new mother in the state." In an earlier article, *The New York Times* (Sack, 1998) attributed this quote to Miller: "*No one questions* that listening to music <u>at</u>

a very early age affects the spatial-temporal reasoning that underlies math and engineering and even chess" (emphases added).

By 2002, the Mozart Effect had been largely de-bunked (McKelvie & Low, 2002). However, even in more recent times, respected researchers (e.g., Pietschnig, Voracek & Formann, 2010; Reuell, 2013) felt the need to continue to drive nails into the Mozart Effect's coffin.

SCN research has had its own research design flaws (particularly with weak or inappropriate statistical analyses), false discoveries and false conclusion-drawing (though the mistake rate seems to be decreasing with the increasing use of multi-modal studies—those that use two or more types of neuroimaging technologies to facilitate more accurate interpretation of data and as a means of within-study replication or confirmation—and with new "corrected" statistical models). Neuroscientists who have made these mistakes must be identified and their research and/or claims should be debunked (as the Mozart Effect has been). At the same time, I believe that neuroscience, in most cases, is taking flak for things that neuroscientists didn't say and didn't do.

In my opinion, most of the misinterpretations, exaggerations and far-overreaching theoretical applications of SCN data for which neuroscience is being blamed are in reality the responsibility of the media (broadly conceived to include social media, blogs and a variety of other online postings such as syndicated science news summary services) rather than with scientists themselves. There are several contributing factors:

1. A large percentage of the people who interpret the results of SCN research for others simply aren't qualified to do so. As a result, they often innocently misconstrue or misapply original findings (Bell, 2013; Quart, 2012).

2a. In our politically and ideologically polarized society (Balz, 2014), many people have incentives to purposely misconstrue or misapply research findings (Abramowitz, 2013). (The "debate" over climate change comes quickly to mind.) Sometimes people are conscious of this distortion and it is their intention to misinform. Other times, people with strong political or ideological beliefs simply aren't aware of their misinterpretations. This can occur at the communication-sending end of the equation and/or at the receiving end. In regard to the latter, Reid (2012) found that most people who viewed themselves as either staunchly conservative or staunchly liberal rated the *same* news articles about various politicians running for office (and even objectively reported poll results) as fair or biased entirely on the basis of whether they had been led to believe that the author shared their political beliefs. In other words, conservatives were more likely to rate (the same) content as biased if they believed that it was written or reported by a liberal or a liberal organization and as "fair" if they believed a conservative or conservative organization produced the work. The same "in-group bias" was true for liberals.

2b. Non-political media professionals can be influenced by other kinds of incentives. In these cases, the incentives might be to gain attention, get that first-page headline or create controversy.

3. Many people who take positions disfavoring (or for that matter, favoring) SCN research do not read original documents or studies. Thus, distortions in "facts" can be caused in a serial fashion (e.g., from blogger to blogger to blogger) just like what happens in the "Telephone Game" that is often played at children's parties.

With these and other similar factors operating, it's no wonder that much of what has been said/written by non-experts—whether the positions taken are positive or negative with regard to SCN research or neuroscience more generally—is rubbish.[8]

As I stated earlier in the prologue, I believe that Change Leaders, followers and consultants can benefit greatly from knowledge of some of the recent, reliably assessed findings of SCN research, as I believe I and my colleagues at TiER1 Performance Solutions have. *However, this Guide is not intended as a blanket endorsement of neuroscience.* The technologies on which most SCN studies are based are still in development and the data they generate are complex and easy to misinterpret. So, SCN research studies must be evaluated individually and rigorously and shown to be reliably repeatable—if only because of a demonstrated tendency of experts and non-experts alike to overvalue work in the field based on its hard-science face alone (Weisberg, Keil, Goodstein, Rawson & Gray, 2008). At the same time, I believe that SCN should be an important contributor to any organization's attempt to practice "evidence-based management"[9] *because of the science itself.* For example, in another part of this Guide, I cite Matthew Lieberman's work demonstrating that talking aloud to one's self (by labeling one's emotions) can cause a nearly instantaneous reduction in anxiety. Lieberman didn't have subjects talk aloud and then ask them if they felt less anxious. Rather, he: 1) measured subjects' Time 1 levels of the stress-producing neurochemical cortisol, 2) asked them to talk about their anxiety levels according to an established emotion-labeling protocol, 3) demonstrated that when subjects were doing so there was increased activity in the right ventromedial prefrontal cortex that had previously been shown to be a source of secretions of DHEA, a cortisol-neutralizing hormone (Tor et al., 2006) and, finally, 4) measured subsequent (Time 2) levels of cortisol and found them to be lower.

The work by Lieberman and others on the use of self-talk, specifically emotion-labeling (called affect-labeling by neuroscientists) to control thoughts and behavior has received much acclaim, as—in my opinion—it certainly should. What is often over-looked, however, is that Lieberman didn't "discover" the calming effect of emotion-labeling. Rather, he used SCN research methods to support—some would say "affirm"—the validity of an hypothesis, developed by psychiatrist Jeffrey Schwartz, that had been tested in clinical practice trials assessing the effectiveness of emotion-labeling vs. traditional therapies (including treatment with medication) with randomly selected patients who were being treated for Obsessive Compulsive Disorder (OCD). Emotion-labeling was found to be far superior in effectiveness.

The Lieberman (SCN)–Schwartz (Psychiatry) connection is an excellent example of how we can best understand human behavior by *combining* the insights of SCN and non-SCN research.[10] Despite being a huge proponent of SCN, I don't see it as a substitute for other research fields or methods. Instead, I believe (as do notable others, e.g., Cacioppo & Cacioppo, 2013; Cikara & Van Bavel, 2014; Mather, Cacioppo & Kanwisher, 2013; Tokuhama-Espinosa, 2011) that it provides support, compelling and often theory/paradigm-busting support, for work being done in all of the social and behavioral sciences.

This Guide itself *combines* a lot of things:

- From SCN research: Powerful, very robustly and reliably demonstrated brain-based influences on behavior that I have found to be most helpful in understanding, initiating and sustaining organization change;
- Observations, insights and practical tips from my 40+ years of consulting experience with over 100 work organizations;
- The discernment, creativity, problem-framing skills and innovative ideas of my colleagues at TiER1 Performance Solutions;
- Established best practices in organizational performance and organizational change management;
- The findings of relevant research in social psychology and organizational psychology;
- The wisdom and business sense of many outstanding organizational leaders in client organizations; and, not least,
- Tips shared with me by other organizational consultants, especially in the area of "things you should never, ever do."

Readers of this Guide will not only learn how to effectively manage the incredibly varied and complex personal and organizational changes that are required for successful implementation of enterprise-wide performance improvement processes. They will learn how to do so in the shortest amount of time, while consuming the fewest resources, and causing the least amount of emotional havoc.[11] They will also be shown how to get the absolute maximum number of organizational benefits from the change. Examples of the last would include using the change process to develop employee skills that will have applications in other settings, to open (and maintain) new communication channels among departments, or to field-test the leadership abilities of particular staff members.

It's a Guide that no large-scale, performance improvement project manager (nor anyone "drafted" into service on such a project) should go without reading (and, I sincerely hope, enjoying)!

Rob Snyder

Notes

1 In *The optimism bias: A tour of the irrationally positive brain* (2011), neuroscientist Tali Sharot documents in everyday language how our brains are hard-wired for seeing the bright

side of things—and the consequent, usually positive but often disastrous outcomes that ensue: A strong optimistic outlook can promote better health and at the same time nudge us to make decisions that ignore the true base rate of their likely success (e.g., assuming that one's marriage will be perfect contrary to the statistics on divorce). This optimism bias can also cause us to neurally record past conversations or events in the way we *wanted* them to occur. In "Remembering what could have happened: Neural correlates of episodic counterfactual thinking," DeBrigard, Addis, Ford, Schacter & Giovanello (2013) believe that they have isolated the specific brain mechanisms that are responsible for this effect.

2 High levels of *cortisol* have been shown to hamper decision-making effectiveness. In addition, high levels of *adrenaline* can virtually shut down the decision-making process, at least the rational part of that process. Interactions between managers and their direct reports are a major, all-too-common source of a "double dose" of these noxious neurochemicals. For example, displays of anger during poorly delivered criticism of performance is associated with rapid increases in both cortisol and adrenaline (see Goleman & Boyatzis, 2008).

3 The same type of positive effects occur when leaders avoid problem-oriented questions (Why isn't this working?) and use solution-oriented questions (What can we do to make this work?) (see Pulakos et al., Forthcoming; Rock, 2006).

4 The U.S. Army has found that training war fighters in war zones not only increases the effectiveness of training, it creates huge savings as well, as many state-side training facilities are no longer needed (Graesser & King, 2008).

5 Brainy- (but not neuro-) scientist Albert Einstein has been attributed the quote, "The monotony and solitude of a quiet life stimulates the creative mind." That turns out to be an hypothesis that has been supported in a number of different SCN studies (see Van Hecke et al., 2010). Thus, "I get my best ideas in the shower" is an aphorism with empirical validity: Whenever the brain is operating on automatic pilot (i.e., basal ganglia are doing all the work), the parts of the brain involved in higher level thinking are free to work together, combining possible ideas. In an HBR Blog Matthew May (2012) provides some tips on "Quick and easy ways to quiet your mind" when you need to ramp up your creativity or keep it active chronically.

6 Obviously, this has to be done with both finesse and subtlety or you could sound like an idiot!

7 *The believing brain*, a book by *Skeptic* magazine editor and frequent *Scientific American* contributor, Michael Shermer (2011), can compete with anything ever written by Stephen King in terms of being totally frightening. Consider: More people believe in angels and the devil than believe in the theory of evolution, the amount of science education college students receive is uncorrelated with whether they believe in paranormal phenomena, and the percentage of U.S. citizens who believe in astrology, extrasensory perception and alien abductions *is increasing*.

8 Criticism of SCN research can be and has been constructive and instrumental in improving research design, interpretation of data and applications/practice. Admittedly, as a strong proponent of applied SCN research, I'm biased. But, within the last couple of years, criticism of SCN seems to have changed tone (toward more radically negative statements) and lost much of the balance that characterized earlier, more valuable punditry.

Beyond negative tone, there's another problem that I see with some of the SCN criticism that's out there these days. In pointing out the flaws in SCN research and in castigating pop culture and pop psychology non-experts for their egregious exaggerations, many journalists, bloggers and public speakers/commentators leave their audiences with the impression that there is nothing of value in the neurosciences, broadly considered. I submit as an example a very influential, often-cited article in *The New York Times* by Alissa Quart (2012) as an example. I doubt that Quart believes that there is nothing good that can be said about neuroscience—but by not saying anything at all about that value, many bloggers and pundits used her article to ring the death knell for the entire field of study.

In a related vein, Bennett and colleagues published a "study" in which they obtained fMRI activity readings from a dead fish. The article was intended to humorously demonstrate that neuroscientists need to "correct" their readings for possible false positives. But whenever I've seen or heard the article referenced, it's portrayed as a condemnation of the methods of neuroscience with no mention of the article's true intent (Bennett, Baird, Miller & Wolford, 2010).

It seems to me that most of the rest of the criticism of SCN research can be sorted into three clusters. One cluster in the mix is represented by the academic in a non-scientific discipline (I'll call the discipline "X") who appears convinced that acceptance of the value of the neurosciences is the equivalent of believing that the study of, or the profession of, X has no value. An example I submit here is Raymond Tallis (the author of several books on philosophy), specifically regarding his very widely read book, *Aping mankind: Neuromania, Darwinitis and the misrepresentation of humanity* (2011). In a review of this book, Garson (2014) calls it "a metaphysical journey to separate consciousness [i.e., "mind"] from the brain and rescue libertarian free will, humanism, and moral progress from a variety of 'pernicious' reductionisms [in the neurosciences]." For an example of negative tone, Tallis condemns researchers who "**grovel before the supposed superiority of science**." (Note that SCN research inclusive of the constructs brain *and* mind is clearly possible (Hannah, Balthazard, Waldman, Jennings & Thatcher, 2013).)

Cluster 2 (perhaps a subset of Cluster 1 above) is represented by people who believe that SCN is an infringement on the basic religious doctrine of free will. It's true that Jeffrey Schwartz, a research psychiatrist who is a proponent of SCN, has popularized among neuroscientists the belief that the concept of "free won't" should replace "free will." (Free won't reflects Schwartz's conclusion that you can't stop your brain from sending you bad ideas and poor advice; but, you can tell it "no.") It turns out that Schwartz is a self-proclaimed "very religious person" and sees no conflict at all with his faith.

The third cluster is represented by people who are concerned with (largely potential, i.e., possible, future) unethical uses of SCN data. For example, Lindebaum (2013) raises concerns that organizations will use sensitive data about brain functioning to make decisions regarding the worth of each individual to the organization (e.g., leader or non-leader?). Articles following Lindebaum's in the same issue of *JMI* refute the position that he has taken (Ashkanasy, 2013; Cropanzano & Becker, 2013). I agree with the rebuttals. But, I guess it's never too early to sound the alarm about possible future ethical issues.

In any case, for a more balanced and nuanced view on the relative strengths and weaknesses of neuroscience research, I recommend that one should "tune in regularly to" the Neuroskeptic blog in *Discover* magazine.

9   Basing your decision-making as a manager on the best available hard evidence of what really works in practice and purposeful avoidance of using strongly held beliefs, the usual way of doing things, or what a famous professor or expert recommends.

10 The continued melding of social psychology and social cognitive neuroscience is reflected in a comparison of reviews of the issue in 2008 vs. 2014 (see Cikara & Van Bavel, 2014; cf., Dovidio, Pearson & Orr, 2008). The melding appears to be well underway.

11 Large-scale organizational change is widely believed to be emotionally disruptive (i.e., highly stressful) for many, often even most, of the people involved. But, studies investigating the relationship between organizational change and stress have usually been based on survey or interview data or archival statistics such as the number of people who voluntarily left the organization while the change was being considered or implemented.

A study by the Danish Social Science Research Council at the Danish Agency for Science, Technology and Innovation (Dahl, 2010) is one of the few to have found objective evidence of the change/stress relationship, independent of the focal organizations: Among nearly 100,000 Danish workers, prescriptions for stress-reducing medications during major organizational changes increased dramatically.

References

All web site URLs accessed on December 12, 2015.

Abramowitz, A. (2013). *The polarized public: Why our government is so dysfunctional*. New York, NY: Pearson Longman.

Altman, L. (2011, February 17). *Why neuroscience should change how we manage people*. Retrieved from http://intentionalworkplace.com/2011/02/17/why-neuroscience-should-change-the-way-we-manage-people/.

Anchors, Z. (2011). *Forget the MBA, managers should study the brain*. Retrieved from www.cbsnews.com/8301-505143_162-40245154/forget-the-mba-managers-need-to-study-the-brain/.

Angier, N. (2009). In pain and joy of envy, brain may play a role. *The New York Times*, February 17 (Science), D2.

Ashkanasy, N. (2013). Neuroscience and leadership: Take care not to throw the baby out with the bathwater. *Journal of Management Inquiry, 22*, 311–313.

Balz, D. (2014). What's left of the political center. *Washington Post*, July 5. Retrieved from www.washingtonpost.com/politics/whats-left-of-the-political-center/2014/07/05/37122966-0447-11e4-8572-4b1b969b6322_story.html?wpisrc=nl_headlines.

Becker, W. & Cropanzano, R. (2010). Organizational neuroscience: The promise and prospects of an emerging discipline. *Journal of Organizational Behavior, 31*, 1055–1059.

Becker, W. & Cropanzano, R. (2011). Organizational neuroscience: Taking organizational theory inside the neural black box. *Journal of Management, 37*, 933–961.

Becker, W., Cropanzano, R. & Sanfey, A. (2011). *Social science research network*. Retrieved from http://papers.ssrn.com/sol3/papers.cfm?abstract_id=1742384.

Bell, V. (2013). Our brains, and how they're not as simple as we think. *The Observer*, March 2. Retrieved from www.theguardian.com/science/2013/mar/03/brain-not-simple-folk-neuroscience.

Bennett, C., Baird, A., Miller, M. & Wolford, G. (2010). Neural correlates of interspecies perspective taking in the post-mortem Atlantic Salmon: An argument for proper multiple comparisons correction. *Journal of Serendipitous and Unexpected Results, 1*, 1–5.

Bennett, D. (2012). When animal spirits attack. *Bloomberg Business Week*, June 4, pp. 4–5.

Cacioppo, J. T. & Cacioppo, S. (2013). Social neuroscience. *Perspectives on Psychological Science, 8*, 667–669.

Carey, T., Mansell, W. & Tai, S. (2014). A biosocial model based on negative feedback and control. *Frontiers of Human Neuroscience*. Retrieved from http://dx.doi.org/10.3389/fnhum.2014.00094.

Cikara, M. & Van Bavel, J. (2014). The neuroscience of intergroup relations: An integrative review. *Perspectives on Psychological Science, 9(3)*, 245–274.

Cooney, R., Joorman, J., Eugene, F., Dennis, E. & Gotlib, I. (2010). Neural correlates of rumination in depression. *Cognitive, Affective, & Behavioral Neuroscience, 10(4)*, 470–478.

Cropanzano, R. & Becker, W. (2013). The promise and peril of organizational neuroscience: Today and tomorrow. *Journal of Management Inquiry, 22*, 306–310.

Dahl, M. (2010). Organizational change and stress. *Danish Social Science Research Council at the Danish Agency for Science, Technology and Innovation: Final report from Grant No. 09-065803*. Retrieved from www.healthatwork-online.de/fileadmin/downloads/Studie-Dahl.pdf.

DeBrigard, F., Addis, D., Ford, J., Schacter, D. & Giovanello, K. (2013). Remembering what could have happened: Neural correlates of episodic counterfactual thinking. *Neuropsychologia, 51(12)*, 2401–2414.

Doidge, N. (2007). *The brain that changes itself: Stories of personal triumph from the frontiers of brain science*. London, U.K.: Penguin.

Dovidio, J., Pearson, A. & Orr, P. (2008). Social psychology and neuroscience: Strange bedfellows or a healthy marriage. *Group Processes and Intergroup Relations, 11(2)*, 247–263.

Farah, M. (2014). Brain images, babies, and bathwater: Critiquing critiques of functional neuroimaging. In J. Johnston & E. Parens (Eds.), *Interpreting neuroimages: An introduction to the technology and its limits. The Hastings Report* (Special Issue) *44(2)*, S19–S30.

Garson, J. (2014). *Aping mankind: Neuromania, Darwinitis and the misrepresentation of humanity*: A review. *Notre Dame Philosophical Reviews (online)*. Retrieved from http://ndpr.nd.edu/news/28270-aping-mankind-neuromania-darwinitis-and-the-misrepresentation-of-humanity/.

Goleman, D. & Boyatzis, R. (2008). Social intelligence and the biology of leadership. *Harvard Business Review, 86*(9), 74–81.

Goode, E. (1999). Mozart for baby? Some say, maybe not. *The New York Times*, August 3, F1.

Graesser, A. & King, B. (2008). Technology-based training. In J. Blascovich & C. Hartel (Eds.), *Human behavior in military contexts* (pp. 127–149). Washington, D.C.: National Academies Press.

Hannah, S., Balthazard, P., Waldman, D., Jennings, P. & Thatcher, R. (2013). The psychological and neurological bases of leader self-complexity and effects on adaptive decision-making. *Journal of Applied Psychology, 98(3)*, 393–411.

Howard, P. (2006). *The owner's manual for the brain: Everyday applications from mind-brain research* (3rd ed.). Austin, TX: Bard Books.

Jacobs, C. (2009). *Management rewired: Why feedback doesn't work and other surprising lesson from the latest brain science*. New York, NY: Penguin Group.

Levitin, D., Gazzanega, M., Saxe, R. & Wang, S. (2009). *Unlocking the secrets and the powers of the brain*. Philadelphia, PA: National Science Foundation Forum at the Franklin Institute.

Lieberman, M. (2010). Social cognitive neuroscience. In S. T. Fiske, D. T. Gilbert & G. Lindzey (Eds.), *Handbook of social psychology* (5th ed., pp. 143–193). New York, NY: McGraw-Hill.

Lindebaum, D. (2013). Pathologizing the healthy but ineffective: Some ethical reflections on using neuroscience in leadership research. *Journal of Management Inquiry, 22*, 295–305.

McKelvie, P. & Low, J. (2002). Listening to Mozart does not improve children's spatial ability: Final curtains for the Mozart effect. *British Journal of Developmental Psychology, 20*, 241–258.

Mather, M., Cacioppo, J. & Kanwisher, N. (2013). How fMRI can inform cognitive theories. *Perspectives on Psychological Science, 8*, 108–113.

May, M. (2012). Quick and easy ways to quiet your mind. *HBR Online*. Retrieved from https://hbr.org/2012/12/quick-and-easy-ways-to-quiet-y.

Medina, J. (2008). *Brain rules: 12 principles for surviving and thriving at work, home, and school*. Seattle, WA: Pear Press.

Nolen-Hoeksema, S., Wisco, B. & Lyubomirsky, S. (2008). Reconsidering rumination. *Perspectives on Psychological Science, 3(5)*, 420–424.

Pietschnig, L., Voracek, M. & Formann, A. (2010). Mozart effect–Shmozart effect: A meta-analysis. *Intelligence, 38(3)*, 314.

Pulakos, E., Hanson, R., Arad, S. & Moye, N. (Forthcoming). Performance management can be fixes: An on-the-job experiential learning approach for complex behavior change. *Industrial and Organizational Psychology: Perspectives on Science and Practice, 8(1)*. Retrieved from Member web site (Society of Industrial and Organizational Psychology).

Quart, A. (2012). Neuroscience under attack. *The New York Times*, November 23, 12. Retrieved from www.nytimes.com/2012/11/25/opinion/sunday/neuroscience-under-attack.html?_r=0.

Rauscher, F. H., Shaw, G. L. & Ky, K. N. (1993). Music and spatial task performance. *Nature, 365*, 611.

Reid, S. (2012). A self-categorization explanation for the hostile media effect. *Journal of Communication, 62*, 381–399.

Reuell, P. (2013). Muting the Mozart effect. *Harvard Gazette*, December 11. Retrieved from http://news.harvard.edu/gazette/story/2013/12/muting-the-mozart-effect/.

Rock, D. (2006). *Quiet leadership: Six steps to transforming performance at work*. New York, NY: Collins.

Rock, D. (2009a). *Why should business care about neuroscience?* Retrieved from www.linkageanz.com.au/uploads/pdf/David_Rock_Why_Should_Business_Care_About_Neuroscience.pdf.

Rock, D. (2009b). *Your brain at work*. New York, NY: HarperCollins.

Rock, D. & Schwartz, J. (2007). *Why neuroscience matters to executives*. Retrieved from www.strategy-business.com/li/leadingideas/li00021.

Rominiecki, J. (2009). Management lessons from neuroscience (Part I). *Associations Now*. Retrieved from www.asaecenter.org/Resources/ANowDetail.cfm?ItemNumber=44068.

Sack, K. (1998). Georgia's governor seeks musical start for babies. *The New York Times*, January 15, A 12.

Sharot, T. (2011). *The optimism bias: A tour of the irrationally positive brain*. New York, NY: Pantheon Books.

Shermer, M. (2011). *The believing brain: From ghosts and gods to politics and conspiracies—How we construct beliefs and reinforce them as truths*. New York, NY: Times Books.

Soon, C., He, A., Bode, S. & Haynes, J-D. (2013). Proceedings free choice for abstract intentions. *Proceedings of the National Academy of Sciences*. Retrieved from www.pnas.org/cgi/doi/10.1073/pnas.1212218110.

Tallis, R. (2011). *Aping mankind: Neuromania, Darwinitis and the misrepresentation of humanity*. Durham, U.K.: Acumen Publishing.

Tokuhama-Espinosa, T. (2011). *Mind, brain, and education science: A comprehensive guide to the new brain-based teaching*. New York, NY: W. W. Norton.

Tor, D., Christian, W., Lindquist, M., Fredrickson, B., Noll, D. & Taylor, S. F. (2006). The role of ventromedial prefrontal cortex in anxiety and emotional resilience. *Organization for Human Brain Mapping International Conference*, Florence, Italy.

Van Hecke, M., Callahan, L., Kolar, B. & Paller, K. (2010). *The brain advantage: Become a more effective business leader using the latest brain research*. Amherst, NY: Prometheus Books.

Vedantam, S. (2010). *The hidden brain: How our unconscious minds elect presidents, control markets, wage wars and save our lives*. New York, NY: Spiegel & Grau.

Wang, S. & Aamodt, S. (2008). Your brain lies to you. *The New York Times*, June 27, A31.

Waytz, A. & Mason, M. (2013). Your brain at work. *Harvard Business Review, 91(7–8)*, 102–111.

Weinberger, D. (2011). *Too big to know: Rethinking knowledge now that the facts aren't the facts*. New York, NY: Basic Books.

Weisberg, D., Keil, F., Goodstein, J., Rawson, E. & Gray, J. (2008). The seductive allure of neuroscience explanations. *Journal of Cognitive Neuroscience, 20*, 470–477.

Whitford, T., Kubicki, M. & Shenton, M. (2011). Diffusion tensor imaging, structural connectivity and schizophrenia. *Schizophrenia Research and Treatment*, v.2011, Article 709523. doi.org/10.1155/2011/709523.

1

INTRODUCTION TO ORGANIZATIONAL CHANGE AND CHANGE LEADERSHIP

Starting Point

Here's what I'm **not** going to do. I'm not going to start out—as so many books and articles on change management do—with a bunch of supposedly awe-inspiring (and panic attack-inducing) statistics or metaphors about change. You know the kind of thing:

> There has been more knowledge created in the last seven seconds than in the previous seven billion years!

> Change is like being in the eye of a hurricane AND in the funnel of a tornado while rats chew off your toes!

None of that for me. I'm not here to scare you. Quite the opposite, really. I hope to comfort you by providing you with insights into the Change Leadership process that will help you deal effectively with change (if not *master* it entirely) in a specific, but vitally important, part of the organizational world: Leading enterprise-wide (or at least large-scale) organizational changes. **These insights focus on both the "big picture" as well as what you should consider, do and say in very specific circumstances.** This is not to claim that, if you become involved with a large-scale change after reading this Guide, your task will be easy. Far from it. Enterprise-wide changes test the sanity and resilience of even the most experienced and competent leaders.

So what if you never become involved with a large-scale organizational change? Well, I think that that's unlikely in today's workplaces. **More importantly, I sincerely believe that the knowledge and skills you develop by reading this**

Guide have wide applicability. And practicing what I'm preaching can even be a key to your overall ability to contribute to your organization. **In fact, change management skills are becoming recognized as so important to the success and overall effectiveness of organizations that many of today's top corporations are making change management skills training a key part of their leadership development programs.** Likewise, change management competencies are finding their way into prominent academic theories of leadership. For example, Zenger and Folkman's (2002) influential and oft-cited model of "Extraordinary Leadership" posits five poles in the "leadership tent": Character, focus on results, interpersonal skills, personal capability and *leading organizational change.* **So, whether viewed in terms of business practice, or purely "theoretically," competency in change management has an extremely high personal and organizational utility.**

What's wrong with this picture? World-wide research by the most respected thought-leaders in leadership development (e.g., Cegos Asia Pacific (Blaine, 2013), Center for Creative Leadership (Leslie, 2009; Gentry, Eckert, Stawiski & Zhao, 2014), Development Dimensions International (Boatman & Wellins, 2011), etc.) consistently find that: 1) change management skills are currently crucial for effective leader performance, 2) the need for high-level change management skills will become much greater in the future and, yet, 3) **change management skills remain among the very weakest competencies of leaders at all levels of organizations today**.

Reading and reflecting on this Guide can help you greatly improve your change management skills whether your current skill level is low or very high. Two experts in change management, both with decades of experience but little knowledge of recent SCN research, each reported that they learned a lot—and a lot that they can use in their consulting—by reading a pre-publication copy of the Guide.

Effective Change Leaders: Characteristic Predispositions and Behaviors

The focus of this Guide is what I call "Change Leadership." The choice of the word "leadership" rather than "management" here has two connotations. First of all, I want to convey that my goal is not to simply help you and your organization survive (i.e., "manage" to get through) the change process. I want to show you how to get the absolute maximum number of organizational benefits from each change initiative. Examples (provided earlier) include using the change process to develop employee skills that would have applications in other settings, to open (and maintain) new communication channels among departments, or to field-test the leadership abilities of particular staff members.

The second connotation is more elemental. Here I want to convey that major change initiatives must be *led*—just as a department, a division or an entire organization is. That is, if you are at the forefront of a major change initiative and hope to be truly effective, **it will be necessary for you to maintain the same attitudes and consistently manifest the very same behaviors that are expected of all outstanding leaders in the performance of their roles**.

Effective leaders come in all sizes, shapes, ages, genders, sexual orientations, nationalities—whatever. But, the vast majority of them share important characteristics. That is, they are predisposed to *consciously* do these eight things with great consistency. They:

- act with integrity;
- focus on performance improvement and adhere to what are called change-facilitative values;
- maintain a positive disposition;
- monitor themselves carefully and are sensitive to how their behaviors are perceived and interpreted by others;
- make things (results) happen;
- help people understand and internalize the organization's overall strategy and how the planned changes are necessary for the strategy's successful execution;
- maintain a high energy level;
- take time to step back/to reflect.

Acting with Integrity

Research in many disciplines and using many methods has determined that **acting with integrity, having character, being honest, etc. is the most critical leader behavior**. However, many people have a limited understanding of the full notion of integrity that is implied in these studies. When asked to provide a meaning for or definition of integrity, most people say that it is consistency between what you say and what you do. No argument there. However, integrity[1] is a lot more than that. Its key dimensions are:

- consistency among words, actions and the ***values of the organization*** (assuming that those values are admirable);
- consistently (i.e., *always*) telling the truth;
- consistently (i.e., *always*) treating people with respect;
- consistently (i.e., *always*) maintaining confidences;
- consistently (i.e., as "always" as circumstances allow) fulfilling promises.

Show this list to managers and the likely response from each would be something like, "Yep, that's me! I know that these things are important and I do them." The *truth* is, however, that virtually all of us—leaders or not—don't do any of these things with real consistency. Let me just use one example: Always telling the truth.

Lying or deceiving others has traditionally been viewed as "bad" or as an aberration or at least as something that shouldn't happen. However, for good reason,

the circuitry of our brains evolved to make lying come easily—as those non-human animals or humanoids who used lies well were more likely to survive, having learned to escape responsibility for behaviors that run counter to the clan's or tribe's or group's norms. The neurophysiological reward for, or instinctual basis of, lying is amusingly demonstrated by higher-order primates who experience what amounts to glee or happiness when they get away with fooling another ape or chimp (Leslie, 2011).[2]

Perhaps more powerfully (and certainly, hypocritically), from our earliest years **we are taught to lie** and that lying can be a "good" thing. Do any of these sound familiar?

*   "It's time to go to bed so that Santa and his reindeer can come."
*   "No matter how you really feel, you have to give grandma a big kiss and tell her that you love the birthday present she sent you."
*   "If the server asks how old you are, be sure to say that you're 12 so we can save half of the cost of your dinner."
*   "If you don't stop acting up I'm going to leave you right here in the airport."
*   "Don't tell the baby sitter that you were up sick all night."
*   "Sticks and stones will break your bones, but words can never hurt you."
*   "Don't tell your teacher how much I helped you with this project."

No wonder that by the time that people are employed, most have become proficient at and quite at ease with lying.[3] Studies have found that lying is not only prevalent in the workplace; there are organizations whose official policies require employees to lie (e.g., Shulman, 2007).[4]

> "And it must follow, as the night the day, thou canst not then be false to any man."
>
> (Shakespeare, *Hamlet*, Act I, Scene III)

Without question, it is extremely difficult to *always* tell the truth *and always* treat people with respect, etc. But, the best/most effective Change Leaders and consultants fully enact the several consistencies listed above. And, I didn't use the word "enact" without conscious intent. **Great leadership has a whole lot in common with great acting on the live stage.** And, that's ironic in a way— because when people are asked to define integrity, the second most common definition they provide runs along the lines of "just being yourself" or "what they see is what they get." Well, Yorick, if you agree, that's an idea that you need to get out of your skull right now.

Hamlet is Shakespeare's longest play and requires a marathon-like performance of the lead. For that reason alone, it is considered a very, very difficult role. Often listed among the greatest performers to play the role are Laurence Olivier, Richard Burton, Derek Jacobi and Kenneth Branagh. Those are four guys that you'd never find on the same bowling team. Definitely not birds of a feather. And, as you might expect, their approaches to the role of Hamlet were as different as their personalities and their world views. In fact, if you were to cut the audio and just watch their recorded performances on four TV screens simultaneously, some people would guess that four different plays were being performed. Again, the approaches of the actors couldn't be much less similar. Yet, one thing is common and most assuredly contributed directly to these actors' reputations for greatness. If you were to watch any one of them perform the play, you would see him hit precise marks, make the same gestures in exactly the same way (etc.) in every one of their more than 200 performances each. They were never out of character for even the twitch of an eyebrow.

Great leaders (not just Change Leaders) know that a reputation for integrity must be painstakingly earned and very carefully managed. **They know that they can only acquire that reputation by** *performing* **the role of the Great Leader, day after day after day, while never stepping out of character.** Great leadership is not just "being yourself," it's being your ***best*** self at all times.[5]

EXPERTS' INSIGHTS: INTEGRITY, VALUES AND BEHAVIOR

Perhaps the most famous quote by former President Richard M. Nixon is, "I am not a crook!" (1973). By all accounts, Nixon truly believed that he wasn't dishonest—despite an impressive amount of evidence to the contrary. Why was he able to remain so self-righteous?[6] Well, part of the reason comes from something that I'll cover in great detail elsewhere in this Guide: The fundamental human drive or need to view ourselves in the most positive light possible. If that's the case, then it makes sense that we'd pay a lot more attention to, and selectively remember, our positive (e.g., honest, courteous, smart, etc.) behaviors than we would the exceptions. That's one of the reasons why such a high percentage of people (usually 75–95 percent) report being above average in leadership skills and in driving ability.

In the same way, a very large percentage of people report that their words are consistent with their behaviors, that they consistently fulfill their promises, and so on. But, just as in President Nixon's case, the evidence usually doesn't support these beliefs. Most of us stray away from our best behaviors fairly often, certainly a LOT more often than we consciously remember. **So, how do we recognize the unintended and undesired variances in our own behavior and change them for the better over time?**

It's been demonstrated to the point of certainty that if you really want to improve your performance on behaviors that, so far at least, have not come about naturally, you are most likely to make those improvements if you use some type of written-goals-with-frequent-review process like the one that I call, "The Pick 3, 3x5 Card Method" or "Pick 3" for short. Quite simply, Pick 3 involves writing down a small number (three or so) of your specific, personal behavioral goals and reviewing them on a twice-daily basis. There are two great things about this method: 1) if you are committed to making behavior changes and you stick to this method, **it will work (!)** and 2) it is very "generalizable," i.e., it works in lots of different circumstances with lots of different kinds of behaviors—whether it's becoming more patient, going to the gym more regularly, whatever.

In the case of leadership skill development, let's say that you want to become better at some of the "consistencies" that demonstrate integrity (listed above)—like always telling the truth, always treating people with respect and always maintaining confidences. Using the Pick 3 method, you would begin by simply writing these three (goal) behavior statements on something semi-durable, like an index card or a note card of some type, and place the card in an obvious place on your desk. (I've found that some people like to stick the card in the space between two rows of buttons on their computer keyboards each evening. That way, they "see" the card right away when they arrive at work.) Next, every morning, every single morning, you take just a few moments to read each of the three statements and think about what each one means. This takes no longer than ten seconds max.

Next comes the real key—**the critical part of the process in terms of actually changing/improving your behavior**. Every evening, every single evening, before you leave the office or plant, you once again grab the card, read each statement and think back over the entire day to review whether there have been any violations or exceptions. No self-mutilation required. Just noting the exceptions will make you less likely to violate your intent to be more consistent. Once you find in your nightly reviews that there are no longer any violations at all, it's time for a new card and three more behavioral statements. Before very long at all, you'll find that you are behaving much more consistently with your very best self.[7]

Doubt what I'm saying? All I can tell you is that I've seen it work, and work well, in over 50 organizations. And, even the oldest dogs can learn to behave differently/more effectively as a leader or follower or whatever. The hardest part is often just coming to the realization that you have control over whether and how much you can improve. It's like the leadership maxim: The first person you have to lead is yourself!

Adhering Consistently to Change-Facilitative Values

It has been well-established that change initiatives (and performance improvement processes in general) are dramatically more likely to succeed when the following conditions are created and maintained:

- Everyone involved respects and works for the benefit of *all* organizational stakeholders.
- Trust is built through honest, open communication and debate.

- Input is broadly based; civil, principled dissent is welcome and respected.
- People are given the information, and the time, that they need to adjust to change, as well as the skills that they need to implement it.
- Contributions of individuals and groups to the success of the change effort are appropriately recognized.

Unlike acting with integrity, the extent to which these values are manifest throughout an organization is not entirely under the control of most Change Leaders or change management consultants. However, the goal for both Change Leaders and consultants should be to: 1) align their behaviors with these values at all times and 2) consciously work toward their full adherence in every part and phase of the change process with the goal of sustaining adherence to these values over the long term (i.e., after the focal planned change process has been completed).

Maintaining a Positive Disposition

Without question, there will be periods during any major change initiative in which people will feel overwhelmed, exhausted and unsure of whether success is even possible. No matter how strongly you share those feelings, no matter how badly things have gone to that point, your obligation is to be a beacon of (rational) cheer. Your best weapon in such circumstances (next to your smile and overall demeanor) is to continually remind the people with whom you're working that their feelings are natural (resulting from the massive challenge that is being faced) and characteristic of all similar change initiatives. **It sounds Pollyanna-ish, but SCN has determined beyond doubt that smiling and optimism (if not irrationally based) are truly contagious.**

Think about the "Eeyore" character from Winnie-the Pooh. Be the opposite.

Effective Self-Monitoring/Sensitivity to Others

When Change Leaders or consultants are ineffective, the arguably most common reason is a lack of awareness of the effects of their behavior on the people around them. In contrast, the most competent leaders/consultants are consistently sensitive to the aspirations, preferences, concerns and the needs of others. This is very diffi-cult to pull off if you lack true respect for the people with whom you are working. But, **being sensitive is a conscious choice**. Once you make that choice, you can teach yourself how to be more aware of the interpersonal effects of your behavior.

BRAIN CONNECTION! MIRROR NEURONS

"She has a smile that will light up a room!" Maybe you've heard someone's smile described like this. Hey. Don't be jealous. A room? No big deal. Just *one* of your smiles can light up hundreds of other people's brains. No joke.

UCLA faculty member, Marco Iacoboni, has done a lot of work (e.g., Iacoboni, 2009, a review article) on what neuroscientists call "mirror neurons." Mirrors reflect images, right? Well, that's just what the mirror neurons in the brain do. Sort of.

When a monkey sees a human making a grasping motion (e.g., picking up a stick), the neurons fire in the monkey's brain as if the monkey were actually making that motion. In the same way, when we see a face, the (mirror) neurons in our brains simulate the emotion we "read" in that face. Or, how about this one: You see somebody doing something really, really embarrassing. How does that tend to make you feel? Embarrassed!! It's those little mirror neurons at work again. Iacoboni says that this makes us "hardwired for empathy."

Let's get back to smiles. When you give a big smile, the mirror (smile) neurons in the brains of the people around you start to light up and that's likely to make them smile, or at least increase the probability that they will. You can even make yourself more likely to smile—just put a pencil or pen in your mouth. (SIDEWAYS, of course, not lengthwise.) Holding a pencil or pen like this starts the muscle movement that is required when you smile. So, catch this, people who hold a pencil-like object in their mouths are more likely to laugh at cartoons or jokes. It's like, once you start toward smiling, it's easier to go all the way.

BTW: Next time that you're seated across a desk or table from someone with whom you've been speaking and you notice that both you and the other person have your hands clasped behind your heads, you'll know what's going on in your brain!

It all starts with what psychologists refer to as *self-monitoring*: **Examining our own behavior from the perspective of others.** Most of us are excellent self-monitors *in retrospect*. For example, there's probably not a soul among us who hasn't become angry with a family member and realized after the fact that we simply should not have said some of the hurtful, inaccurate or irrelevant things that we did. (If this has never happened to you, go straight to heaven; do not pass "Go.") So, we all know how to self-monitor. But, timing—as usual—is all. **Great self-monitors are able to turn the clock ahead and evaluate what they say and what they do <u>as it is being said or done</u>.**[8] How do they do that? I recommend three commonly applied means of self-monitoring:

- Establish a practice of mentally imagining that you are "looking down" on the room in which you are interacting with others thereby creating the ability to "watch yourself in action."
- After a meeting, mentally play it back and focus on "prosecuting" each of your statements for rudeness, lack of respectfulness, etc. **You are much less likely to repeat such behaviors once they have been identified and "labeled" as undesirable.**
- Become alert to passing expressions, shifting postures or "side-ways looks" that might be signs of irritation or discomfort and so on.

These methods have been shown to be quite helpful. However, the most effective Change Leaders/consultants never rely entirely on their own abilities to judge situations. **They frequently solicit feedback from colleagues or clients about how they are being perceived.** These conversations can also be used to rectify misunderstandings. Plus, there is yet another notable bonus. Asking for, graciously accepting and acting upon personal feedback has a wonderful side effect. **People who solicit feedback about their <u>own</u> behaviors are also seen as being more caring and concerned about <u>others</u>.**

Making Things (Results) Happen

In 1999, Ulrich, Zenger and Smallwood published a book entitled *Results-based leadership*. I think that it's fair to say that this book had influence of some type on almost all of the leadership theories developed since then. I'm greatly oversimplifying things here. But, the core of that book is the idea that "leaders make things happen." They challenge people to reach difficult goals. They turn ideas into action steps. They persuade people to take the next step and to keep stepping. They work hard to identify and eliminate barriers to progress on goals. They work with speed and intensity. They bounce back from setbacks; they don't become discouraged.

They're like Energizer Bunnies, but with their "eyes" always "on the prize." Oh, but what's the prize, you say? It's: 1) strategy, 2) strategy execution and 3) maintaining alignment with changes in strategy. But, most of all, the prize is having a real understanding of why 1, 2 and 3 are so very important.

Helping People Understand and Internalize the Organization's Overall Strategy and How the Planned Change(s) Are Necessary for the Strategy's Successful Execution

My experience has been that managers at all but the highest levels understand quite well the strategies of their individual units.[9] Understanding the overall organization's strategy, much less being able to articulate it, is a whole other story. And, because of that lack of understanding, the overall strategy's "story" gets told much too infrequently.[10]

In a long-term, comprehensive study of barriers to the successful execution of strategy, Sull, Homkes and Sull (2015) found that only slightly more than half of senior executives reported having a clear sense of how major priorities and initiatives were interrelated while less than one-third of their direct reports could say the same. At the supervisory and team leader level, the "clear sense" percentage dropped to 16 percent. Typically, upon being fed back the results for their particular organization, executives were dumbfounded or incredulous or both.

Nadeau (2014a, 2014b) believes that most employees lack, but need to gain, a deep understanding of strategy. She argues that that understanding can be the emotional "spark" that "builds meaning and purpose for people at work" and therefore is one of the two prerequisites for engagement (the other being trust). But, how can managers provide that understanding of strategy. She suggests that they should 1) **develop and share stories of successful outcomes** resulting from execution of strategy through excellent customer service, knowledge of competitors, accomplishments in other departments, or whatever is at hand and 2) **never miss a teaching moment**[11] that can help someone gain a more nuanced understanding of the strategy. Then managers can:

- help employees envision how they can make contributions to strategy execution themselves—and recognizing and celebrating the occasions when they do;
- involve people in improving alignment between work procedures and processes with strategy;
- ask employees to be alert for and resolve any obstacles that prohibit or slow down strategic execution, etc.

Lacking a "true personal understanding about the organization and its strategy," Nadeau (2014a) argues, employees really can't be expected to develop a "sense of meaning and purpose" in what they do day to day. "In order for strategy to guide priorities, actions and decisions," employees must first have that understanding and be confident that they do.

Based on three global workforce effectiveness studies conducted in 2014, Towers Watson (2015) argues (similarly to Nadeau) that a "crucial" part of every leader's job today is to "clarify what strategy means at the unit level," "consistently reinforce how local contributions add up to enterprise success" and "demonstrate through actions and words the types of behaviors the organization needs to make a well-executed strategy a real source of competitive advantage." In short, the role of the leader "is to make what seems broad and general become concrete and actionable for individual employees."

Maintaining a High Energy Level

If you want to keep "going, and going, and going" like an Energizer Bunny, **you can't neglect your health—as so many leaders/managers do during super-challenging, long-term, large-scale changes.** They work longer hours, their sleep is often fitful and their opportunities to consume vast amounts of sugar and processed foods (whether it be working lunches or unconscious snacking) are virtually unlimited. If they don't manage to give themselves ulcers, it won't be because they haven't tried. So, consider this: Like any activity that requires extraordinary stamina (marathons, mountain climbing, Dancing with the Stars), you should *train* for—be in shape for—leading a major change initiative.

One important aspect of training to lead major change initiatives is to increase the amount of **exercise** . . . blah blah blah blah blah blah blah blah blah blah blah blah blah blah blah blah blah blah.

I knew that as soon as you read the word "exercise" in the previous paragraph you would tune me out. So, I'm not going to even try to go there. **Instead I'm going to suggest one simple way you can train for Change Leadership while you're sitting in your desk chair or in your car: Get more oxygen to your brain!**

Neuroscientist and corporate consultant, Robert Cooper (2002), contends that the majority of people who work in "office jobs" (or, really, any job involving long periods of sitting or stress) typically suffer from somatic contraction. (Picture an accordion with the bellows partly compressed.) This problem, like most, starts with your head (ha, ha) and most people's heads weigh 12–15 pounds, just about the same as bowling balls. Without enough strengthening of specific muscles, our neck and shoulders and back get awfully tired of holding up the old Brunswick for hours on end, and so we "slump" at our desks and at the conference table. When we do that, we cut off as much as 30 percent of the oxygen (and the blood that carries it) that is supposed to go to our brains. This is a shame, as our brains are particularly fond of oxygen. In fact, our brains are so oxygen-fond that the darn things will die on us if they go without oxygen for even a few minutes. And, here we are cutting off the supply of oxygen by 30 percent ALL DAY LONG, EVERY DAY!

Now, the fix for this is really rather simple and can actually be fun. Cooper says that in order to reverse somatic contraction, you have to strengthen the cervical anterior muscles in the back of your neck. And, how do you do that? Well, I'll give you one example. First, you pretend that you have a book or a beanbag or something sitting on top of your head. Now, raise your head and stretch your neck by pushing that book or beanbag closer to the ceiling. (You should immediately feel more air rush into your lungs!) Next, with your head held high, nod very slowly three times, turn your head to the far left, nod slowly three more times, and then turn your head to the far right and nod yet three more times (all the while with your neck stretched as much as possible). Repeat the whole thing maybe half a dozen times each day at work. Pretty soon, your heavy, old Brunswick will feel like an Ebonite Light. (What's fun about that, you say? Well, I did say that it was fun, didn't I? Okay. I confess. I like to do this drill when I pull up next to another car at a stop sign. It's impossible not to have fun when you see the reaction that it gets.)

Taking Time to Step Back/to Reflect

> We do not learn from experience . . . we learn from reflecting on experience.
> —John Dewey (quoted in Burke & Noumair, 2015, p. 279)

With the daunting scope and complexity of many organizational changes today, it's so very, very easy to get caught up in the "now," the present. And the "now" usually means fighting fires, herding stray cats, resolving conflicts, correcting mistakes, finding more resources—in general, keeping things in line (or, perhaps, keeping things from imploding), high stress tasks all. **But, the deeper you allow yourself to get into the "now," the further the "now" tends to diverge from the "should be."**

Yes, you need to make things happen. Yes, you should be action-oriented. Yes, you have to be responsive and available. Yes, you have to be on top of things. Yet, within the "now," you have to make sure that you regularly step back, step away, get out of the line of fire and take the time to reflect, to calmly look hard at the big picture, or what John Candy might have called, "the WHOLE enchilada, the WHOLE ball of wax, the WHOLE megillah," the *whole* organizational change.

A considerable amount of research (c.f., Di Stefano, Gino, Pisano & Staats, 2014; Paese, 2007) has shown **change managers (and top managers in general) characteristically have grossly insufficient opportunities to focus on the big scheme of things and their ability to reflect thoughtfully is often lost completely.** Many change managers think that this is simply a sacrifice that they have to make (even as they see a spillover of stress and anxiety into their personal lives). They think that every moment they might spend in reflection takes away from their job performance—when just the opposite is true. **When key leaders don't force themselves to reflect, the result is almost always significant lapses in judgment and performance, with objectives critical to business and personal success being compromised as a result.**

Rid yourself of any guilt associated with making and taking the time for quiet reflection. <u>All great (change) leaders do</u>.

So far, I've covered some key behaviors that you need to manifest if you are going to be highly effective as a Change Leader. **Now, I'm going to draw your attention to a classic behavior pattern that you need to avoid.**

Unbridled Achievement Orientation

If you find yourself called upon to be a manager (or perform another key role) in leading a major organizational change, chances are it's because you've been a high performer over time in your organization. Many, but certainly not all, high performers are classic over-achievers. They don't want to reach their goals for the quarter, they want to pulverize them. Being average or even "good" is a painful experience. They don't want to be anything but the best at what they do. They're high-energy (that's good), driven from within (that's good up to a point) and highly competitive (that might or might not be good depending upon the situation).

Many classic over-achievers find satisfying and lucrative careers in sales, science and engineering. There's always a potential new customer out there, another important discovery to be made or some beautiful new thing to build. Usually, over-achievers make excellent individual contributors. It's only when recruited (or drafted) into management/leadership positions that their Achilles' Heels start to radiate and their strong drives need to be dampened or re-directed.

The primary doubled-sided blind-spot for over-achievers as managers is a very strong self- (rather than other-) focus and a corresponding belief that all others are like (i.e., similar to) them or want to be. As a result, they work at a pace that is too fast for most of their reports and are widely impatient with poor performance. They typically have too much of some things and not enough of others (just like the rest of us). Most often, they have too much focus on goals (rather than on people) and on their immediate work units (rather than on the organization as a whole). Generally, they don't particularly value feedback from their bosses, as they like to "keep score" in other ways, such as sales volume and size of bonuses or pay raises. And, they don't like to be told how to do something; they feel hemmed in by directions or detailed guidance. So, you guessed it: They don't bother to provide much feedback/encouragement to others, nor do they provide much in the way of structure or guidance on how-to.

The good news is that over-achievers are "trainable" and often make great managers/leaders. **The key is to be able to focus their attention on "achieving" great performance** *as a manager/leader of others*, **rather than on only "making their numbers" or winning whatever particular competition in which they are engaged.**

What's the reason for talking about this possible leadership liability of over-achievers in a book on enterprise-wide change? There are two. **First, if you happen to be a world-class over-achiever and are asked to play a major role in a change effort, I hope that mentioning this Achilles' Heel here might help you recognize some of these tendencies in yourself and motivate you to cool (actually, redirect) your jets a bit accordingly. Second, if you don't fit the classic over-achiever profile, I'd like you to be prepared for the fact that you're going to be working with several leaders on the**

team who do. Virtually every change management team with which I've worked over the last 40 years has included several over-achievers drafted into leadership positions—some for the very first time. Forewarned is forearmed; remember the key is to redirect their special energies toward people and toward the change process as a whole and away from taking someone else's Bishop off the board.

Notes

1 In *Managing the dream: Reflections on leadership and change*, Warren Bennis (2000, p. 58) famously wrote that:

> Character [integrity, etc.] is the key to leadership, a fact confirmed by most people's experiences, as it is in my 15 years of work with over 150 leaders, and in the other studies I've encountered. Research at Harvard University indicates that 85% of a leader's performance depends on personal character.

2 Leslie also shows that effective lying is regrettably related to the likelihood of being promoted or being seen as a good performer in the workplace.

3 Dan Ariely (e.g., Ariely, 2012), a behavioral economist at Duke, has conducted many well-designed studies that demonstrate (sometimes quite amusingly) how we deceive ourselves into believing that we're much more often truthful than we really are.

4 A notorious example of the latter is Staples' store managers who had been found to instruct employees that if they didn't think that they could sell at least $200 worth of peripherals or useless warranties (that covered the same possible problems as the manufacturer) with the purchase of a computer, they were to tell the customer that the computer was not in stock (Siegal, 2012). The incentive was to avoid lowering the average sales receipt—a key metric for evaluating managers.

5 In many management training programs I've conducted, this recommendation to "be your best self at all times" is contested by a few participants who argue that it is "deceitful" (or "it's just putting on a show" or "putting on an act"). I usually respond by arguing that it's role-appropriate behavior that is similar to patiently listening to an employee who is having difficulty communicating something that is not of great importance to you or to being nice to in-laws or customers whom you don't like. Further, I indicate that "deceit" implies trickery or taking advantage of the other party—neither of which applies here. When managers are their best selves, even if they don't come by it naturally; it works to the benefit of all parties.

6 History repeats itself: NJ Gov. Chris Christie made the same sort of gaffe at a press conference when he declared in response to a reporter's question, "I am not a bully!"

7 **So**, what happens with New Year's Resolutions? They're almost always "broken" and, usually, they are broken embarrassingly early in the new year. Why? Is it simply because people lack appropriate resolve? Well, commitment is definitely a factor. But, even high levels of commitment/resolve can be trumped **when your brain is working against you sticking to what you have resolved to do**.

   As you'll see in Chapter 2, a fundamental operating imperative of the human brain is to conserve energy. So, your brain—the part that controls "automatic" behaviors unconsciously at least—prefers to take the easier of any two options. What's easier, going to the gym right after work or going directly home or out for a beer with friends?

   On the other hand, if used as designed, processes like the Pick 3 method get your brain working on "your side." That's because—at least twice a day—you give your brain reminders of what you have resolved. That takes decision-making out of the automatic mode allowing you to deal with your choices more consciously.

8 At the Center for Creative Leadership (CCL), they refer to this type of self-monitoring as "Conscious Engagement." CCL staffers have written an excellent white paper on the concept of conscious engagement and how it fits in the overall CCL Leadership Model and how "leadership is all in your mind" (Clerkin, Ruderman & Connolly, 2014).
9 If those unit-level strategies exist—which often they do not.
10 Keller and Price (2011, Kindle location 2623) note that another story, the story of the focal organizational change itself, must also be retold frequently:

> To have a sustained effect, the change story must be told over and over again to remind employees where they are heading, and to highlight places where the transformation is already achieving results. Recognizing how important this is, organizations such as technology company 3M and NASA (National Aeronautics and Space Administration) go to the lengths of building storytelling skills into the curriculum of their leadership development programs.

11 In his book, *The leadership engine* (2002), Noel Tichy, used the phrase "a teachable point of view." Sales literature accompanying the book indicates that he "coined" the term.

References

All web site URLs accessed on December 12, 2015.

Ariely, D. (2012). *The honest truth about dishonesty: How we lie to everyone including ourselves.* New York, NY: HarperCollins.

Bennis, W. (2000). *Managing the dream: Reflections on leadership and change.* Cambridge, MA: Perseus Press.

Blaine, J. (2013). Leading and managing in the 2020 multi-dimensional workplace. *Cegos-Temasek Polytechnic-STADA Partnership Research Report.* Retrieved from www.slideshare.net/JeremyBlain/leading-and-managing-in-the-2020-workplace-challenges-for-gen-x-leaders-in-waiting.

Boatman, J. & Wellins, R. (2011). Time for a leadership revolution. *Development Dimensions International Global Leadership Forecast.* Retrieved from www.ddiworld.com/glf2011#.VBtAghbl-PU.

Burke, W. & Noumair, D. (2015). *Organization development: A process of learning and change.* Upper Saddle River, NJ: Pearson Education.

Clerkin, C., Ruderman, M. & Connolly, C. (2014). *Outstanding leadership: It's all in your mind.* Center for Creative Leadership, White Paper. Retrieved from www.leadingeffectively.com/outstanding-leadership-its-all-in-your-mind/.

Cooper, R. (2002). *The other 90%.* New York, NY: Crown Business.

Di Stefano, G., Gino, F., Pisano, G. & Staats, B. (2014). Learning by thinking: How reflection improves performance. Harvard Business School. Working paper. Retrieved from http://hbswk.hbs.edu/item/learning-by-thinking-how-reflection-improves-performance.

Gentry, W., Eckert, R., Stawiski, S. & Zhao, S. (2014). *The challenges leaders face around the world.* Center for Creative Leadership, White Paper. Retrieved from www.ccl.org/leadership/pdf/research/ChallengesLeadersFace.pdf.

Iacoboni, M. (2009). Imitation, empathy, and mirror neurons. *Annual Review of Psychology, 60,* 653–670.

Keller, S. & Price, C. (2011). *Beyond performance: How great organizations build ultimate competitive advantage.* Wiley: Kindle Edition.

Leslie, I. (2011). *Born liars: Why we can't live without deceit*. London, U.K.: Quercus.

Leslie, J. (2009). *The leadership gap: What you need, and don't have, when it comes to leadership talent*. Center for Creative Leadership, White Paper. Retrieved from www.ccl.org/leadership/pdf/research/leadershipGap.pdf.

Nadeau, R. (2014a). *The #1 mistake managers make*. Prism Perspectives Group, July 14, White Paper. Retrieved from https://prismperspectivesgroup.wordpress.com/2014/07/08/the-1-mistake-managers-make/.

Nadeau, R. (2014b). *Leaders: Do your people really understand the business strategy?* Prism Perspectives Group, April 14, White Paper. Retrieved from www.hrcsuite.com/understanding-the-business-strategy/.

Nixon, R. (1973). Speech transcript. *President's Address to Attendees at the Annual Convention of the Associate Press Managing Editors Association*. November 17. Orlando, FL: Contemporary Hotel at Walt Disney World.

Paese, M. (2007). *Managing complexity at the top*. Development Dimensions International, White Paper. Retrieved from www.ddiworld.com/resources/library/articles/managing-complexity-at-the-top.

Shulman, D. (2007). *From hire to liar: The role of deception in the workplace*. Ithaca, NY: Cornell University Press.

Siegal, D. (2012). Selling it with extras or not at all. *The New York Times*, September 8. Retrieved from www.nytimes.com/2012/09/09/your-money/sales-incentives-at-staples-draw-complaints-the-haggler.html?pagewanted=1&_r=0&ref=staplesinc.

Sull, D., Homkes, R. & Sull, C. (2015). Why strategy execution unravels – and what to do about it. *Harvard Business Review*, *93(3)*, 57–66.

Tichy, N. (2002). *The leadership engine: How winning companies build leaders at every level*. New York, NY: HarperCollins.

Towers Watson. (2015). *Effective managers: Your crucial link to successful strategy execution*. Towers Watson, White Paper. Retrieved from www.towerswatson.com/en-US/Insights/IC-Types/Ad-hoc-Point-of-View/Perspectives/2015/effective-managers.

Ulrich, D., Zenger, J. & Smallwood, N. (1999). *Results-based leadership*. Cambridge, MA: Harvard University Press.

Zenger, J. & Folkman, J. (2002). *The extraordinary leader: Turning good managers into great leaders*. New York, NY: McGraw-Hill.

2

THE BRAIN AND HUMAN BEHAVIOR AT WORK (AND EVERYWHERE ELSE)

This is by far the longest chapter in the entire Guide. There are several reasons for that:

1. The **"human element" in organizational change is typically the major impediment** to unqualified success and it's definitely the component of change that is least understood by the people who are responsible for implementing major change initiatives (Fugate, Kinicki & Prussia, 2008; Jorgensen, Owen & Neus, 2008; Savolainen, 2013; Seo et al., 2012).
2. To be effective as a Change Leader or change management consultant, **you have to be very good at persuasion**, i.e., getting other people to do what should or needs to be done, despite any initial or continuing opposition on their part. And, **it's virtually impossible to be a great persuader unless you have a thorough understanding of why people behave the way that they do at work**.
3. **Human behavior is extremely complex. At the same time, it is highly predictable** *if you have an appropriate (and relatively easily learned) lens through which to view it.* (I'll get back to this lens-concept in a later section.)

In this chapter, I'm going to present some behavior basics, the understanding of which I believe to be critical to successful change management, much less true Change Leadership. **I'm going to approach the neural (brain-controlled) basis of human behavior from three primary (psychological, physiological and evolutionary) perspectives.** At present, there are no contradictions or incompatibilities among the three approaches. However, in the last decade, the mainstream psychological perspective has had to make some self-corrections to account for a number of recent findings in SCN research (i.e., the knowledge well-spring of the physiological perspective).

Internal and External Influences on Behavior

Kurt Lewin, about whom much information follows in later sections, came up with a formula that is considered the most basic building block in understanding human behavior:

$B = f(P, E)$ **[Behavior is a function of both the person and the environment.]**

That is, there are internal and external causes of behavior. If you want to influence behavior, you can attempt to change the person or change the environment (or both) (Shoda, 2004).

> Q. Of the two, person or environment, which one is easier to change?
> A. The environment.

> Q. Of the two, person or environment, which one do most managers concentrate on when they are attempting to change someone else's behavior?
> A. The person.

> Q. Is that smart?
> A. No.

Consider this: I have a 9″ × 9″ solid wooden beam in a 15-foot length. I place the beam on the floor in the lobby of the building where you work. I then ask you and nine of your physically unhampered colleagues to come to the lobby and, forming a single line, walk on the beam from one end to the other. This would likely be a very simple thing for each of you to do. Some may wonder why they were asked to do it. But, it's likely that none would refuse.

Now consider this: I place two, 10-foot, sturdy stepladders approximately 13 feet apart and securely bolt each of them to the floor of the lobby. I then take the same 9″ × 9″ × 15′ beam and secure it atop the ladders. (For visualization: This would result in a structure somewhat akin to a tall, very solidly built saw-horse. Imagine that there is no chance that it will fall or even sway the tiniest bit.) This time, the task I ask the ten of you to accomplish is to climb a ladder, stand on the beam, walk across the beam to its other end and then climb down the second ladder.

What would happen this time? In all likelihood:

- some people would refuse to even try;
- those who attempt to complete the task would suffer some amount of anxiety or fear, whether a little or a lot;
- one or more of you might fall from the beam and seriously hurt yourselves.

Hah! I know what you are thinking. You're thinking that, yeah, well, of course the task of walking across the beam would be tougher in the second "environment" than in the first. But, it's a preposterous example. Work environments don't inhibit performance . . .

But, they do. Every day. Every single day. In every large organization. The truth is that most work environments don't lend themselves very well to . . . Well, they don't lend themselves very well to work! Brain and behavior expert, John Medina (2008, p. 5) says that:

> If you wanted to create an education environment that was directly opposed to what the brain was good at doing, you probably would design something like a classroom. If you wanted to create a business environment that was directly opposed to what the brain was good at doing, you probably would design something like a cubicle. And if you wanted to change things, you might have to tear down both and start over.

How common are *environmental* problems such as these? (**Very**; I've seen all of them myself):

- Gail's computer has a 17-inch screen and at any one time, she can see a maximum of 50 percent of the spreadsheets with which she must work.
- Bill can't complete his daily work because he is continually interrupted by others who need his help.
- Jean and Phil are supposed to keep each other informed of all developments in their respective departments. But, their departments aren't located in the same building and they almost never see each other by chance.
- The training manuals for the new software system provide generic instruction. The materials haven't been tailored to the version of the software as customized for Joann's company.
- Janet's cube is near the copier and vending machines where everyone hangs out to chat.
- The monthly reports that Sam obtains don't include the kind of metrics he needs to improve any of the production processes in his shop.
- Gary is the CFO of a company that has recently been acquired by a German firm that uses a completely different kind of enterprise-wide software/information/accounting system.

Bottom line: If you want to change (improve) performance, look FIRST at what you might helpfully change (fix) in the environment (E) before you start trying to change the people (P) involved. And, it's so easy to remember:

Before you go to P, think about E! (small joke)

EXPERTS' INSIGHTS: A "GOOD" WORK ENVIRONMENT IS NOT INTUITIVELY OBVIOUS

Effective Change Leaders and consultants know that environmental problems are not always as obvious as those in the bulleted list shown previously. **In many cases, you can't simply look at the work environment and decide whether it (or any part thereof) is "good" or "bad."** In fact, what really works for the best is often counter-intuitive. Police patrol units are a good example.

What do you think is safer for police officers who are assigned to neighborhood patrols: One officer per car or two officers? Which do you think is safer for criminals and non-criminal citizens: One officer or two per car?

Well, if you said two per car, you'd certainly be in agreement with patrol officers themselves. When given the option, patrol officers overwhelmingly choose to work in pairs. Partner officers provide conversation that makes time on uneventful patrols pass more quickly, they provide second opinions when there is time to consider options and any officer will say that their partner "has my back."

Nonetheless, evidence supports the opposite. That is, one-person patrols have lower incidences of injury to both officers and citizens (criminal or non-) than do two-person patrols. Why? Well, it's pretty complicated. But, at the simplest level, the answer is that officers working together take more chances because they "feel safer" in pairs. Officers working alone are less confrontational and more cautious, at least in part because they feel more vulnerable when they must operate without a partner (Boystun, Sherry & Moelter, 1977; Scoville, 2011). Go figure, huh?

So how do you tell what works? Ideally, you'd do just what police departments all around the country have done, **try different variations, in different kinds of situations, and carefully record performance on as many objective measures as is practical. Then, let the data speak.**

A Psychological Perspective on Behavior

Please read the following list carefully!

- Maslow's Hierarchy of Needs
- Herzberg's Motivator-Hygiene Theory
- Attribution Theory
- Expectancy Theory
- Equity Theory
- (Need for) Achievement Theory
- Behavior Modification
- Theory X and Theory Y
- The Theory of Cognitive Dissonance
- Goal-Setting Theory.

Now, and this is very important, **forget everything you've ever heard about these things**. (Yes, I am totally serious.)

Why? Pick up any textbook on work motivation and you'll likely find that this is the format:[1]

I. Theory 1

   a. Explanation of the theory
   b. Example of a study or two where the theory seemed to "work" (i.e., accurately predict the behavior of some of the participants)
   c. Example of more than one or two studies where the theory didn't seem to work
   d. Possible explanation for why the theory doesn't work in many circumstances.

II. Theory 2

   a. Explanation of the theory
   b. Example of a study or two where the theory seemed to "work" (i.e., accurately predict the behavior of some of the participants)
   c. Example of more than one or two studies where the theory didn't seem to work
   d. Possible explanation for why the theory doesn't work in many circumstances.

III. Theory 3...

Get the idea? Well, even if you do, this is a dead horse that I'm going to continue to beat. But, first . . .

BRAIN CONNECTION! METAPHORS AND STORIES

It's said that we *learn through metaphors* (Lakoff, 2008) **and we remember through stories** (Gottschall, 2013). That is, **our brains store all information in the form of stories**. So, here's a story. (**Remember it!**)[2]

Once upon a time . . .

. . . at Harvard, there was a famous professor by the name of David McClelland. He was hired by some insurance companies to help them do a better job of selecting sales people. McClelland predicted that people who have a high need for achievement (i.e., those who preferred to work toward and accomplish challenging goals) would make better sales people than those who have this need to a lesser extent or not at all.

The insurance companies started using the "test" of need for achievement that McClelland proposed. In the test, candidates for sales jobs were asked to make up a story about each of several pictures. One picture showed a man sitting at a drawing table on which there were architectural and design tools. The man was looking out of the window next to the table and he was smiling.

Stories that applicants told about this particular picture, at the extremes, tended to fall into two categories:

1. The man is thinking about a (building, bridge, whatever) that he is designing and he knows that it's going to be the best (building, bridge, what-have-you) ever designed. That's why he's smiling.
2. The man is thinking about the vacation he is going to take next week with his family. He can picture himself having fun doing (whatever) and that's why he's smiling.

As you might guess, the job applicants who told a story more like number 1 than number 2 were thought to have higher needs for achievement and were awarded higher test scores. The insurance companies then began hiring only those applicants with the best scores. And, guess what? McClelland's theory worked! That is, people hired on the basis of their need for achievement scores sold more insurance on average than did people who had been hired on the basis of other criteria. But . . .

Q. Did everyone who obtained a high test score have above average sales?
A. No.

Q. Was an individual's sales revenue on average proportional to the size of that person's need for achievement score?
A. No.

Yet, on average, overall sales increased when applicants who had the highest need for achievement scores were hired. Given this bottom-line success, the theory and the need for achievement test were applied elsewhere.

Eventually, this selection method was tried in a Japanese company. Did it work there? Nope. Japanese were found to be extremely likely to meet their need for "achievement" by collaborating with others, not by competing with or beating them (as American sales people might) (Colon, 2011; Holloway, 1988). Thus, they uniformly scored very poorly on McClelland's test. In fact, there was so little variance (variation) in the scores that it would have been impossible to use them to separate out prospective employees into likely to succeed vs. unlikely to succeed categories.

So ... Like almost all the other theories of human motivation, Need for Achievement Theory **can predict—with marginal accuracy—the behavior of some people in some circumstances**. But, when you are trying to get hundreds or thousands of people to change from Behavior A to Behavior B across a wide variety of situations (as you must in an enterprise-wide change project), **none of these theories taken individually is going to help you much.** And, trying to keep them all in your head and figure out which one applies best in one situation vs. another would certainly be an impossible task.

As alluded earlier, many psychologists and other motivational theorists believe that there is one need (or "motive") that is trans-personal, trans-situational and trans-cultural. Meaning that this need is applicable to almost every person, in almost every circumstance, in almost every part of the world. This is the need to either enhance (whenever possible), or at least to protect or maintain, one's self-image (i.e., how positively or negatively one views one's self).

Today, most psychologists believe that people in every culture around the world have this fundamental drive to think favorably of themselves (rather than unfavorably) and that positive self-images are strongly and consistently associated with both psychological well-being and effective performance (both job performance and "life" performance). In contrast, threats to self-images often result in direct and powerful negative effects on general psychological well-being and on everyday behavior (Snyder & Williams, 1982). (In fact, many psychologists believe that when people commit suicide, it's because those people can think of no other way to stop the downward spiral of their self-images (Baumeister, 1990).)

Saying this in another, simpler way, **people's brains are powerfully attracted to situations in which they believe they will "look good" ... and, they avoid situations—sometimes even at great personal cost—where they expect that they will "look bad"** (or even "not good"—as seen through their own eyes).

Now, as you read the previous sentence, you might have been thinking that the point being made could be nominated for a prize at the International Championship of the Obvious. But, the implications of the point are not obvious as all.

Here's how it all gets applied to work performance: Don't view poorly performing employees (or colleagues or bosses) as unmotivated or un-influenced by their managers. Instead, **focus on the fact that humans are always motivated to maintain or enhance their self-images** (i.e., the personal view of ourselves that is our mental image or self-portrait; it's a collective representation of our assets and liabilities as we see them).

The difference between high-performing employees and low performers is not in the levels of their motivation. All workers are fully motivated at all times. However, high performers perceive good performance as a means of maintaining or enhancing their self-images,

whereas low performers see poor performance (or not trying hard to perform well) as providing this fundamental function (Snyder & Williams, 1982).

A common example of the latter is the person who is recently promoted to first-line management and who fails to train subordinates to do certain parts of their jobs or who fails to delegate appropriate levels of authority to subordinates. These behaviors might not be effective in the eyes of the organization, but they might be highly effective in allowing this new manager to retain personally desired levels of power or control (i.e., part of a positive self-image, as defined by this particular employee) (Snyder, 1998a, 1998b).

Okay, now let's apply these concepts to major change initiatives. Your role as a Change Leader or change management consultant is to get people to adopt the newly expected/required behaviors as quickly and as willingly as possible. **Your ability to succeed at this challenging role will be significantly enhanced if you keep reminding yourself to operate within a self-image maintenance or enhancement framework.** That is, focusing on how you can help people feel better about themselves if they work hard to implement and adopt the new system. **On the other hand, if people don't move in the direction in which you're trying to "herd" them, try to identify the possible threats to their self-images that might be involved and do whatever you can to reduce or eliminate those threats** (Snyder & Williams, 1982). A lot more on this is forthcoming.

EXPERTS' INSIGHTS: MAKING PEOPLE FEEL GOOD ABOUT THEIR PERFORMANCES

A big part of aligning self-image enhancement and high performance involves the judicious use of feedback. Here are some things to keep in mind as you provide feedback to colleagues or customers—whether a high-level executive or the lowest-paid person in the organization. (It's just a "teaser," there's lots more on feedback to come.)

1. **One old maxim certainly holds true: "Praise in public, criticize in private."** For most people, few things are more threatening to one's self-image than being criticized in front of co-workers—or worse still—in front of the "boss." In addition to looking for a private way of providing corrective feedback, you have to be sure that you can provide it calmly. Sometimes, this might even mean waiting until the next day to address an issue. Although, when your emotions aren't involved, feedback (whether positive or negative) should be as close in time to the actual performance as possible.

When you must provide corrective feedback, make sure that it is specific (e.g., ". . . when these kinds of invoices arrive in your system, the very first thing that needs doing is . . .") and focused entirely on performance, not the person.

2. **If you want your praise to have the intended impact, watch out for "blanket recognition."** Example: Ann, Mark and Courtney work on delineating

each of the steps in a complicated manual process that will soon be automated. Their report turns out to be excellent. However, you are aware that Mark and Courtney did almost all of the work and Ann, if anything, was more of an obstacle than an asset. In these circumstances, you should try to avoid situations in which you need to praise the group for its work. If you were to do that, it's likely that it would greatly decrease the impact of the praise on Mark and Courtney and it sends a clear message to other change-project team members that you don't have to contribute to a sub-project to get by (with flying colors, even). So what do you do?

In public you can focus on the quality of the work product and use phrases like, "this was a really outstanding job," without specifically mentioning any of the individuals. It's usually best to follow up a situation like this by telling Mark and Courtney individually how much you appreciate their fine work. (Guidelines for dealing with Ann will come later.)

3. **Another old saying that applies well to effective feedback: "Don't kill the messenger."** To be successful at leading change, you have to find ways to encourage people to voluntarily inform you of things that aren't going as planned. Likewise, you have to be prepared to handle bad news in a positive way. Be aware that even "off-hand" comments can be misperceived. For example, if you respond to bad news with a negative exclamation (e.g., "Oh, crap!!!"), this might seem to you to be simply and entirely a result of your frustration—or perhaps even a self-condemnation (e.g., "Why didn't I see that coming?"). However, to the people who provide the news, it will often "feel" as a criticism of **their** behavior.

4. **Praise given at the completion of a major project task should be an "automatic."** However, task completion is sometimes a reward in itself. With difficult tasks, it is often the case that people more dearly need praise and encouragement while the effort is still underway. So, don't wait until end-points to "make people feel good about their performance."[3]

5. From expert-on-human-behavior, Maya Angelou: "I've learned that people will forget what you said, people will forget what you did, but people will never forget how you made them feel."

A Physiological Perspective on Behavior

And, now, for something entirely different . . .

The "psychological" perspective on human behavior that I covered in the preceding section has been around for a long time. Much more recently, an entirely different (but, totally compatible) view of behavior has evolved, primarily through the work of neuroscientists. It focuses on "brain wiring," i.e., the electro-chemically based circuitry in the brain.[4]

Through the use of a variety of brain activity recording devices, it has now been established beyond all doubt that **every time you learn something, the circuitry in your brain undergoes a measurable, physiological change**.

That is, the circuitry reprograms itself in much the same way that a computer can be reprogrammed.[5]

Consider this example: You see a story in your daily newspaper entitled, "World's Most Widely Recognized American." You read the story and find out that it is Muhammad Ali who holds this distinction. Instantly, in a way similar to how electrons flow across computer circuitry, your brain now sends an electro-chemical impulse from the neuron that has just stored the concept "World's Most Widely Recognized American" along a neural pathway to the neuron(s) in which your knowledge of "Muhammad Ali" has been stored. That is, a new (yet relatively weak) circuit is hard-wired within your brain's (neural) network.

To continue with the same example: Six months later, a friend of yours wonders aloud who the most globally well-known American might be. If you think immediately of Ali, it is a result of the previously created circuit (connecting "Muhammad Ali" and "World's Most Widely Recognized American") being reactivated. However, the brain tends to "**prune**" connections (circuits) that aren't used frequently—especially if the circuit hasn't been used many times in total. So, if this same question arises five years later (yet did not arise in the interim), you might not think of Ali as a possibly correct answer. That once-active connection is no longer retrievable (i.e., it is forgotten).

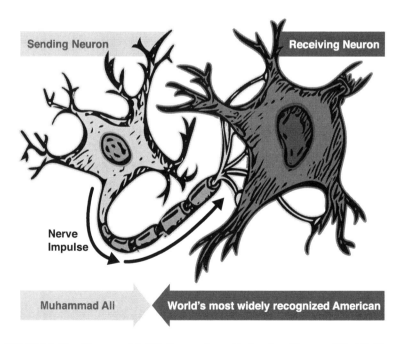

FIGURE 2.1 One Concept (M. Ali) Connecting with Another Concept (World's Most Widely Recognized American) Electro-Chemically in the Brain

> ## BRAIN CONNECTION!
>
> Why are there some things that you don't ever forget (e.g., your SSN, your middle name)? Later, I'll provide a fuller explanation. But, for now, I'd like you to know that REPETITION plays a huge role. With this "Ali" example, suppose you obtained a job as a guide for the Muhammad Ali Museum in Louisville, KY. If you told 6–8 groups of visitors each day (possibly for years on end) that Ali is the world's most widely recognized American, it would be very unlikely that that link would ever be pruned by your brain (i.e., you'll likely remember it until the day you die).
>
> The format of this Guide takes advantage of the power of repetition: Any given important concept or consulting tactic will appear in more than one section and will be expressed in more than one way (e.g., a different example of the same phenomenon).

Let's look at another example of a simple, neuron-to-neuron, physiological connection being created: Jen, your friend whom for years you have called frequently, changes her phone number to 545.9718. She calls you while you're driving to work (your phone is in your briefcase just out of reach, but you can talk with Jen through the dashboard speaker) and reports the change. If you say the new number aloud several times, you have a better chance of remembering it than if you listened only. When you hear the new number, your brain creates a circuit between "Jennifer" and "545.9718." However, when you repeat the number three times, that circuit gets used again, then again, then a fourth time. So, it has become a stronger, faster (ever so slightly more durable) circuit.

A few days later, (using your land line at home which lacks a call directory) you decide to call Jen. You "automatically" punch in her old number. Why? Because the "Jen to old number" circuit has been reactivated hundreds of times and so it is much stronger (and faster to activate) than the newer one for Jen's current number (Duhigg, 2012).[6]

Now, here's an example of a really, really strong circuit: Back in the day, most Americans had a cigarette and coffee after dinner. Do this most days for ten years and you have a circuit that has been reactivated over 3,500 times. As a result, people who are attempting to quit smoking often find that sticking to their pledge is hardest right after dinner. Behavior associated with very strong circuits such as these can be extremely difficult to change. For example . . .

In work organizations, managers often assume that if they explain clearly and compellingly the need for change, then the behavior of reasonable people will fall in line. Clear and compelling communication is undoubtedly an important part of any behavior change campaign. However, a single communication is the equivalent of your friend, Jen, telling you her new phone number. **The communication creates** a circuit, but it's likely to be weak in comparison with competing cir-cuits—especially when ultra-strong, often-used brain circuits are already in play, as they typically are in "routinized" work behavior patterns.

BRAIN CONNECTION! THE BRAIN IS A CONSERVATIONIST

For reasons detailed later in the section "An Evolutional (that is, Evolution-Based) Perspective on Behavior," the human brain is designed to conserve its energy. After many repetitions of a specific behavior in a specific cir-cumstance, the brain no longer has to "work" to decide what to do in that circumstance—it simply initiates the behavior that is wired to it. As a result, in the everyday course of events, you don't have to think about how to open your car door or how to tie your shoes. When *complex patterns* of behavior are repeated often enough, those patterns (switching from speaking one language to another) can also become "automatic."

Conservation of the brain's energy is critical for survival. So, the brain "protects" its strong circuits—the ones that result in automatic behaviors—by releasing noxious neurochemicals if we try to substitute a different behavior. Thus, people who are prevented from performing their routine work behav-iors due to a prescribed organizational change can easily suffer as much (often much, much more) psychological *and* physiological discomfort as those who are trying not to have a cigarette after dinner.

The Infrastructure of Brain Circuitry (**Greatly** Oversimplified and **Metaphor**-Based)[7]

Our senses are continuously bombarded with stimuli (things we see, hear, touch, etc.). Before making their way to the brain, these stimuli must pass through the equivalent of a spam filter. This enables the brain to put aside the vast majority of (apparently useless) stimuli and keep itself from being overloaded. **(In any given** *second*, **the sensory system sends the brain about** *11 million bits of information but it can actively process less than 50 of them* (Mlodinow, 2012).)

Most of the remaining stimuli are encoded to the brain's largest storage area called long-term memory. This is where the brain maintains hard-wired (i.e., strong, fast and durable) circuits. That is, all the things we know—but which we are not actively considering or thinking about. Long-term memory has a colossal capacity and requires very little energy to do its job of being a storage facility. (For someone living in a cold-weather state, it would be analogous to keeping an extra case of sodas in the garage during the winter. You don't need those sodas right now; yet, you know that you can go and get them if you do—and they will be cold. Yet, it doesn't require any additional energy to store the sodas in an already chilly garage like it would in a refrigerator.) This is a very important advantage of long-term memory because, as indicated above, **the brain overall is biologically programmed to be as energy efficient as possible**.

Recent SCN research has demonstrated conclusively that the brain hardwires every connection that it can. To conserve energy, the brain sends stimuli to the apparently appropriate "folder" in long-term memory as soon as it detects an absolute minimum level of similarity to an established set of connections/circuits. Of course, this results in many **erroneous connections being stored together**. These include **mistaken beliefs** (e.g., all dogs shed), **misunderstandings** (e.g., thinking that an appointment was set for 4 p.m., when 3 p.m. was actually the appointed time), **misperceptions** (e.g., "hearing" someone say one thing when another thing was actually said) and so on. Furthermore, information stored in long-term memory is consistently undergoing de-fragmentation as apparently related data are compressed and compacted—**making it more difficult for the brain to identify bits of data that do not belong in a particular set of connections** (i.e., in that folder).

Stimuli that are not filtered out as spam or sent to long-term memory are sent to an area of the brain called **working memory** (very roughly the equivalent of system memory in a computer). Here, in temporary residence, are the stimuli that the brain wants to actively consider; those that are perceived as new or relevant or important for decision-making or problem-solving or other types of **connection-making**. Again, classification mistakes can be made and, as a result, (irrelevant or incorrect) information can be held in short-term memory that only interferes with accurate connection-making or decision-making.

In terms of fuel (energy) consumption, working memory is a 1957 Cadillac hearse and long-term memory is a brand-new Vespa motor scooter. So to reduce its energy usage, working memory tends to "jump to conclusions" (i.e., make decisions very quickly; **it strongly favors speed over accuracy**). (The evolutionary basis of this speed-over-accuracy function is explained later in the section "An Evolutional (that is, Evolution-Based) Perspective on Behavior.")

Brain circuits become faster, stronger and more durable the more times they are activated.

Attention and action activate the brain's circuits. That is, you can activate a circuit by thinking about the connection it represents or by acting out the connection. For example, most people learned multiplication by focusing on "multiplication tables" or flash cards and by saying "multiplication facts" aloud (over and over; **attention**) and solving multiplication problems (**action**). Each time, we saw "3 × 4 = 12" or recited that equality or filled in the number 12 next to "3 × 4 = ," we reactivated the circuit between this specific pair of factors and their product. As these individual circuits are reactivated repeatedly, a myelin sheath (a white, fatty substance generated by the brain) grows over the connection increasing the speed with which it is activated. The effect is much like what happens when a CAT-5 cable is replaced with a CAT-6.[8]

In the same way, the more often you repeat a relatively complex behavior pattern, the stronger the associated brain circuits become and the less you have to think about them in order to successfully re-manifest the behaviors involved. The lower need for focused thinking occurs with strong circuits because you do not need to search in long-term memory for connections, retrieve them to working memory, check their relevance and decide how to apply them. It's all "automatic." Hundreds, sometimes thousands, of our behaviors are controlled directly by strong circuits in long-term memory every day. We tend to only "notice" this happening when circuits in long-term memory control behaviors that we assume must be governed by conscious thinking, such as driving a car. For example, you drive from home to work or vice versa and when you turn off the ignition, you have an experience similar to waking up. You suddenly realize where you are. But, you "don't know how you got there." You actually do know how, but not at a conscious level because the focus of your attention was diverted (Mlodinow, 2012). Again, the more you repeat a complex behavior pattern (and reactivate the associated brain circuits), the more easily you can re-manifest that pattern of behaviors because the circuitry in your brain has created a "program" to direct it. This strengthen-by-reactivation programming function is so cumulative, in fact, that the level of measurable brain activity of long-time assembly workers while on the job is similar to that of people who are unconscious (Rock, 2006). It seems that the phrase, "operating on automatic pilot," applies as fittingly to many people in their daily work routines as it does to guidance systems for airplanes.

BRAIN CONNECTION! PHONES—THE REAL "WEAPONS OF MASS DESTRUCTION"

Do you think that the "don't know how you got there" experience could simply be a case of multi-tasking? Well, stop thinking like that! Despite common beliefs, your brain cannot multi-task because it can only focus on one thing at a time. Imagine a teenager "studying" while listening to high volume Death Metal. He's not studying&listening simultaneously. In nanoseconds, his brain is doing this: Read-listen-read-listen-read-listen over and over. If the goal is learning, to the brain the music is a distraction; the only possible value of which is that it might keep the kid from being distracted by one or more OTHER things.

Okay. Now, feature yourself driving and talking on your phone. Again, it's not multi-tasking. In this case, it's drive-talk-talk-drive-talk-talk-talk-drive-on-autopilot-talk-talk-talk, etc. As the conversation develops, your brain falls back on a driving "program" and devotes more focus to the conversation. No wonder research shows that using a phone while driving is the equivalent of driving while "under the influence" in most states. Of course, texting causes much greater performance degradation (Medina, 2008)!

So, WMD really DO exist. We just never thought to look for them in our cars!

"Programmed driving" is an example of how a practiced pattern of brain connections can control perceptions and behavior in a specific incidence or domain. However, our complete brain circuitry houses hundreds of thousands of massive, dynamic (i.e., changeable) and extremely complex sets of interconnections that collectively control all of our thoughts, memories, skills and more. Scientists refer to these sets of interconnections as cognitive maps (or schemas or mental models). Any given cognitive map can be labyrinthine (e.g., a mathematician's understanding of quadratics), but is nonetheless comprised by the same kinds of circuits that structure much less complex ideas. There are simply many more and more intricately interwoven connections.

"Belief system" is the lay term for *each one* of these sets of interconnections of concepts, assumptions, values and knowledge (i.e., each cognitive map or schema). Our belief systems can be shared (i.e., with other people) partially or in full. For example, McCandless and Posavec (2009) have illustrated that members of the "political left" (broadly defined) share many beliefs throughout the western world and their resulting belief systems can be contrasted with those typical of the "political right." Table 2.1 shows an adapted excerpt.

Once a belief system is established (repeatedly activated, compressed and compacted), **it is self-validating and very difficult to change**. Contributing factors include:

Confirmation bias. When confronted with information that contradicts an existing belief system, the brain could struggle to resolve the inconsistency, a major energy drain. Or it could: a) ignore the inconsistent information and/or b) seek out other information that fits with established beliefs. The brain has a strong tendency to take the latter, energy-saving course (Tavris & Aronson, 2007) while "enjoying" the additional benefit of keeping individual beliefs fitting together compatibly. In fact, that's why they are called belief *systems*.

In the book *The Political Brain* (2007), neuroscientist Drew Westen reported studies that demonstrated another determinant of confirmation bias: Euphoria.

Much like Reid's (2012) study reported earlier, Westen and his colleagues had participants read essays with purposely inserted contradictions. Few contradictions were noticed when an essay was attributed to a representative of their own political party. But when statements were said to be made by a member of the opposition, many more contradictions (in the same content) were identified. The kicker: **When participants ignored same-party contradictions *and* when they identified other-party contradictions, their brain activity was equivalent**

TABLE 2.1 Common Political Belief Systems in the Western World

Political left believes . . .	Focal construct	Political right believes . . .
Based on ethics	**Community**	Based on morals
Equality	**Equality or Freedom**	Freedom
Scientific, non-organized, unconventional	**Religion**	Theistic, organized, traditional
Others must observe	**Rights**	Others must not interfere
Social and economic victims	**Criminals**	Choose to be criminals
Downtrodden, lack opportunities, victims of the system	**Homeless**	No work ethic, no values, no shame
One for all and all for one	**Society**	Each to their own
Utopianism, things can be better, bring in the new	**World view**	Preservation, protect of the good things around the world
Multicultural, inclusive, evolving	**National view**	Nationalistic, exclusive, established

to the experience of elation (Westen, 2007; Westen, Blagov, Harenski, Kilts & Hamann, 2006). That is, during the enactment of confirmation bias (below the level of conscious awareness), **strong neurochemicals are secreted in the brain that make the performance of _bias_ highly satisfying**.

Maintenance of self-image. Under the "psychological basis of behavior," I argued that people, in every culture around the world, have a *very strong need* to maintain (or enhance) their views of themselves, i.e., their self-images. In fact, our self-image is our most complex and elaborate belief system. **Our brains are particularly sensitive to situations or experiences in which our self-image is threatened.**

For example, most people have a strong belief that their mothers love them. Any new information that is consistent with that belief will be fired immediately to the neurons in long-term memory that house the set of connections relating to your "mother" and "loves me." **Information *inconsistent* with the belief that your mother loves you would be handled quite differently for three reasons.**

1. Anything pointing to the fact that your mother doesn't love you is, for most people, incompatible with their fundamental need to maintain or enhance their self-images. (What kind of person must I be if even my mother doesn't love me?)
2. There is no strong, established circuit on which this information can travel electro-chemically.

3. As with confirmation bias, ignoring discrepant information conserves the brain's energy.

Thus, people are able to continue to believe that their mothers love them, sometimes even when a mammoth amount of evidence (e.g., harmful and hurtful belief-contradicting behaviors manifested by their mothers, counter-intuitive insights provided by siblings, friends and perhaps therapists or counselors, and so on) strongly suggests otherwise. (People who endure domestic violence (DV) over the long term is a current worrisome example—although there are certainly additional factors (e.g., safety of children, etc.) involved in DV.)

Confirmation bias and maintenance or enhancement of the self-image are processes in which the physiological basis of behavior becomes intertwined with the psychological basis, resulting in what are sometimes referred to as the "neuro-emotional" causes of behavior. Here, "neuro" refers to the physiological part of the equation, while "emotional" reflects the psychological dimension at play. **<u>These dual forces (neuro and emotional responses) assure that strong beliefs will be repeatedly re-validated and maintained.</u>**

One of the most common frustrations I've heard expressed by managers over the years is their inability to "get through to" poor performers. They conclude that "she just doesn't get it," "he's completely unmotivated," "Chris is thick as a brick!" Yet, **the behaviors that lead to these condemnations are simply the result of these poor performers' neural spam filters working properly**. Again, telling people that their performance is poor is one of the best ways of influencing poor performers to resist change, thereby maintaining their current performance levels!

How about this example of attempted-but-failed behavioral change that scientists have only recently begun to understand. People who have very serious heart attacks and yet survive are typically prescribed both physical (exercise) therapy and a form of mental therapy. The mental therapy is designed to help them to understand that they can dramatically reduce the likelihood of a second heart attack simply by changing their eating habits. (For simplicity's sake, I'll focus on eating habits here. But, of course, other lifestyle factors such as exercising frequently and cessation of smoking are relevant as well.) This mental therapy was assumed to be effective because patients who complete it and then take a test on the relationships between diet and heart healthiness generally score very well. Yet, all that these high test scores really tell us is that the patients who undergo mental therapy know intellectually (at one point in time) that there is a strong relationship between poor eating habits and the reoccurrence of heart attacks. This **passively learned** brain circuit is simply no match for the stronger and faster circuits between eating or overeating pizza/candy/ice cream and immediate physiological feelings of satisfaction. In fact, only 11 percent of the participants in this type of therapy actually change their eating habits—despite the fact that, as a result, they are putting their lives at much higher risk. (More on this kind of "irrational" behavior shortly.) The stronger, more frequently activated circuitry simply wins the competition to control behavior. It is important to note that, in this example, the majority of patients did not change their behaviors even though: 1) they are likely to believe what they are told by cardio-therapists and that the therapists have their best interests at heart, 2) making the change is clearly to their immediate, personal advantage, 3) they have the skills needed to make the change, and 4) they are not in a heightened emotional state at the time the information is provided—**highly favorable conditions for altering behavior that are far from typical in most large-scale organizational changes**.

Why do people refuse to change their behavior when most of the conditions and circumstances (including self-interest) favor making a prescribed change? Four of the primary <u>person-centered</u> (i.e., non-organizationally specific) reasons are:

1. **People didn't draw their own conclusions.** When people in cardio-therapy are only *told* what they should (not) do, **rather than being allowed to make their own new connections**, they simply continue to follow established patterns, habits, etc. (the old, strong circuitry). Looked at another way, the patients have not created new strong circuitry (perhaps involving preparing, eating, enjoying, sharing healthy foods) to replace the old circuitry (Pulakos, Hanson, Arad & Moye, Forthcoming; Rock, 2006).[9] So, the old circuitry continues to control their behavior.

Note that the failed change strategy for cardio patients is repeated frequently in the pre-execution stage of major organizational changes. We tell employees that it's not good for the organization to continue to do X (whatever represents the organizational equivalent of eating artery-clogging foods) or something bad is going to happen (the organization will have a financial heart attack). Instead, people need to do Y (e.g., collaboratively implement a major reorganization). **We've made all the connections and drawn all the conclusions for people. They just need to change (and suffer the neuro-emotional consequences)!**

2. **People aren't always rational.** As much as we'd like to believe that we behave rationally (in our own best interests) virtually all the time, well, we just don't. Much of our behavior is controlled by secretions and counter-secretions of neuro-chemicals that do their "work" below the level of our conscious awareness. For example, do you know that when heavy fog rolls into an area, **the average speed of the traffic on interstate highways increases** which greatly amplifies the danger of deadly, many-vehicles-involved crashes (Culham, 2012; Pretto, Bresciani, Rainer & Bülthoff, 2012; Rogers, n.d.)? What could cause such irrationality?

In heavy fog, our brains recognize that the situation is dangerous. And, because of that perception of danger, our brains release neurochemicals designed to help us survive that we experience as primitive instincts: Flee, fight and/or freeze. The subconscious flee response tells us that we need to get through the fog as quickly as possible. The subconscious fight response causes us to focus on the source of the danger (the fog) and ignore seemingly non-dangerous elements of our environment (like the speedometer). The subconscious freeze response (in this case, the easiest one of the three to ignore) sends us a conflicting signal that we need to stay right where we are until we can figure out the exact nature of this particular danger. Unfortunately, a very small percentage of drivers do, in fact, stop in the midst of the fog virtually guaranteeing that they will be hit from behind.

Mathematical *physicist* turned expert on the unconscious, Leonard Mlodinow (2012, p. 5) exhorts:

> To gain a true understanding of human experience, we must understand both our conscious and our unconscious selves, and how they interact. Our [unconscious self] is invisible to us, yet it influences our conscious experience of the world in the most fundamental of ways: how we view ourselves and others, the meanings we attach to the everyday events of our lives, our ability to make the quick judgment calls and decisions that can sometimes mean the difference between life and death, and the actions we engage in as a result of all these instinctual experiences.[10]

3. **Their current emotional state overloads their brain circuitry.** The brains of employees must deal with incoming stimuli from many sources, not just from the workplace. Prior to the pre-execution stage of an organizational change, many employees have already run out of processing space in their working memories. Perhaps they are facing foreclosure on their houses or they have sickly parents for whom to care. **Unfortunately, none of these people has a unique working memory that can be dedicated to work-related issues only.** When they arrive at the workplace each day, the brains of these employees are literally "tired" from overwork. They are tired in the sense that: 1) their spam filters are over-reaching—casting aside useful stimuli in an attempt to conserve the brain's energy, i.e., reduce the load on working memory, 2) with shorter processing time, greater numbers of stimuli are being misclassified to and within long-term memory, again in the service of workload reduction (i.e., speed-over-accuracy) and 3) electro-chemical impulses from working memory are sending out warning signals that way too much energy is being expended.

Change implementers (especially senior managers) often completely overlook, or grossly underestimate, the size of this brain-weary subset of employees. How sizable is this group? One inkling: Large national studies (Attridge, Cahill, Granberry & Herlihy, 2013; Mahieu & Taranowski, 2013; Taranowski and Mahieu, 2013) have found that the average combined services utilization rate for Employee Assistance Programs is in the range of 6–13 percent. Actuarial evidence suggests that there are 3–4 employees who should use these programs for every one that does; utilization rates of minorities are especially low (Albrecht, 2014; APA Practice Research and Policy Staff and Communications Staff, 2007; Bouvard, 2012; Fleming, Lee & Dworkin, 2014). If we do the math, those findings suggest **conservatively that 20–30 percent of the employees who will be asked to undergo a major organizational change might have extremely limited neural ability to effectively do so**. Yet, in Change Leadership programs that I've facilitated over the past 25+ years, **nine out of ten**

managers who are asked to estimate the percentage of people in their organizations who might be dealing with at least partially debilitating emotional issues at the present moment give answers in the range of 2–9 percent—most often at the low end of that range.

Yet, it's not only people's current emotional states that can hamper the implementation of organizational change, **the emotional histories that people bring with them to the workplace are often equally or more important**. That's why Kaiser and Kaplan's work on "overcoming sensitivities" is absolutely "MUST READING" for Change Leaders and consultants.

A brief summary of their work is presented in the box at the end of this section. But for now, let's stick a bit longer to the focal question: Why do people refuse to change their behavior when most of the conditions and circumstances (including self-interest) favor making a prescribed change? So far, I've covered three of the primary reasons:

1. **People didn't draw their own conclusions.**
2. **People aren't always rational.**
3. **Their current emotional state overloads their brain circuitry.**

And, here's No. 4 . . .

4. Strong, pre-wired emotions (such as "inequity aversion") are driving behavior. I've proposed a couple of times now that people in every culture have a fundamental need (or "motive" or "drive") to maintain or enhance their self-images. Perceptions of fairness or equity seem to be imbedded (hard-wired) in the maintenance or enhancement function. That is, if we believe we are being treated unfairly, it is very difficult to maintain (much less enhance) our self-images. Could this fundamental concern with fairness be "pre-wired"? It certainly looks that way.

Anyone who has spent any time at all around young siblings knows that perceptions of fairness are either pre-wired into our brains or they evolve at a very early age. Kids seem to have acute mental calipers that can detect microscopic

Grapes of Wrath

In a clever experiment at Emory University, Sarah Brosnan (Brosnan & de Waal, 2003) was able to demonstrate that even young, lower primates (in this case, Capuchin monkeys) manifest severe forms of "inequity aversion." In her study, Brosnan trained monkeys to complete a task in order to obtain a reward—a slice of cucumber handed by the experimenter to each appropriately performing monkey. At this point, there was every reason to conclude that the monkeys were more than happy to "work" for cucumber "pay." Then, however, Brosnan began to reward some monkeys with a grape rather than a cucumber slice. Well, if you don't know much about monkey cuisine, I need to tell you that grapes are MUCH preferred over cucumbers.

When the monkeys who were receiving the cucumber slices saw other monkeys receiving grapes, they reacted in different ways—but all of those ways reduced their "work performance." Some worked more slowly, some stopped working completely. Many monkeys began to screech at the experimenter; a few threw their cucumber slices at the experimenter while doing so.

(perceptual) differences in the sizes of two pieces of cake or two bowls of ice cream. And, whether it's kids in the home or employees at work, people who think that they received the "short end of the stick" often suffer severe distress that, as with cases of social rejection to be covered in the section below, "An <u>Evolutional</u> (that is, Evolution-Based) Perspective on Behavior," some psychologists have likened to a punch in the stomach.

We now know that when we believe we are being treated unfairly, brain regions that register pain are highly activated. I'm going to write that again. **When we believe that we are being treated unfairly, brain regions that register *physical* pain light up like the proverbial Christmas tree.** Yet, the real neuro-emotional kicker here is that brain regions that register pleasure (via secretions of dopamine) are highly activated if we see bad things happen to someone whom we perceive to have been advantaged by the inequity we experienced. **The bad-der, the better, in terms of the amount of dopamine secreted** (Cikara & Fiske, 2013). In all likelihood, these types of automatic pain and pleasure responses came about as a physical, evolutionary defense mechanism (e.g., the need to make sure that you get your fair share of the Wooly Mammoth you helped kill). Yet, psychologists believe that this particular, pre-wired circuitry has not only lost its bright side, it might well be a fundamental cause of violence in the world today. (Think school shootings, etc.)

EXPERTS' INSIGHTS: UNCOVERING PERCEIVED INEQUITIES

In several places throughout this Guide, I recommend that if you want to understand performance, you have to talk to the performers (i.e., the people who actually do the work) because they're the best source of information about what is contributing to and/or prohibiting desired work outcomes. There are some times, however, when the performers are going to be less than open about what is really going on and you can usually count on perceptions of inequity/unfairness to be one of those areas.

One of the everyday-language names for perceptions of inequity is "envy." And, if we were to rank order the negative emotions (e.g., anger, sadness, disgust, fear, etc.) on how "shameful" they are, envy would be right up there vying for the top spot. Due to the shamefulness of envy, we find it difficult to recognize it in ourselves and, even when we do, we don't like to own up to it. People can admit to being angry, or even fearful, more easily than they can admit to being envious. **Self-perceptions of enviousness seem to strike at the core of the maintenance or enhancement function.** Bottom line: If you ask Mary directly why she doesn't get along with Paul (and even if she recognizes at some level that envy is at the root of the interpersonal problem), she is likely to attribute the problem to a more self-image-friendly cause.

This means that you often have to uncover perceptions of inequity **indirectly**. One way to do that is to **focus on others rather than the employee at hand**.

Statements and questions like the following can often be used to open the trail to deeper emotions:

"In most organizations, there are people who are under-rewarded in comparison with their contributions and others who are over-rewarded. Would you say that that is true here?" If the respondent agrees . . . "Would you mind giving me an example or two of how that works here?"

OR—"When you think about the people with whom you work on a day to day basis, who do you admire the most? Why?"

There's another possible trail that involves getting the focal performer to talk about himself without directly asking any questions about envy or related feelings:

"All things considered (not just pay—but recognition, opportunities for advancement and learning and so on), do you think that you are fairly rewarded for all that you contribute to this organization?"

OR—"When you feel that you have a particularly good day here, what might be the kinds of things that would make you to feel that way?" Followed by: "When you have a day that's not so good . . ."

It's a crap shoot. But, relationship and equity issues often come to the fore in answer to questions like these.

BRAIN CONNECTION! "HOT BUTTONS" AS IMPEDIMENTS TO ORGANIZATION CHANGE (AND TO PSYCHOLOGICAL SAFETY AT WORK)

. . . Rob Kaiser and Bob Kaplan, of the consulting firm Kaplan DeVries, have authored a large and important body of work (e.g., Kaiser & Kaplan, 2006) that examines how psychological wounds that we suffer as children can sensitize us as adults to be anxious about getting hurt again and that anxiety is often what underlies emotional outbursts in the workplace. **What in office jargon might be called "hot buttons" or "issues" that cause people to "fly off the handle" without apparent justification, Kaiser and Kaplan refer to as "deep sensitivities."**

They define a "deep sensitivity" as "a set of emotionally charged beliefs and expectations generalized from experience *[but operating below the level of awareness]* that serve to protect the individual from repeating a painful psychological or physiological injury from the past" (Kaiser & Kaplan, 2006, p. 466). **That is, people who have had extremely hurtful experiences, most likely occurring in childhood, are unconsciously ever-alert, at less than a conscious level, for the possibility of the same kind of thing happening again.** This causes people to react *intensely* to any situational cues—not noticed by others—that might signal a forthcoming reoccurrence of the previous hurt, regardless of how objectively dissimilar the present and past circumstances may be. Common sensitivities include being perceived as intellectually inadequate, being extremely dependent upon a person who will "let you down," or being seen as weak and unable to stand up to authority.

When such a sensitivity is activated via exposure to a proposed change in the psychological comfort or safety of the organizational status quo, there is likely a two-phase response. At first, the focal person will overestimate the demands of the change or underestimate his ability to deal with it or both. Unless something occurs that disarms the brewing emotions, the attack of anxiety that results leads to highly emotional behaviors designed to stop the change from occurring (i.e., fight) or getting away from/out of the situation entirely (i.e., flight). **The person who manifests this type of behavior may recognize that it is inappropriate, perhaps afterward even sincerely apologizing for the outburst. But, recognition of the occurrence without an understanding of the underlying dynamics makes the behavior no less likely to reoccur.**

Kaiser and Kaplan have developed sophisticated "desensitization" programs that have proven highly effective in eliminating these behavioral explosions. Unfortunately, the programs require that the offending person voluntarily participate and actively work to eliminate the sensitivity. What is more likely, however, is that the offender will not learn the true extent of the problem because the organization will ignore, excuse or decide to "work around" the issue, particularly if the focal employee is an otherwise solid contributor. **In fact, sensitivity-based outbursts by executives are often considered to be not only acceptable, but normal!**

An <u>Evolutional</u> (that is, Evolution-Based) Perspective on Behavior

Why Deal with Evolution in a Book on Leading Large-Scale Organizational Change in the 21st Century?

For quite some time, I've been helping clients employ SCN research findings to increase the likelihood that: 1) their large-scale organizational change projects would be more successful and 2) their organizations would become more effective overall. As indicated earlier, some of this research has demonstrated that much of what we thought to be true about the causes of human behavior was both wrong *and* counter-intuitive to accepted (and deeply ingrained) management practices. In many cases, especially in the early going, helping managers come to their own conclusions that a new, very different and strikingly better way to manage people is available to them has been a very demanding task. **Over time and by trial and error, I have found that the means by which people most quickly "see the light" and gain the deepest understanding of the true reasons why people behave the way they do is by describing a simple relationship that explains a whole lot:** <u>The exceedingly *strong* and *constant* impact on current work behavior that results directly from the way in which the human brain evolved over hundreds of thousands of years.</u> If that statement is hard for you to believe at the moment, that's good. It means you have a lot to gain by giving consideration to this fresh, potent and rich evolutional perspective.

Please take a moment and try to imagine what the brain of our ancestor (Figure 2.2) was like. Then think about the ways that your brain is likely to be different.

Perhaps you're thinking that there must be so many and such extreme differences that the two types of brains can't be truly or meaningfully compared. But, in fact, from a structure and function standpoint, there is only one major difference: The outer-most layer of your brain is thicker than those of our friend in Figure 2.2.

In the western world today, most non-scientists have what could be called a vaguely "morphological" view of how the human brain evolved. For example,

FIGURE 2.2 How, and In What Ways, were the Brains of Our Primitive Ancestors Different from Ours?

their visual metaphor for the change might be the transformation of a caterpillar into a butterfly, the result of the transformation being something completely different from the original. Metaphors such as this one aren't even close to being accurate.

A more fitting metaphor I use to help people understand the evolution of the human brain is a motorcycle that has been customized with external metal cladding, an extended seat with a back brace, a sound system and a side car. **The now largely hidden (original) motorcycle can barely be seen but it's still there and it still performs the same elemental functions.**

A second metaphor, one that is more faithful to the true evolutionary process, is "animal adaptation." That is, the process by which animals increased the likelihood of their survival by adapting to their environments. For example, ducks developed webbed feet, rams developed horns and hedgehogs developed external spines. The ducks remained ducks but they developed new functionality. Same for the rams and hedgehogs. Likewise, **the human brain adapted/evolved by adding functionalities to its most primitive form while that primitive form** *remained intact during all later phases of evolution.*

It's often said the modern humans have three brains. It's more accurate to say that the human brain has three parts[11] but those parts operate **independently as well as interactively**.

Brain 1

The oldest part of the brain is commonly called the primitive or reptilian brain; let's call it "Brain 1." **Brain 1 evolved in a highly precarious environment with life-threatening forces lurking in abundance and survival in the balance.** Survival over time in the reptilian era was determined by how quickly each animal was able to detect sources of danger (such as a predator) or reward (such as food) and how quickly that animal could respond to what had been detected. In this environment, the consequence of failing to detect danger was, more often than not, fatal. So, speed of decision-making in detection was paramount. **As a result, Brain 1 favors speed over accuracy. It would rather be wrong than a predator's breakfast.** (Ultra-fast decision-making also serves the brain's biologically programmed need to conserve energy by, for example, not using further effort to evaluate more information.)

Let me break down this detection/decision-making process a bit further. While it's an oversimplification to say, Brain 1's job has two primary parts. One is to constantly monitor the environment, essentially "asking itself" five questions simultaneously and repeatedly about anything encountered in its environment:

- Can I eat it? (aka **"fight,"** should I try to kill it?)
- Will it eat me? (aka **"flight,"** should I run from it?)
- Should I **"freeze"** (until I figure out if I'm in danger)?

- Can I ignore it? (the brain's "spam filter," described previously)
- Can I procreate with it?[12]

The second part of Brain 1's job is to provide a warning (for danger) or an alert (for an available reward) and initiate the appropriate response, such as kicking in specific neurochemicals to provide the energy and focus needed to escape from a predator. A key to understanding much of human behavior is to know this: **Brain 1, that ancient reptilian organ, remains intact and largely unchanged in humans today and it continues to perform those same primitive, survival functions as it has for hundreds of thousands of years.** Brain 1 can still be a life-saver today, as when it provides a blast of adrenaline that enables a mother's strength to be increased to extraordinary levels when it is needed to save a child. The problem is that (for most people) the environment in which they live is no longer so precarious nor as frequently life-threatening. Yet, Brain 1 remains alert for just such a problem anywhere and everywhere. **Essentially, it presses a panic button much more frequently than is appropriate (resulting in such behaviors, as you will recall, like speeding up when dense fog covers interstate highways).**

When I first started covering the evolutional perspective in management training programs, I found that several people would express disbelief about the (current) existence of Brain 1 and the discussion would devolve into arguments for and against. So, I developed another tactic. I now have a number of 10–20-second videos that present different versions of essentially the same content (some pleasant or relaxing scene that is unexpectedly and loudly interrupted by, for example, the noise from an unseen explosion or the sudden appearance of a horrible-looking monster unleashing a frightening scream). At the point of surprise in the video, inevitably almost all of the trainees exhibit a strong, visible startle response usually accompanied by shrieks of various sorts (from both men and women). Immediately thereafter, trainees start looking at others around them and chatting rapidly (if only to themselves)—seemingly seeking assurance that everything is okay (a further automatic response to this type of situation which serves the purpose of returning their heart rates to normal and re-establishing composure). Since I started using these videos, I have never once had a trainee argue that Brain 1 isn't alive and well—and inarguably operative.

Brain 2

With the evolution of mammals, several things changed. Three of the most important changes were that a) newly born offspring needed extended periods of nourishment, general care and protection[13] (Broad, Curley & Keverne, 2006), b) neural mechanisms had to evolve that would assure that those offspring would seek this care and protection and that the relevant parent (or both parents) would provide it (Power & Schulkin, 2013) and c) the probability of the survival of a species became greatly enhanced by within-species cooperation, the hunting behavior of wolves being one example (Bailey, Myatt & Wilson, 2012). Thus evolved Brain 2—the "mammalian" or "social" brain[14]—whose job it is to flood the nervous system with chemical secretions (neurotransmitters) that guarantee a strong, systemic, self-defensive response to any possible threat to the hard-wired emotions that this part of the brain monitors including "fear" of social rejection/loss of affiliation.

Naiomi Eisenberger (2012a, 2012b, 2012c; Eisenberger & Cole, 2012; Eisenberger & Lieberman, 2004), an inventive and prolific SCN researcher at UCLA, has done a long series of neuroimaging studies that **demonstrate very well how primal and strong Brain 2's social affiliation/fear of social rejection drive is**.[15] One of the common methods that Eisenberger has used is as follows:

Each subject was equipped with a brain activity recording device and was led to believe that two other (unseen) subjects were participating simultaneously in the study. Subjects were shown a screen in which appeared two cartoon characters supposedly representing each of the other subjects that were part of the three-some. A drawing of a hand represented the focal subject herself (see Figure 2.3).

Subjects were told that they should participate in a ball-tossing game with the other two subjects. In reality, there were no other subjects and the cartoon characters representing the mythical subjects were controlled by a computer program.

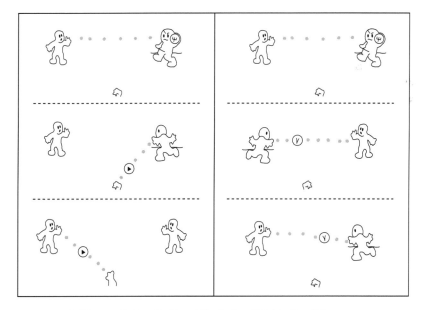

FIGURE 2.3 Subject Inclusion (Left) and Exclusion (Right) Conditions

Source: Eisenberger & Lieberman, 2004

In different conditions, the true subjects were a) able to fully participate in ball-tossing throughout many trials (social inclusion condition) or b) had their ability to participate gradually reduced until the two mythical subjects tossed the ball back and forth only between themselves (social exclusion condition).

The brains of subjects in the social inclusion condition responded as though they were in a reward state (i.e., their brains were registering a mild "fun" effect). The activity of the brains of subjects in the social exclusion condition manifested a firing pattern equivalent to physical pain.

After the neuroimaging part of the study was completed, subjects in the social exclusion condition also self-reported experiencing various kinds of physical discomfort. These same results have been obtained in a variety of related experimental, neuroimaging studies (e.g., use of still photographs of humans bearing expressions of "disapproval" for which no cause was provided—instead of the cartoon characters) (Kross, Egner, Ochsner, Hirsch & Downey, 2007).

The now accepted conclusion drawn from this (quite large and varied) collection of studies is that the reaction to social rejection (broadly defined), as well as to many other emotion-based, negative experiences (e.g., perceived inequity or unfairness) "piggy-backs" on the brain's circuitry for physical pain and causes the same experience (i.e., emotional pain felt physically) (Eisenberger & Lieberman, 2004).[16] (Yes, even when the subjects are "rejected" by cartoon characters or photographs of unknown people, it *still hurts*. You might want to keep this in mind the next time you ask some, but not all of the people within earshot, to go to lunch, etc.)

Conversely, social acceptance has been found to relate positively to self-esteem, ability to regulate stress and self-perceived well-being/quality of life (while social rejection has been associated with depression, susceptibility to PTSD, wounding and inflammation dynamics) (Eisenberger, 2013; Eisenberger & Cole, 2012).

BRAIN CONNECTION!

Lieberman (2010) suggests that the link between social rejection and physical pain evolved for mammals because being rejected by their caretakers was usually fatal. This link remains functional today. Recent SCN research consistently replicates this rejection/pain relationship thereby leading to the label of the brain as "a social organ" (Rock, 2008). In fact, even when the brain is at rest, most of the unconscious processes that continue to operate are related to "thinking" about yourself and your relationships with other people (Rock, 2009).

Brain 2 houses all of the evolutionarily pre-hard-wired emotions (i.e., ones that are built into the brain prior to learning taking place).[17] There are five of these "built-in" emotions that are particularly relevant to Change Leadership/ employee behavior in the workplace. In addition to a) the need for social accept- ance or attachment (just covered), I've previously introduced two of the others: b) the drive or need[18] to maintain or enhance one's self-image and c) the drive or need to receive equitable or fair treatment. The remaining two are **d) the drive or need for certainty/elimination of ambiguity and e) the drive or need to have a sense of control or be free from constraints**. (These two drives or needs (d, e) are interactive/reciprocal in that, for example, dealing with ambiguity can reduce one's sense of control in or over the situation. And, for both (d) and (e), Brain 2 gets a lot of "enforcement" help from Brain 1.)

The Drive or Need for Certainty/Elimination of Ambiguity

You've already learned that Brain 1 is decision-driven. It would rather be wrong than not come to a quick conclusion—in the primitive service of not making a fatal mistake as well as to conserve energy by limiting the amount of processing that is being done by working memory. When Brain 1 deals with very familiar events, it can "relax" by going into its automatic mode, such as the aforementioned driving-while-not-consciously-thinking-about-driving example. Were something unusual/unexpected to happen while your Brain 1 is in that automatic (driving) mode—let's say that you hear a siren and realize that a police officer is ordering you to pull off the road—Brain 1 will instantly adapt by going into an *anticipation of danger mode*. When the same unexpected stimulus (siren, police car) is received by Brain 2, it is recorded in a small part of Brain 2's emotional system called the ACC[19] that is responsible for emotional and cognitive processing (in this case, fig- uring out what the heck is going on and how bad it is going to be) and as a result, it creates a tension or uneasiness in the brain that can only be eased by achiev- ing certainty/eliminating ambiguity. Lieberman (2010) *metaphorically* compares the ACC to a smoke alarm. A smoke alarm has to be able to *detect* when a dangerous level of smoke particles is present—and, if it is—the alarm sounds a *warning* and the warning continues (unless turned off) until the smoke level has dissipated below a programmed threshold, i.e., when there is no longer any danger. Of course, not all uncertainty is dangerous. The point is that your brain (Brains 1 and 2 working in concert) are ever on alert for problems that can be caused by uncertainty, with a hair-trigger connection to a possible declaration of danger and a quick response. In Chapter 6, you'll see that uncertainty—on many levels—is rampant in organizations today and a major suppressor of performance (Ash, 2013; Damon, Harackiewicz, Butera & Quiamzade, 2007). **Of course, <u>additional</u> high levels of uncertainty/ ambiguity are typically inherent in large-scale organizational changes and are close correlates of resistance to change.**

The Drive or Need to Have a Sense of Control or be Free from Constraints

This drive or need works in exactly the same way as (d), the drive or need for certainty/eliminate ambiguity and most likely evolved for the same reason: Being constrained (e.g., not being able to flee from a dangerous predator) in prehistoric times was usually paramount to death (Leotti, Iyengar & Ochsner, 2010). There is certainly evidence that this drive is every bit as strong in animals, including humans, today. You're probably aware that both wild and domesticated animals have been known to chew off their own limbs to escape from a trap. There have been many documented cases of the same phenomena with humans, though a cutting tool is usually involved rather than teeth. The 2013 movie, "127 hours," tells the story of just such a case.

There is an entire storehouse of research documenting the relationship between employee autonomy (usually defined by being free to make choices/employees have input on decisions that affect them) and engagement (Trinchero, Brunetto & Borgonovi, 2013), job performance and self-regulation (Legault & Inzlicht, 2013), self-efficacy and customer service (Sousa, Coelho & Guillamon-Saorin, 2012), work satisfaction and organizational commitment (Graves & Luciano, 2013), organizational citizenship (Peng, Hwang & Wong, 2010), innovation (Lu, Lin, Leung, 2012), relatedness (Van den Broeck, Vansteenkiste, De Witte, Soenes & Lens, 2010), favorable perception of procedural justice (Gillet, Colombat, Michinov, Provost & Fouquereau, 2013), psychological health and satisfaction (Moreau & Mageau, 2012), initiative (van der Kaap-Deeder et al., 2014) and **(negatively) to resistance to change** (Thomas, Walker & Musselwhite, 2014). Such findings seem relatively free of cultural moderators (Wichmann, 2011).

Brain 3

The last major part of the brain to evolve is its thick, outer layer called the neo-cortex. This is the most distinctively "human" part of the brain and is usually what people are thinking of when they use the term "brain" in everyday language. It's also almost all of what can be seen in a picture of the brain's exterior. **It's the part of the brain that is responsible for higher-level thought (e.g., language acquisition, conception of past and future, planning and goal-setting, self-reflection, etc.). A second important function of Brain 3 is to accept or reject (usually the latter) electro-chemical impulses (communications) from Brains 1 and 2.** The accept/reject function of Brain 3 will be explained shortly.

It's often said that Brain 3 is the most complex organism in the universe. Unfortunately, that complexity is inversely related to how much is known with certainty about it, even though Brain 3 evolved some 25 million years ago (Rakic, 2009).

One thing we can be sure of is that much of what is said and written about Brain 3 is pure hyperbole, often without any scientific basis. Famously, science-popularizer, Carl Sagan, was quoted many times in saying that the human neocortex is more complicated than an entire galaxy, quite a claim for an astronomer-astrophysicist-cosmologist to make. How did he measure THAT? Well, he didn't. Dr. Sagan was speaking metaphorically, with purpose—as you will see in Chapter 5, using metaphors in this way helps complex ideas "stick" in people's minds. It's like an icon on the desktop of your brain's filing system.

Some of the hyperbole is beginning to be tested. For example, the most common estimate of the number of neurons in the brain is 100 billion (a number you'll see confirmed on the very highly regarded MIT McGovern Institute for Brain Research's web site). However, Suzana Herculano-Houzel, a neuroscientist at the Federal University of Rio De Janeiro, says she has looked at the relevant literature long and hard and can find no evidence on which the 100 billion number could be based. Hard to believe, but she and her students came up with a way to actually count the neurons in the brains of four deceased men and found the average number of neurons to be 87 billion (Herculano-Houzel, 2009). So, it might be best to take many of the super-complexity-claims about the brain with a couple of billion micrograms of salt.

Michael Shermer (2011, p. 113), the respected physicist and middle-of-the-roader on such estimates, offers his view of the brain's complexity:

> [It] consists of about a hundred billion neurons of several hundred types, each of which contains a cell, a[n] . . . axon cable, and numerous dendrites and axon terminals branching out to other neurons in approximately a thousand trillion . . . connections between those hundred billion neurons. . . . The number of connections in the brain is equivalent to the number of seconds in 30 million years.

Remember the graphic from earlier in this chapter (see Figure 2.4)? **It represents just ONE of those thousand trillion connections in the typical human brain.** Those connections collectively represent all of the pieces of data/ideas/concepts that have been connected together, that is, shared between neurons—from a simple idea to a complex belief system.

Note the "connecting electro-chemically" in the box. I didn't explain this concept earlier; I wanted to develop other ideas about how the brain works before I did that. I did, however, provide this example in the Prologue:

> [Lieberman's work has demonstrated] that talking aloud to one's self (by labeling one's emotions) can cause a nearly instantaneous reduction in anxiety. Lieberman didn't have subjects talk aloud and then ask them if they felt less anxious. Rather, he: 1) measured subjects' Time 1 levels of the stress-producing neurochemical cortisol, 2) asked them to talk about their anxiety

FIGURE 2.4 One Concept (M. Ali) Connecting with Another Concept (World's Most Widely Recognized American) Electro-Chemically in the Brain

levels according to an established emotion-labeling protocol, 3) demonstrated that when subjects were doing so there was increased activity in the right ventromedial prefrontal cortex that had previously been shown to be a source of secretions of DHEA, a cortisol-neutralizing hormone (Tor, Christian, Lindquist, Fredrickson, Noll & Taylor, 2006) and, finally, 4) measured subsequent (Time 2) levels of cortisol and found them to be lower.

Neurochemicals in the brain (like cortisol and DHEA in this example) are called *neurotransmitters* because they communicate (i.e., transmit) information between and among neurons. The brain doesn't "experience" life directly; rather it does so via these neurotransmitters. For example, we touch a pot on the stove that we didn't know was very hot. The heat from the pot is detected by sensors (nerve endings) in the skin on our hand and those sensors send out a signal that travels along a peripheral nerve in the arm to the spinal cord. Once in the spinal cord, the signal is converted a couple of times, resulting in the activation of neurotransmitters that carry the converted signal to the pain receptors in the brain. The brain translates that information and sends a "move your hand" command back to the hand along a similar pathway.

This response to a hot pot is multi-faceted and quite complex. Yet, for the neurons involved, it is just one of perhaps hundreds of signals sent by each neuron every second. Please recall from earlier in this chapter that **the sensory system alone sends the brain about 11 million bits of information but it can actively process less than 50 of them** (Mlodinow, 2012). And, filtering out the 10,999,950 bits of information that it's not going to consider is an active process. No wonder the brain needs to conserve its energy![20]

The Three Brains Often Work at Cross-Purposes

Okay, now you know that the brain is crazy-busy having to process millions of bits of information, communicated by neurotransmitters, every second. The perception-decide-act process is actually even more complicated than that **because much of the information the brain receives is contradictory**.

In Chapter 1, you learned about mirror neurons, those brain cells that help us understand the experiences of others. (Recall the example of seeing someone embarrass themselves often causes us to "feel" embarrassed.) Those mirror neurons also work in reverse. That is, they help us use other people's actions to make our choice of how to act (or respond) (Jarrett, 2012). Earlier in this chapter, you also learned that when we feel we have been treated unfairly (inequitably), that experience often creates a desire to see that the other person "will get what's coming to him" and that typically means something worse than the unfair

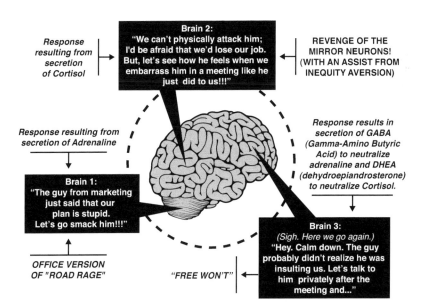

FIGURE 2.5 Human Behavior Results from Constant "Battles" Among Neurotransmitters

treatment we experienced. **This is a case where two (albeit similar and closely related brain functions) coproduce an amplified reaction** (cf., Brain 1 and 2 co-conspiring in Figure 2.5).

Chapter 2 Wrap-Up: Making All This Complicated Brain-and-Human-Behavior Stuff *Simple*

To my knowledge, there is only one holistic theory of human behavior that has been both broadly and specifically applied to the workplace and is based 100 percent on neuroscientific findings: David Rock's (2008) theory/model that he calls SCARF (explanation of the acronym forthcoming). Rock acquired his knowledge of these findings initially by interviewing prominent neuroscientists from, literally, around the world.

These are some of the theory's basic premises:

• the primal, primary and "overarching" organizing principle of the brain is "minimize danger and maximize reward"—in that order;
• the brain, operating below the level of conscious awareness, immediately identifies each new person, circumstance or situation (PCorS) it encounters as potentially dangerous/bad or potentially rewarding/good;
• the brain is repelled by danger and attracted to reward;[21]
• the traditional inducements (money, promotion, perks, etc.) used to get employees to be attracted to a PCorS or a way of performing are usually ineffective and frequently counterproductive;
• the traditional inducements (e.g., punishment, threats, etc.) used to get employees away from a PCorS or a way of underperforming are usually ineffective and frequently counterproductive;
• contrary to traditional business practice, the best way to induce desired performance is to provide rewards that affect an employee's drive or need for **S**tatus, **C**ertainty, **A**utonomy, **R**elatedness and **F**airness (thus, SCARF) and avoid any possible threats to those same drives or needs.

So, once you have this SCARF thing, what do you do with it? The most effective leaders constantly self-monitor their behaviors to make sure that they do as little as possible that would elicit "threat" responses in the people who report to them. At the same time they must do as much as possible to elicit "reward" responses during their interactions with those reports (Rock, 2008). I think of this as "managing by SCARF."

Table 2.2 presents a number of possible managerial behaviors that can, and usually do, lead to reward expectations or threat expectations for each of the elements of SCARF. Here are a few things to note about the table:

1. I chose unique examples of behaviors that lead to reward-expectations vs. threat-expectations. However, the opposite of behaviors that lead to reward-

expectations are also likely to elicit threat-expectations (e.g., being truthful vs. being dishonest);

2. Some behaviors can activate the brain's response to more than one element of SCARF. For example, being truthful can influence others' sense of certainty and sense of fairness—though I haven't represented that in the table; and

3. **Some behaviors can activate the brain's response to all of the elements of SCARF.** These multi-impact behaviors are so important that I devoted two of the rows in the table to examples of them. If you look at the last two rows under possible rewards, you'll see that "Building plans with someone; allowing someone to choose among options" and "Delegating an important task or responsibility" are likely to impact status, certainty, autonomy, relatedness *and* fairness perceptions. Think about delegation for example. If your boss selects you (rather than others) to do something important, that's going to affect your self-perceived status in relation to co-workers. You'd get an increase in certainty and autonomy perceptions because you get to decide how some things are going to be done. Being chosen for the task and spending more time with your boss might lead to a sense of being closer to her (relatedness). And, people almost never think it is unfair to be chosen among others for something desirable (though those not chosen might). Of course, things that should have positive impacts can lead to the opposite effects. If by "delegating" a task, you really just dump a bunch of extra work on someone, react emotionally to any mistakes made, micro-manage the work, abdicate your own responsibility for the work, etc., you'll be creating highly compounded threat-expectations.

In my view, SCARF is irrefutably supported by every related neuroscience study with which I'm familiar. So, why did I devote so much (previous) space to the critical importance of the maintenance or enhancement of the self-image drive or need? Here's the short-hand version: First, I believe that (Rock's) status and (my concept of) self-image are similar enough so that they can be considered the same concept.

Second, I believe that when Rock talks about a threat state and I talk about the need to protect one's self-image or when Rock talks about a reward state and I talk about an opportunity to enhance one's self-image, we're talking about precisely the same things.

At the same time, there are some differences between the two perspectives: Rock views the five variables (S-C-A-R-F) as *roughly equivalent in impact.* I see self-image (or Rock's notion of "status") as more fundamental. Why? **One reason is that I can't come up with a situation in which the brain sees the self-image as irrelevant. But, I can imagine many theoretical situations in which one or more of the other variables are less than central, if operative at all.** For example, if certainty (C) is as powerful as self-image, why would anyone ever go sky-diving or volunteer for hazardous warfare or want to become an astronaut? On the other hand, learning how to sky-dive and surviving several jumps, serving your country in ways that most other people wouldn't dare,

TABLE 2.2 Setting Reward-Expectations Rather Than Threat-Expectations with SCARF

	Status	*Certainty*	*Autonomy*	*Relatedness*	*Fairness*
POSSIBLE REWARDS	Providing any form of public or private recognition for good work, good decisions, special effort, etc.	Providing real-time, honest, open communication especially information about the future	Where possible, allowing people to set their own priorities, to organize their own work and schedules	ALWAYS treat every person in the workplace with respect, civility and cordiality; CARE about people as individuals	Aligning rewards, recognition and desirable opportunities with performance levels
	Selecting someone for a job, a desired promotion, training or enjoyable tasks	Being authentic, transparent and truthful; remaining calm in the face of crises and unexpected events	Organizing your meetings and communication to show respect for the value of others' time; don't distract them unnecessarily	Keep reminding people how what they do fits into the "big picture" (i.e., organizational or work unit strategy)	Basing your decision-making on the best available hard evidence; avoid knee-jerks
	Asking someone for an opinion, particularly if it's based on knowledge or skills	When some major outcome is unknown, giving someone information about when it will be known	Where possible encourage/ allow people to evaluate their own performances	Recognize/reward collaboration; tell stories about teamwork and supporting others	Giving credit for the work of others; owning up to your own mistakes
	Building plans with someone; allowing someone to choose among options	Building plans with someone; allowing someone to choose among options	Building plans with someone; allowing someone to choose among options	Building plans with someone; allowing someone to choose among options	Building plans with someone; allowing someone to choose among options
	Delegating an important task or responsibility	Delegating an important task or responsibility	Delegating an important task or responsibility	Delegating an important task or responsibility	Delegating an important task or responsibility

Pitting employees or groups against one another	Behaving inconsistently, unpredictably, moodily or out of line with goals or organizational values	Micro-managing; telling someone exactly how things must be done; over-checking work	Not including someone in planning, discussions or even lunch invitations if extended to others	Failing to address performance problems, ethical violations or undesirable behaviors
Responding emotionally to bad news or to the discovery of mistakes	Frequently changing goals, priorities, practices without apparent cause	Countermanding someone's decisions or authority to make them	Creating work spaces for some that elicit a sense of isolation	Failing to explain the reasons or logic behind decisions
Ignoring someone's opinions, concerns or preferences	Providing inadequate training or preparation for new tasks, technologies or responsibilities	Ignoring or failing to act on feedback about your own performance or behavior	Criticizing some employees in the presence of other employees	Establishing uneven workloads; asking top performers to do more than their share

and being picked as one of 50 applicants for the "job" of astronaut most assuredly would affect one's self-image. Likewise, if autonomy (A) is always crucial, why would anyone have six children or become a Buddhist Monk or even endure football training camp?

So, is SCARF at odds with the primacy-of-self-image view? No. As depicted in Figure 2.6, **I see our self-image as a _LENS_ through which we view all of our experiences, our own behavior and other peoples' reactions to our behavior**. For example, if we don't get to choose how we do something or if we are micro-managed, that hurts not because it's a threat to our need for autonomy (A) per se. **It hurts because of how that threat affects our self-image.** Most people in work organizations today simply can't feel good about themselves if they have zero impact on decisions that are being made about how the work is to be done and have the level of oversight usually extended to kindergarteners.

Likewise, if we don't feel that we are being rewarded in line with our contributions (F—fairness) that hurts not because it's a threat to our need for fairness/equity in itself. When people say, "It's not fair!" what they really mean is that "I am **(i.e., my self-image is)** hurting because I don't feel like an equal in this situation" (in Rock's parlance—one's **status** is being threatened!).

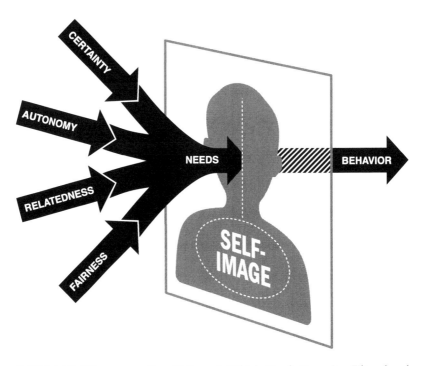

FIGURE 2.6 Self-Image as a "Lens" Through Which Needs/Fears Are Filtered and Processed Into Behavior

For all of these reasons, I recommend that Change Leaders take the simpler route: <u>Focus on the lens</u>: **How all experiences affect employees' self-images!**

Okay. If you're presently telling yourself that there doesn't seem to be much difference between Rock's theory and my approach, you're right. In the end, Change Leaders who follow my recommended course of action—and Change Leaders who follow Rock's—do pretty much the same thing day-to-day. The difference is primarily in the focus.

Of course, it **<u>IS</u>** easier to **FOCUS** with a **LENS**!

Notes

1 Readers interested in what a college textbook would be like if it were designed around SCN learning principles can find out here: Snyder (2014).
2 Milligan (2014) provides an interesting interview with Jonathan Atwood who explains how Unilever uses stories to build brands and promote sustainability issues.
   Melcrum Communications (*n.d.*) has a model for collecting and refining organizational stories to support change projects.
3 Bob Nelson has written several books about using a wide variety of recognition tactics as rewards. You can find an overview of his work in Nelson (*n.d.*).
4 McGill University (*n.d.*) maintains an excellent primer on brain circuitry and neural networks.
5 In many ways, the TED talk by Sebastian Seung (2010), a computational neuroscientist at MIT, is out of date. It was made *way back in 2010*—which is a long time ago by SCN standards. However, the graphics he created for that talk are the best I've seen in terms of giving a lay person insight into the wondrous nature of the process by which the brain reprograms (i.e., physiologically changes) itself.
6 Duhigg (2012) describes the *power* that these circuits have over the decisions we make and the ways that we behave in life and in business. It's a fascinating book; one that has woken up many people to the possibility of the fact that they are behaving automatically (i.e., without thinking) in circumstances where thought/consideration would make an important difference.
7 What I mean by metaphor-based should be obvious (you'll see spam filter, garage, system memory, folder, 1957 Cadillac hearse, etc. used in this section). "Oversimplified" isn't as transparent, so I'll provide an example. For the sake of understanding and retention, I've made it sound as though data from our senses are being processed in a linear fashion by stand-alone entities: Spam filter > working memory > long-term memory. This description of the process would make a neuroscientist cringe; the process is far from linear and several parts of the brain are usually doing their *jobs* (yet another metaphor) simultaneously and reciprocally. In fact, it is now believed that data are processed by neural networks that are widely distributed throughout the brain. For a more technically accurate description of the process, you might want to take a look at Cikara and Van Bavel (2014).
8 Knowledge of the nature and function of myelin sheaths has come full circle (something that only rarely occurs in neuroscience). Earlier on, myelinization was believed to function like insulation that kept signal quality from decaying during transmittal. At other times, sheaths were likened to amplifiers, then later to "repeaters" in the sense of how radio frequency transmissions can be made to go faster via intermediate placement of devices that essentially resend the same signal.
   Most recently, the insulation view is back in vogue—albeit with a much more complex understanding of how the sheaths function. A sound technical explanation can be found at Bechler and ffrench-Constant (2014).

9 If you aren't familiar with the training programs developed by Gordon Graham, you should be. That is, I think that everyone can benefit from the insights on human behavior that he developed (long before the very same ideas were being validated by SCN). Graham was a (very) hardened criminal who served 19 years in prison, including 12 months of "bread and water only" in a tiny, isolated cell in Walla Walla Federal Prison. (That sounds medieval, but it occurred during the 1960s.) Graham was able to turn his thinking and his life around and he became a management trainer with many Fortune 500 firms as clients.

Videos of many of his programs are still available on YouTube. The one that provided the most valuable insight for me is called "Effective Feedback" (Graham, *n.d.*). Today, it would likely be called "Performance Management."

The means by which Graham was able to change his life is described in this six-minute, low-budget shoot. More importantly, Graham explains that if you want to change someone's behavior, never tell them what you don't want them to do—because of how the brain records and replays that directive over and over and that interferes with acceptance of the new, desired behavior. Likewise, Graham emphasizes that people only change when *they decide* to change and *they decide how* to change. So if, for example, one of your reports doesn't make her sales quota, you could ask, "Why didn't you make your quota this month?" That only leads to defensive excuse making. Rather, he suggests: "What would have to be different so that you could make your quota every month?" and then let the report "paint the picture" of how to change.

10 It wasn't SCN research and the study could be considered "cute" rather than impactful. But, Melissa Bateson and her colleagues (Bateson, Nettle & Roberts, 2006) randomly rotated a picture of flowers or a picture of human eyes on a sign above the "kitty" for an honor coffee stand. All other possible variables were the same throughout the study. When the eyes, rather than the flowers, were present, revenues were 2.76 times as great. Of course, people would be more honest when they were being "watched!"—apparently, even if they were being watched by a picture.

11 Some experts talk about a fourth part of the brain with No. 4 being the pre-frontal cortex (PFC). I believe that, for my purposes here, it's fine to include the PFC in the neocortex because: a) it is a part thereof and b) inclusion is the more common practice. When the three-part approach is taken, the term "Triune Brain" applies.

12 First, procreation is essential to the survival of the species, not the individual animal; second, in one way, ancient reptiles were smarter than contemporary humans. Reptiles never procreated with any creature from which they should flee.

13 The ability of offspring to quickly learn to recognize their primary care-giver has survived the millennia. There's evidence (Medina, 2008) that human babies can recognize their mother's face within four to five hours after birth if, that is, the biological mother is the predominant person to provide care.

14 Brain 2 is called the Limbic System in the neuroscience literature.

15 Among social animals, there is protection in numbers. Aged, sickly or injured members of a herd, for example, struggle mightily to keep up with the herd's movement because they know instinctively that otherwise they will die.

16 Eisenberger and Lieberman (2004, p. 295) also report:

> Perhaps most surprising, though, is that even when participants are told they are playing with a computer program and that the computerized players are going to stop throwing the ball to them, participants still report lower self-esteem following the game.

17 I'm oversimplifying here for ease of presentation. Emotion-related neural activity occurs throughout the entire brain, not just in Brain 2.

18 I'm using both of these words so as to include two divergent scientific perspectives. It's

beyond the scope (and intent) of this section to explain the arguments for and against each of these labels.

19 This is the anterior cingulate cortex.

20 The human brain averages about 2 percent of the body's weight but consumes about 20 percent of the energy used each day.

21 Personally, I would add a qualification to this premise: "So long as other factors don't interfere."

References

All web site URLs accessed on December 12, 2015.

Albrecht, S. (2014). Why don't employees use EAP services. *Psychology Today Online*, February 14. Retrieved from www.psychologytoday.com/blog/the-act-violence/201402/why-dont-employees-use-eap-services.

APA Practice Research and Policy Staff and Communications Staff. (2007). Reaching out to diverse populations: Opportunities and challenges. *American Psychological Association*, July 12. Retrieved from www.apapracticecentral.org/ce/courses/diverse-populations.aspx.

Ash, B. (2013). What happens when employees are left in the dark? *Florida State 24/7*, February 20. Retrieved from http://news.fsu.edu/More-FSU-News/24-7-News-Archive/2013/February/A-question-of-accountability-What-happens-when-employees-are-left-in-the-dark.

Attridge, M., Cahill, T., Granberry, S. & Herlihy, P. (2013). The national behavioral consortium benchmarking study: Industry profile of 82 external EAP providers. *Journal of Workplace Behavioral Health*, *28(4)*, 251–324.

Bailey, I., Myatt, J. & Wilson, A. (2012). Group hunting within the Carnivora: Physiological, cognitive and environmental influences on strategy and cooperation. *Behavioral Ecology & Sociobiology*, *October 112*. DOI: 10.1007/s00265-012-1423-3.

Bateson, M., Nettle, D. & Roberts, G. (2006). Cues of being watched enhance cooperation in real-world setting. *Biological Letters*, *2(3)*, 412–414.

Baumeister, R. (1990). Suicide as escape from the self. *Psychological Review*, *97(1)*, 90–113.

Bechler, M. & ffrench-Constant, C. (2014). A new wrap for neuronal activity. *Science*, *344(6183)*, 480–481.

Bouvard, M. (2012). *The invisible wounds of war: Coming home from Iraq and Afghanistan*. Amherst, NY: Prometheus Books.

Boystun, J., Sherry, M. & Moelter, N. (1997). Patrol staffing in San Diego—One or two officers units? *National Criminal Justice Reference Center*. Retrieved from www.ncjrs.gov/App/Publications/abstract.aspx?ID=41454.

Broad, K., Curley, J. & Keverne, E. (2006). Mother-infant bonding and the evolution of mammalian relationships. *Philosophical Transaction of the Royal Society B: Biological Sciences*, *361(1476)*, 2199–2244.

Brosnan, S. & de Waal, F. (2003). Monkeys reject unequal pay. *Nature*, *425*, 297–299.

Cikara, M. & Fiske, S. (2013). Their pain, our pleasure: Stereotype content and schadenfreude. *Annals of the New York Academy of Sciences*, *1299(1)*, 52–59.

Cikara, M. & Van Bavel, J. (2014). The neuroscience of intergroup relations: An integrative review. *Perspectives on Psychological Science*, *9(3)*, 245–274.

Colon, D. (2011). *Achievement values: Puerto Rico and the United States*. Pittsburgh, PA: RoseDog Books.

Culham, J. (2012). New ideas on how drivers perceive speed emerge from the fog. *eLife* (*National Institutes of Health's National Library of Medicine*). DOI: 10.7554/eLife.00031.

Damon, C., Harackiewicz, J., Butera, F. & Quiamzade, G. (2007). Performance-approach and performance-avoidance goals: When uncertainty makes a difference. *Personality and Social Psychology Bulletin, 33(6)*, 813–827.

Duhigg, C. (2012). *The power of habit.* New York, NY: Random House.

Eisenberger, N. (2012a). The pain of social disconnection: Examining the shared neural underpinnings of physical and social pain. *Nature Reviews Neuroscience, 13*, 421–434.

Eisenberger, N. (2012b). The neural bases of social pain: Evidence for shared representations with physical pain. *Psychosomatic Medicine, 74*, 126–135.

Eisenberger, N. (2012c) Broken hearts and broken bones: A neural perspective on the similarities between social and physical pain. *Current Directions in Psychological Science, 21*, 42–47.

Eisenberger, N. (2013). Social ties and health: A social neuroscience perspective. *Current Opinion in Neurobiology, 23*, 407–413.

Eisenberger, N. & Cole, S. (2012) Social neuroscience and health: Neuropsychological mechanisms linking social ties with physical health. *Nature Neuroscience, 15*, 669–674.

Eisenberger, N. & Lieberman, M. (2004). Why rejection hurts: A common neural alarm system for physical and social pain. *Trends in Cognitive Sciences, 8(7)*, 294–300.

Fleming, P., Lee, J. & Dworkin, S. (2014). "Real men don't": Constructions of masculinity and inadvertent harm in public health innovations. *American Journal of Public Health, 104(6)*, 1029–1035.

Fugate, M., Kinicki, A. & Prussia, G. (2008). Employee coping with organizational change: An examination of alternative theoretical perspectives and models. *Personnel Psychology, 61(1)*, 1–36.

Gillet, N., Colombat, P., Michinov, E., Provost, A. M. & Fouquereau, E. (2013). Procedural justice, supervisor autonomy support, work satisfaction, organizational identification and job performance. *Advances in Nursing, 69(11)*, 2560–2571.

Gottschall, J. (2013). The science of story-telling: How narrative cuts through distraction like nothing else. *Fast Company*, October 16. Retrieved from www.fastcocreate.com/3020044/the-science-of-storytelling-how-narrative-cuts-through-distraction.

Graham, G. (*n.d.*). Giving effective feedback. Retrieved from www.youtube.com/watch?v=k2Hob21_HPU.

Graves, L. & Luciano, M. (2013). Self-determination at work: Understanding the role of leader-member exchange. *Motivation and Emotion, 37(3)*. DOI: 10.1007/s11031-012-9336-z.

Herculano-Houzel, S. (2009). The human brain in numbers: A linearly scaled-up primate brain. *Frontiers in Human Neuroscience.* DOI: 10.3389/neuro.09.031.2009.

Holloway, S. (1988). Concepts of ability and effort in Japan and the United States. *Review of Educational Research, 58(3)*, 327–345.

Jarrett, C. (2012). Mirror neurons: The most hyped concept in neuroscience? *Psychology Today (Brain Myths)*, December 12. Retrieved from www.psychologytoday.com/blog/brain-myths/201212/mirror-neurons-the-most-hyped-concept-in-neuroscience.

Jorgensen, H., Owen, L. & Neus, A. (2008). *Making change work.* IBM White Paper. Somers, NY: IBM Global Services.

Kaiser, R. & Kaplan, R. (2006). Outgrowing sensitivities: The deeper work of executive development. *Academy of Management Learning and Education, 5*, 463–483.

Kross, E., Egner, T., Ochsner, K., Hirsch, J. & Downey, G. (2007). Neural dynamics of rejection sensitivity. *Journal of Cognitive Neuroscience, 19*, 945–956.

Lakoff, G. (2008). *Metaphors we live by*. Chicago: University of Chicago Press.

Legault, L. & Inzlicht, M. (2013). Self-determination, self-regulation, and the brain: Autonomy improves performance by enhancing neuroaffective responsiveness to self-regulation failure. *Journal of Personality and Social Psychology, 105(1)*, 123–138.

Leotti, L., Iyengar, S. & Ochsner, K. (2010). Born to choose: The origins and value of the need for control. *Trends in Cognitive Sciences, 14(10)*. DOI:10.1016/j.tics.2010.08.001.

Lieberman, M. D. (2010). Social cognitive neuroscience. In S. T. Fiske, D. T. Gilbert & G. Lindzey (Eds.), *Handbook of social psychology* (5th ed., pp. 143–193). New York, NY: McGraw-Hill.

Lu, L., Lin, X. & Leung, K. (2012). Goal orientation and innovative performance: The mediating roles of knowledge sharing and perceived autonomy. *Journal of Applied Social Psychology, 42*, 180–197.

McCandless, D. & Posavec, S. (2009). *Left vs. right political spectrum*. Created for *Science Maps for Kids* (K. Borner & M. Stamper, Eds.) Online learning aids repository for teachers: http://scimaps.org. Originally appeared in McCandless, D. (2009). *The visible miscellaneum*. New York, NY: HarperCollins.

McGill University. (*n.d.*). The brain from top to bottom. Retrieved from http:///thebrain. mcgill.ca.

Mahieu, K. & Taranowski, C. (2013). External employee assistance program vendors: A study of RFI Data from 2009–2010. *EASNA Research Notes, 3(3)*. Retrieved from www.google. com/url?sa=t&rct=j&q=&esrc=s&source=web&cd=1&ved=0ahUKEwiZkM-Gp9fJA hUFRyYKHQwTBnQQFggcMAA&url=http%3A%2F%2Fwww.easna.org%2Fwp-content%2Fuploads%2F2010%2F08%2FEASNA-Research-Notes-Vol-3-No-3.pdf& usg=AFQjCNH040K8HGEfEcNr-qCNI1qK9qM9uA&sig2=BxvmuykDjCPH_ y7tDeYXVQ&bvm=bv.109910813,d.dmo&cad=rja.

Medina, J. (2008). *Brain rules: 12 principles for surviving and thriving at work, home, and school*. Seattle, WA: Pear Press.

Melcrum Communications. (*n.d.*). Using story-telling to change behavior. Retrieved from www.melcrum.com/research/engage-employees-strategy-and-change/using-storytelling-change-behavior.

Milligan, B. (2014). Using story-telling to change consumer behavior. *Marketing: Green*, January 16. Retrieved from www.mediapost.com/publications/article/217509/using-storytelling-to-change-consumer-behavior-q.html.

Mlodinow, L. (2012). *Subliminal: How your unconscious mind rules your behavior*. New York, NY: Pantheon Books.

Moreau, E. & Mageau, G. A. (2012). The importance of perceived autonomy support for the psychological health and work satisfaction of health professionals: Not only supervisors count, colleagues too! *Motivation and Emotion, 36*, 268–286.

Nelson, R. (*n.d.*). Why managers don't use recognition. Retrieved from www.google.com/url?sa =t&rct=j&q=&esrc=s&source=web&cd=1&ved=0ahUKEwijlLHhqtfJAhXLJx4KHRIB BsAQFggcMAA&url=http%3A%2F%2Fwww.dhmh.state.md.us%2Ftsd%2FDocuments% 2Frewards.pdf&usg=AFQjCNF63_mpbz1LsW3u0H503iJwbwAskA&sig2=dN_whycTjs gZ3ylp-f-ulg&bvm=bv.109910813,d.eWE&cad=rja.

Peng, Y.-P., Hwang, S.-N. & Wong, J-Y. (2010). How to inspire university librarians to become "good soldiers": The role of job autonomy. *Journal of Academic Librarianship, 36(4)*, 287.

Power, M. & Schulkin, J. (2013). Maternal regulation of offspring development in mammals is an ancient adaptation tied to lactation. *Applied & Translational Genomics, 2(1)*, 55–63.

Pretto, P., Bresciani, J., Rainer, G. & Bülthoff, H. H. (2012). Foggy perception slows us down. *eLife* (*National Institutes of Health's National Library of Medicine*). DOI: 10.755/eLife.00031.

Pulakos, E., Hanson, R., Arad, S. & Moye, N. (Forthcoming). Performance management can be fixes: An on-the-job experiential learning approach for complex behavior change. *Industrial and Organizational Psychology: Perspectives on Science and Practice, 8(1).* Retrieved from Member web site (Society of Industrial and Organizational Psychology).

Rakic, P. (2009). Evolution of the neocortex: Perspective from developmental biology. *Nature Reviews Neuroscience, 10(10),* 724–735.

Reid, S. (2012). A self-categorization explanation for the hostile media effect. *Journal of Communication, 62,* 381–399.

Rock, D. (2006). *Quiet leadership: Six steps to transforming performance at work.* New York, NY: Collins.

Rock, D. (2008). SCARF: A brain-based model for collaborating with and influencing others. *NeuroLeadership Journal, 1,* 44–52.

Rock, D. (2009). Managing with the brain in mind. *strategy+business, 56* (Autumn). Retrieved from www.strategy-business.com/article/09306?gko=5df7f.

Rogers, M. (*n.d.*) Safety trips for driving in the fog: Fight your subconscious. *Drive Safely.* Retrieved from www.drive-safely.net/driving-in-fog.html.

Savolainen, T. (2013). Change implementation in intercultural context: A case study of creating readiness to change. *Journal of Global Business Issues, 7(2),* 51–58.

Scoville, D. (2011). Lone-officer patrols: Going solo. *Police* (March), 51–61.

Seo, M., Taylor, M., Hill, N., Zhang, X., Tesluk, P. & Lorinkova, N. (2012). The role of affect and leadership during organizational change. *Personnel Psychology, 65(1),* 121–165.

Seung, S. (2010). I am my connectome. Retrieved from www.ted.com/talks/sebastian_seung.

Shermer, M. (2011). *The believing brain.* New York, NY: New York Times Books.

Shoda, Y. (2004). Individual differences in social psychology: Understanding situations to understand people, understanding people to understand situations. In C. Sansone, C. Morf & A. Panter (Eds.), *The Sage handbook of methods in social psychology* (pp. 117–142). Thousand Oaks, CA: Sage Publications.

Snyder, R. (1998a). What bad impressions tell us about employees (Part I). *Human Resource Development Quarterly, 9(1),* 71–79.

Snyder, R. (1998b). What bad impressions tell us about employees (Part II). *Human Resource Development Quarterly, 9(2),* 179–186.

Snyder, R. (2014). Let's burn them all: The learning-inhibitory nature of Introduction to Management and Introduction to Organizational Behavior textbooks. *Journal of Management Education, 33,* 733–758.

Snyder, R. & Williams, R. (1982). Self theory: An integrative theory of work motivation. *Journal of Occupational Psychology, 55(4),* 257–267.

Sousa, C., Coelho, F. & Guillamon-Saorin, E. (2012). Personal values, autonomy, and self-efficacy: Evidence from frontline service employees. *International Journal of Selection and Assessment, 20(2),* 159–170.

Taranowski, C. & Mahieu, K. (2013). Trends in Employee Assistance Program implementation, structure and utilization, 2009 to 2010. *Journal of Workplace Behavioural Health, 28(3),* 172–191.

Tavris, C. & Aronson, E. (2007). *Mistakes were made (but not by me): Why we justify foolish beliefs, bad decisions, and hurtful acts.* Orlando, FL: Harcourt, Inc.

Thomas, G. O., Walker, I., Musselwhite, C. (2014). Grounded Theory analysis of commuters discussing a workplace carbon-reduction target: Autonomy, satisfaction, and willingness to change behaviour in drivers, pedestrians, bicyclists, motorcyclists and bus users. *Transportation Research Part F, 26,* 72–81.

Tor, D., Christian, W., Lindquist, M., Fredrickson, B., Noll, D. & Taylor, S. F. (2006). The role of ventromedial prefrontal cortex in anxiety and emotional resilience. *Organization for Human Brain Mapping International Conference*, Florence, Italy.

Trinchero, E., Brunetto, Y. & Borgonovi, E. (2013). Examining the antecedents of engaged nurses in Italy: Perceived organisational support (POS); satisfaction with training and development; discretionary power. *Journal of Nursing Management*, *21(6)*, 805–806.

Van den Broeck, A., Vansteenkiste, M., De Witte, H., Soenens, B. & Lens, W. (2010). Capturing autonomy, competence, and relatedness at work: Construction and initial validation of the Work-related Basic Need Satisfaction Scale. *Journal of Occupational and Organizational Psychology*, *83(4)*, 981–1002.

van der Kaap-Deeder, J., Vansteenkiste, M., Soenes, B., Verstuyf, J., Boone, L. & Smets, J. (2014). Fostering self-endorsed motivation to change in patients with an eating disorder: The role of perceived autonomy support and psychological need satisfaction. *Journal of Eating Disorders*, *47(6)*, 585–600.

Westen, D. (2007). *The political brain: The role of emotion in deciding the fate of the nation.* New York, NY: Public Affairs.

Westen, D., Blagov, P., Harenski, K., Kilts, C. & Hamann, S. (2006). Neural bases of motivated reasoning: An fMRI study of emotional constraints on partisan political judgment in the 2004 presidential election. *Journal of Cognitive Neuroscience*, *18(11)*, 1947–1958.

Wichmann, S. (2011). Self-determination Theory: The importance of autonomy to well-being across cultures. *The Journal of Humanistic Counseling*, *50(1)*, 16–26.

PART I

The Infrastructure of Enterprise-Wide Organizational Change Management

3

SPONSORSHIP, GOVERNANCE AND IMPLEMENTATION STRUCTURE

The Sponsorship Team

Typical composition: Mostly upper level managers[1] who have the necessary, formal authority to enact the change, who are committed to the success of the change and who are able and willing to champion the change process over the long term. Other members of the team might include people with central and relevant content knowledge or technical expertise and yet others who are known for their trustworthiness or straight-shooting or are held in high regard for any number of other reasons. Some members of the Sponsorship Team (along with appropriate members of the Implementation Team (see below)) will be directly involved in the creation of the change plan. While different members of the Sponsorship Team will have different roles (i.e., some will be more out front on certain issues and play more of a support role on other issues), all team members are responsible for:

- making sure that the change plan fits well with and strongly supports the organization's strategic plan;
- steadfastly engaging employees throughout the organization to explain and compellingly promote the change and to help them visualize the desired future state;
- assuring that adequate resources to implement the plan are readily available;
- staying abreast of progress and problems and intervening to remove obstacles;
- adapting and monitoring reward systems to assure that change-facilitative high performance is recognized and rewarded;
- actively interacting with resistors while showing strong support for civil, reasoned disagreement;
- demonstrating knowledge and commitment to the change while modeling the behaviors expected of others (i.e., patient listening, consistent optimism, etc.).

Governance Structure

A formal statement of the operating policies and practices of the Sponsorship Team and (primarily) the Implementation Team. Its purposes are to guide the teams' work, assure control and accountability, and indicate how potential conflicts (among people, about the allocation or reallocation of resources, etc.) will be resolved. Obviously, the Governance Structure for a change project should not be in conflict with the policies and practices of the larger organization. I prefer that Governance documents include values to guide *how* the change plan will be executed (e.g., "civil, principled dissent is welcome and respected"; "reductions in staff will be a final and last resort," etc.).

There is nothing more important to the successful implementation of a major organizational change initiative than the development of the Sponsorship Team and the internal governance structure. While sponsorship and governance are <u>always</u> important, they are even more critical to success when the focal organization doesn't have such a great track record of accepting and adapting to change. <u>In fact, there are several conditions that simultaneously increase the importance of effective sponsorship and governance and decrease the overall likelihood of success from the outset</u>:

- past changes were started and then dropped (perhaps even after full implementation);
- past changes often or typically failed to meet important goals;
- past changes led to widespread negative outcomes for some or many of the employees affected;
- past changes led to hostilities among organizational departments or units;
- past changes were made more frequently than people could deal with them;
- employee participation in decisions that affect them has been limited to non-existent;
- and, especially, the culture of the organization doesn't support change (lack of trust, poor interdepartmental or vertical communication deficiencies, as covered below).

The more of these conditions that are present (or the more widely spread they are throughout the organization), the more thought and effort needs to be invested in Sponsorship Team member selection, development and support.

Implementation (or Project) Team

Typical composition: Perhaps a third of the Sponsorship Team members also serve on the Implementation Team; other Implementation Team members are chosen from throughout the organization to represent the divisions, departments and units[2] that are involved with or affected by the change and to provide the knowledge and skills necessary to "do" the change. Membership-wise, the Implementation Team is typically three or more times the size of the Sponsorship Team but size itself is not a specific criterion for team composition. Rather, the main selection criteria are usually the demonstrated ability to "get things done" and to work effectively in large and small teams. Most often, Implementation Team members are assigned to subgroups (perhaps called "action teams" or some such) that work on specific goals or tasks, with a leader designated for each. Sometimes one or a few members of the Sponsorship Team who are also serving on the Implementation Team might be appointed to lead a subgroup that will work on implementing particularly important tasks.

The primary responsibility of the Implementation Team is to execute the change plan and assure completion of deliverables effectively, on time and within budget (Higgins, Weiner & Young, 2012).

Ideally, members of the Sponsorship and Implementation Teams will be selected in large part because they consistently manifest the outstanding leadership behaviors (acting with integrity, consistent adherence to change-facilitative values, etc.) covered previously. Other valuable characteristics of team members include:

- personal dissatisfaction with the status quo;
- outstanding communication skills;
- empathy for, and patience with, people who disagree;
- time to devote to the team roles (in this case, "time to devote" refers to the ability to carve out enough time from other important duties. Generally, you should be wary of individuals who are recommended for team membership because they have plenty of "time to devote" to the change process[3]);
- reasonably likely to remain with the organization during the entire course of the change;
- have control over finances/resources necessary to support the change and the willingness to expend those finances/resources in an appropriately supportive manner; and
- personal interest in a successful outcome; personal performance objectives that are aligned with the goals of the change (and with the organization's strategy and primary business goals, of course).

EXPERTS' INSIGHTS: MORE ON TEAM MEMBERSHIP

While, again ideally, all team members would have most of the characteristics bulleted above, it is absolutely vital that at least some do. And, "some" is not one. A great way to doom a major change project from the outset is to create a dependency for success upon a single individual. If you do, you can be virtually guaranteed that that individual will take a job with another company, move to Malaysia or be hit by a bus.

Other considerations regarding the Sponsorship Team:

- Try to avoid having team members who:

  - have a history of disagreement with each other;
  - are jockeying with each other for power or a particular position/promotion;
  - are closely associated with past changes that were considered unsuccessful.

- When possible, represent all groups or units/departments that are affected—negatively or positively—by the change. This, of course, must be preceded by a careful identification of all internal and external stakeholders, including those who can influence the success of the project even if they won't be affected by the implementation or its outcomes. An important part of conducting this "stakeholder analysis" is obtaining some reasonable assessment of how important each group is to the success of the project. This assessment is very useful when final decisions have to be made (at the margin) for inclusion or exclusion of particular groups.
- When it is impossible for team representation to mirror the entire organization, one option is to designate a team member who is from Department A as the official representative of Departments A and B. That way, employees in both of those departments have an official liaison that can advocate for their interests and communicate their concerns. In the same way, while senior-most Sponsors are more desirable, representation from more than one level (if not several levels) in the organization is usually a good idea.
- The size of the Sponsorship Team should be determined in some part by the number of "things" that the team must do. If you are going to expect a lot of certain team members, it's best not to have such a large group (perhaps in the interest of representation) that there is nothing or nothing much for some team members to do. Unequal workloads can be a source of major irritation to the more heavily burdened members.
- Don't assume that smart, articulate managers necessarily are aware of the roles and responsibilities of Sponsorship Team members. Sponsors should undergo training for their forthcoming roles and responsibilities and, if possible, make some kind of public commitment to undertake them.
- Furthermore, don't assume that smart, articulate managers will necessarily <u>remember</u> their roles and responsibilities during the entire course of the change. It is an important part of the Change Leader's or consultant's role to coach and otherwise shape the behavior of Sponsors on a <u>continuing basis</u>.
- Finally, I've often found it helpful to have the people who will choose/approve Sponsorship Team members rate potential candidates on specific skills or characteristics. I do this when I feel that the "choosers" are down to the last couple of choices and are being overly dependent on their gestalts or general impressions of candidates. I might have a form at the ready that requires choosers to evaluate candidates on several dimensions:

- Communication:

  - Writing skills
  - Presentation skills
  - Talking (one-on-one) skills

- Level of interest in the success of the change
- Willingness to meet/talk directly with staff
- Likelihood of lending sincere and strong endorsement
- Etc.
- Etc.
- Etc.

Sometimes, I collect the ratings, collate them and feed them back; sometimes I don't even collect them. I just use them to start a "deeper" conversation about each candidate: "Okay, what do we think of Laura's writing skills?" "Anyone have any evidence of good or poor skills?"

Notes

1 Some Sponsorship Teams will include vendors or customers/clients and/or Board members with appropriate knowledge and skills.
2 Additional selection criteria vary widely. As but one example, I consulted on a project in which some Implementation Team members were chosen because of the personal influence they had with other team members—who by their role had to be chosen—but were expected to be strong resistors.
3 Have you ever heard the prescription, "If you want to get something done, ask a *busy* person to do it!"? Well, with the notable exception of a few future stars who were under-utilized at the outset of major organizational changes on which I consulted, my experience is that the key players and drivers of those changes had their hands full when I walked in the door. The real do-ers in organizations, maybe 10–20 percent of employees, are not only the ones who get things done; they are the ones who work on the greatest number of things simultaneously. As a Change Leader or change management consultant, you will find that some of the busiest people in the focal organization will make the best Sponsorship Team members. So, if candidates seem really committed to working with the team and to making a real impact, the "busy-ness" of their current schedules shouldn't necessarily be a deterrent to their membership.

Reference

Higgins, M., Weiner, J. & Young, L. (2012). Implementation teams: A new lever for organizational change. *Journal of Organizational Behavior, 33*, 366–368.

4

DEDICATED RESOURCES

Without dedicated resources and funding, change management will not happen.
—Prosci (2012, p. 12)

Large-scale, significant organizational change requires significant investment of time, effort, and dollars. . . . Successful changes are characterized by a willingness on the part of the changers to invest significant resources.
—Nadler & Tushman (1989, p. 201)

In extensive studies, each involving hundreds of organizations, nearly every major change management consulting company (e.g., de Jong, Marston, Roth & van Biljon [McKinsey], 2013; IBM, 2014; Prosci, 2012, 2014; Wagner, Foo, Zablit & Taylor [Boston Consulting Group], 2013; etc.) has found that **ample, dedicated resources are necessary for the success of large-scale organizational changes**. Likewise, consulting company reports (e.g., Hitachi Consulting, 2014; Ojjeh, Fischbein & Murray [Ernst & Young], 2014; pwc, 2014, etc.) of intensive, multi-year change management projects within single businesses have found the same.

Despite irrefutable evidence that you can't implement large-scale changes in organizations successfully with fairy dust and good intentions, I've seen little change over the years in the high percentage of organizations that take on such changes while astonishingly underfunding them. Given the high level of on-going internal competition for resources in most organizations today, I guess that's not surprising. On the other hand, it's insane to condemn a change to failure from the outset.

One of the things that *has* changed over time is the melding (here and there) of organizational change management and the field of project management, a merger that I believe has improved both (historically separate) endeavors (Pollack & Adler, 2015). Perhaps as a result, organizational change management has largely adopted the "Iron Triangle" (i.e., the three traditional measures of success in large-scale projects) from project management: Scope, budget and time.[1] Let's take a look at each of these, consider how difficult they are to derive or estimate in large-scale change processes and cover some suggestions I have for increasing derivation/estimation accuracy.

Scope

> Enterprise-wide change has a major impact on the entire organization and is
> usually strategic, large-scale, chaotic, complex, and/or radical in nature.
> —Haines, Aller-Stead & McKinlay (2005, p. 11)

Surveys of "worst practices" in large-scale organizational changes (i.e., the things that change managers most frequently mess up) consistently point to an underestimation of scope and complexity as a frequent and serious problem.

Consider Procter & Gamble which:

- has over 100,000 employees in over 70 countries;
- provides/sells about $4 billion worth of products in over 180 countries each day;
- manages relations and financial transactions with over 80,000 suppliers and external partners;
- provides benefits, services and support to retirees in 90 percent of the countries in the world;
- spends $2+ billion on Research and Development each year;
- in the relatively recent past, decided to eliminate around 100 of its 180 brands (in addition to the 40+ it had divested previously);
- contributes to social and community development in over half the countries in the world;
- has facilities and real estate holdings in over 70 countries;
- has spent as much as $9 billion annually on advertising;
- is a dominant global force in energy conservation and environmental protection;
- maintains over 200 company-destination web sites.[2]

I'd say it's impossible for the human brain to realistically understand and appreciate this level and breadth of complexity. It's even difficult to envision the number of changes that need to be made at P&G when, for example, the Sarbanes-Oxley Act became law, or when Venezuela, Argentina and Turkey unexpectedly devalued their currencies, or when production, sales and communication were disrupted during the "Arab Spring." The amount of complexity and the number of within-company adjustments that have to be made to multiple external influences is mind-boggling.

Now, with an estimation of scope (and eventually budget and time to completion) in mind, let's consider the possible impacts of a *single* large-scale change (such as an ERP[3] implementation for a specific, describable example) *in a much more manageable, middle-sized company* (say, 5,000 employees and $50 million in annual revenues). Like most enterprise-wide changes, but to an extreme, major ERP installations add substantially to daily workloads, usually for long periods of time. But, workload is only one dimension of the scope of such changes. These types of initiatives can touch every aspect of the organization:

*   Jobs can be added, eliminated or drastically changed;
*   Bosses, work groups and co-workers can be re-organized;
*   Responsibilities can increase or decrease or become shared;
*   Access to information is dramatically widened;
*   Organizational and work unit boundaries often fade in importance;
*   Vertical communication usually decreases while horizontal communication increases;
*   Processes become standardized, leaving less room for discretion;
*   Response times become more critical;
*   Authority moves downward, leaving some managers with less; and, of course,
*   There are many new things to learn.

Imagine how hard it would be to anticipate the impact of all of these kinds of organizational stresses occurring at once. If you feel that this is a relatively easily doable task, let me say that, in my personal experience, I have **never** seen the predicted scope of an ERP installation be even close to on target. Almost always, the scope is underestimated—and by a huge factor.[4]

Budget

There's a line from a poem by Longfellow that ends, "but when she was bad, she was horrid." Old Henry W. wasn't writing about IT implementation budgets. But, he might as well have been. A study by Loudhouse Research (reported in Krigsman, 2007) in the United Kingdom found that "only" one-third of IT projects there came in over budget. But, most of those came in at least 50 percent over budget. That's pretty horrid!

A more recent, global study (Panorama Consulting, 2014) found that 37 percent of implementing organizations came in on budget and another 9 percent managed to come in under budget. Of course, that leaves 54 percent coming in over budget with almost half of those spending over 25 percent more than anticipated. It's hard to argue that things have gotten much better as experience with ERP systems has grown tremendously. But, a qualification worth noting is that the estimated percentage of IT- and non-technology-focused projects that come in over budget varies dramatically from study to study. Likewise, the percentage-over-budget estimates vary. **But, the undeniable conclusion is that MANY projects overspend their budgets and MANY of the overages are astronomical.**

Okay. So, what lies behind these budgeting errors? **Most studies conclude that underestimation of project scope is the primary cause.** I'm going to point out a few others:

1. "Ballparking"—There is often a lot of pressure on IT project planners to get to the implementation stage as quickly as possible. That pressure often results in Work Breakdown Structures being underdeveloped. (A Work Breakdown Structure is one of several possible ways of delineating each individual task required by the implementation and combining them into "families" or groups of similar kinds of tasks (Fuller, 1997).) Planners then pull numbers out of the air, perhaps inflate them by a safety net of 5–10 percent and subsequently assign those cost estimates to the various task families. Inevitably, with the necessary detail absent, many costs remain unrecognized in the planning stage.

2. Undue vendor influence—Difficult as it is to believe, research has shown that long-practicing physicians often rely primarily on the advice of non-medically trained pharmaceutical sales people in making decisions about which drugs to prescribe for their patients (Groopman, 2007). Is it any wonder then that some IT project planners/leaders would also be subject to substantial influence by their vendors? While these vendors are no more honest or dishonest than representatives of other professional groups, they certainly have no motive to make the estimated total price tag for the implementation look any more gigantic than necessary.

3. Unbridled exuberance—In their entirely well-intended efforts to "sell" the new system or software to their colleagues, internal change champions often become caught up in their own enthusiasm. Operating with this sort of head wind, it's easy to believe that goals will be less difficult to accomplish than they actually are.

Time

When IT projects aren't delivered on time, there are three primary reasons. One, it takes longer than expected for employees to work through the resistance-to-change stage to the acceptance-of-change stage and/or two, it takes employees longer than expected to learn how to use the new system or software, and/or three, third party vendors don't meet the deadlines to which they've agreed. The presence of any one of these (much less the more likely presence of all three) can metastasize the dreaded "performance dip" (which is explained in the Experts' Insights section just below).

EXPERTS' INSIGHTS: SCOPE, BUDGET, TIME

1. If you underestimate the scope of an enterprise-wide organizational change, you're going to underestimate budget and time as well. **For this reason, many project planning and measurement experts recommend gathering input on scope from as many people/units as possible as early as possible. While this practice increases both the overall budget and the amount of time needed for planning, the more perspectives that are included on the front end, the greater the probability that the full scope of the project will be identified at that time.** Furthermore, broader front-end involvement in these discussions usually results in money- and time-savings in the implementation stage. And, it's just easier emotionally for people to deal with issues that they see coming (through early, broad-based input) rather than ones that come as a surprise later in the implementation.

2. The means by which you obtain input from people is extremely important. Here are two tricks master Change Leaders frequently use:

A. Most often, employee input is obtained simultaneously from individuals or from groups representing the same work unit. This is easier from a scheduling perspective and people who know one another are often more comfortable speaking out. However, it's very useful to have at least some groups include representatives from more than one work unit or department. In part, that's because groups from different organizational "homes" usually represent different perspectives and needs. **As those different viewpoints are expressed, they will many times trigger good ideas or important insights that would not be brought to the surface in (same-old, same-old) one-unit-only groups.** In addition, some employees are more likely to give you the "real scoop" when they are not in the presence of certain colleagues with whom they must work and interact daily.

B. Employee interviews are usually conducted in a conference room, in an interview room, or in the cafeteria—namely any available open space away from the job. The limitation encountered here is that it is difficult for some people to talk about their jobs in the abstract. That's why it is usually a good idea to conduct at least some interviews while people are in their work stations. For those with less abstract thinking ability or lower articulation skills, "walking someone through the job" helps them collect and convey their thoughts.

3. The more complicated the planned change, the more things that can go wrong, right? Especially if technology is involved! **So, why do so many managers promise that things will get a lot better for everyone as soon as the change is implemented?**

Well, that's one of the dilemmas of having to "sell" the importance of the change to the troops. Sometimes we get so wrapped up in our vision of the future—or in the process of selling the change itself—that we underestimate how long it will take until we'll see the benefits of our efforts.

Forewarning: After the "go live" or date of large-scale change implementation, **things usually get worse before they get better**. This phenomenon is so common it's been given a name: "The Post-Organizational Change Performance Dip."

So, without taking any juice from your promotion of the change, **it's usually best to take a conservative stance on how quickly desired outcomes will be attained**. As I've already argued, major organizational changes can result in a lot of stress for the involved (and affected) employees. That stress itself can put a big limitation on short-term performance subsequent to the implementation. **Once you add in a learning curve, possible equipment down time and the time that it takes many employees to understand and accept the need for the change—and a hundred other factors—the likelihood that things will get worse before they get better is quite high.** So, be smart and lead people to expect that the rose garden you're promising isn't going to be in full bloom by a week from Tuesday.

Meanwhile, your job is to effectively manage the change process so that the depth of the dip and the time to improved performance are each as small/short as possible. In terms of the illustration in Figure 4.1, you're looking to make the "not unusual" line get as close to, or preferably higher/faster than, the "norm" line. That's no easy task. But forewarned is forearmed, so anticipate the dip. Don't be a dip and not build it into your timetable.

4. A major contributing factor to underestimates of budget and time is the failure to identify "dependencies" in the implementation plan. While there are usually many action steps that can be taken simultaneously, there will undoubtedly be steps that need to be taken sequentially. For example, Work Group A must produce Outcome X before Work Group B can begin working on Outcome Y. Each dependency in an implementation plan creates a possibility of delay. So, the more of them

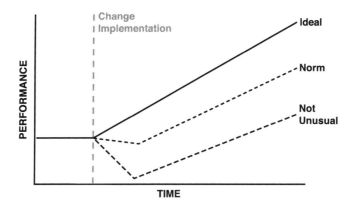

FIGURE 4.1 The Post-Organizational Change Performance Dip

that are identified in advance, the more likely budget and time estimates will be able to take them into account.

5. Here's a wild one: Your initial estimate of project scope can be right on the money and still end up being far off the mark. What? Yep, it's true. Not only true, but common. Why? Because of "scope creep," the likelihood that goals will be added and others expanded during the course of multi-year, large-scale organizational changes. Scope creep usually results in extremely inflationary costs. For example, the addition of goals can create many more dependencies whose effects are difficult to foresee, much less accurately estimate cost-wise, in the midst of the chaos of the on-going change.

Admittedly, add-ons are sometimes counteracted by goals or outcomes that are dropped during the implementation stage. Regardless, in order to maintain control of the project, it's very important to establish on the front end the mechanism through which potential add-ons will be evaluated and approved (or not). Likewise, it's critical that all parties with governance responsibilities understand from the beginning that approval of each "creep" has a likely associated cost.

6. Finally, here's a seldom-used idea that helps keep budgets in line. When large-scale change projects get to the implementation stage, there is typically little attention paid to the budget as things get going (i.e., in the early stages of work). There's plenty of money in the "bank" at that point and cost estimates for the early parts of implementations tend to be fairly accurate. However, it's not a good idea to be content with staying on budget in the first 25 percent or even 50 percent of a project. You can bet that there WILL be unexpected costs coming down the road and the best way to deal with them is to focus on the budget from the very beginning and **try to come in below plan (i.e., under budget) in the early stages to create a resource or cash reserve that can be applied to "surprises" that are surely in store**.

Notes

1 In addition to scope, budget and time, a fourth criterion is often used: End user/doer satisfaction. This criterion is covered in another chapter.
2 P&G statistics were compiled from a variety of (official) P&G web pages and presentations that can be found on the Internet.
3 An enterprise-wide computer system and accompanying software providing governance over a single database that acquires information in real time rather than on the basis of multiple, periodic inputs. ERPs enable all units in the organization to inter-operate fully.
4 Underestimation of project scope is frequently caused by "scope creep," a phenomenon covered later in this section.

References

All web site URLs accessed on December 12, 2015.

de Jong, M., Marston, N., Roth, E. & van Biljon, P. (2013). *The eight essentials of innovation performance.* McKinsey & Associates. White Paper. Retrieved from www.google.com/

url?sa=t&rct=j&q=&esrc=s&source=web&cd=1&ved=0ahUKEwjQub_6kNfJAhXCg j4KHWieCvkQFggiMAA&url=http%3A%2F%2Fwww.mckinsey.com%2F~%2Fmedia %2FMcKinsey%2Fdotcom%2Fclient_service%2FStrategy%2Fpdfs%2Fthe_eight_ essentials_of_innovation_perfomance.ashx&usg=AFQjCNGg6vmgBvh6suk1my4ByT 1Obq34tg&sig2=S4a8p6vHNus3TPale0uN8A&bvm=bv.109910813,d.eWE&cad=rja.

Fuller, J. (1997). *Managing performance improvement projects*. San Francisco, CA: Pfeiffer.

Groopman, J. (2007). *How doctors think*. New York, NY: Houghton Mifflin Company.

Haines, S., Aller-Stead, G. & McKinlay, J. (2005). *Enterprise-wide change: Superior results through systems thinking*. San Francisco, CA: Pfeiffer.

Hitachi Consulting. (2014). *Case study: Aerospace and defense supplier*. White Paper. Retrieved from www.hitachiconsulting.com/sites/catalog/Lists/Collateral/Aerospace%20and%20 Defense%20Supplier-CS.pdf.

IBM (Institute for Business Value). (2014). *Making change work . . . while the work keeps changing*. IBM White Paper. Retrieved from www-935.ibm.com/services/us/gbs/bus/html/gbs-making-change-work.html.

Krigsman, M. (2007). New research into IT project failures. *ZDNet*, September 26. Retrieved from www.zdnet.com/article/new-research-into-it-project-failures/.

Nadler, D. & Tushman, M. (1989). Organizational frame-bending: Principles for managing reorientation. *Academy of Management Executive, 3(3)*, 194–204.

Ojjeh, S., Fischbein, K. & Murray, C. (2014). *Launching a hedge fund – building the operational foundation for success*. Ernst and Young. White Paper. Retrieved from www.ey.com/ Publication/vwLUAssets/EY-Webcast-Launching-a-successful-hedge-fund/$FILE/ EY-Hedge-Fund-Launch-whitepaper.pdf.

Panorama Consulting. (2014). *Scope overruns and suboptimal benefit realization continue to plague ERP implementations*. Retrieved from http://Panorama-Consulting.com/ resource-center/2014-erp-report/.

Pollack, J. & Adler, D. (2015). Emergent trends and passing fads in project management research. *International Journal of Project Management, 33*, 236–248.

Prosci. (2012). *Best practices in change management – 2012 Edition (Prosci Benchmarking Report)*. Loveland, CO: Prosci Research.

Prosci. (2014). *Best practices in change management – 2014 Edition (Prosci Benchmarking Report)*. Loveland, CO: Prosci Research.

pwc. (2014) *Best practices: The elusive benefit*. pwc. White Paper. Retrieved from www.pwc. com/us/en/insurance/publications/adopting-best-practices-successfully.html.

Wagner, K., Foo, E., Zablit, H. & Taylor, A. (2013). *The most innovative companies, 2013: Lessons from leaders*. Boston Consulting Group. White Paper. Retrieved from www. bcgperspectives.com/content/articles/innovation_growth_most_innovative_companies_ 2013_lessons_from_leaders/.

5

COMMUNICATION, CULTURE AND CAMPAIGNS

Applying Social Cognitive Neuroscience (SCN) Findings to Basic Communication Issues

The human brain learns by *metaphors* and remembers by *stories*. So, *both are essential* components of effective change-related communications.

Let's Start with Metaphors

In Chapter 2, you discovered that we can only relate one concept to another when those two concepts are physiologically *connected* in our neural circuitry. Recall the example of a person *learning* that Muhammad Ali is the world's most widely recognized American? That person had pre-existing knowledge of Muhammad Ali but had not yet considered who the world's most widely recognized American might be. Upon reading that Ali was the most widely recognized, a physiological change took place in the person's brain and the neuron with existing Ali information connected electro-chemically with another neuron in which "world's most widely recognized American" was then established.

In order to understand a new concept, we have to have some existing related or relatable neurons to which a new circuit can be connected. Imagine trying to learn algebra if you hadn't first learned multiplication or trying to learn multiplication if you hadn't first learned about numbers. We can only learn new things by connecting those new things to things we already know. And, **that's exactly what a metaphor is; it's something that allows us to learn a new thing in terms of or in comparison to something else** that is already known (Lakoff, 2003).

Metaphor expert, James Geary (2009), has found that we use a metaphor on average about six times per minute. If that number seems unrealistically high, pick up a major city newspaper and skim a couple of pages of article headlines. I just did that with this morning's *The New York Times*. Ten of the first 13 headings I came upon used a metaphor including "A Cuban Brain Drain, Courtesy of the U.S.," "Medical website experiences some hiccups" and "College-bound high school seniors hedge their bets."

Metaphors are used no less often in non-newspaper businesses. One of the best examples of the utility of metaphors for effective communication in a business setting comes from the book, *The myth of the garage* (Heath & Heath, 2011). (The Heath brothers are also the authors of an important book on making messages compelling called *Made to stick* (Heath & Heath, 2008).) The Heaths want you to imagine being the owner of a community bank that needs to differentiate itself from the bigger financial players in the area. Your marketing manager comes to you with the idea of re-designing the lobby and services area of your operation. He says that "We need to have a hipper, more relaxed feel—that will appeal to our younger, upscale professional customers."

Did your brain just conjure up a picture of what "hipper, more relaxed feel" would look like? Are you already picturing certain kinds of chairs and accessories? Probably not. That's because, in all likelihood, you don't have a pre-existing, standardized, cognitive map (or mental model) of what "hipper-more-relaxed" is exactly. And, if you do, my conception of it is extremely likely to be different than yours. However, (per the Heaths) what if your marketing manager said that we need our space to look "less like a bank and more like a Starbucks." Now, we're getting somewhere. You already have a conception of a Starbucks—and so your marketing manager's proposal communicated this way is much more likely to be understood. We have a "visual starting place" for honing the idea.[1]

Good metaphors can convey a lot of abstract information compactly and memorably (Heath & Heath, 2008) and

Mobilizing the Change Process with Metaphors and Symbolism: A Second Chance at Change

Roberto and Levesque (2005) present a case of a successful second attempt to implement large-scale change at a Fortune 500 *auto parts* retailer. In an earlier unsuccessful attempt, the need for change was presented purely in business terms. The second attempt was framed by a metaphor comparing store staff with a NASCAR racing team, NASCAR being a strong, common interest of many employees. The Change Leaders even produced a video that enacted the metaphor by having actual employees, in NASCAR gear, perform the roles of "drivers," "pit crews" and "pit managers" in a store setting. For example, actor-employees portraying pit crew members were shown working quickly and in a highly coordinated fashion re-stocking merchandise on the shelves, thereby drawing a comparison to how actual pit crew members would "re-stock" tires, gasoline and water for the driver in a race car. As with real pit crews, only precise, highly coordinated *team* behaviors could result in a "checkered flag." The metaphor turned out to be a "winner" in the entire "circuit" of the company's nearly 1,000 stores.

they can provide a **shared** *image* **across large numbers of people** (Lakoff, 2003). I use the word "image" purposefully because established metaphors are stored in our brains very much like visual images (or photographs) (Schmidt & Augart Seger, 2009). *Metaphorically speaking*, you could say that familiar metaphors are like icons on the desktop of our brain's visual center. That is, they act as symbols or summaries for the belief and behavior patterns they represent (Ritchie, 2013).

Good metaphors are also effective because they can activate many regions of the brain simultaneously (i.e., not only the visual center). **Amazingly, the brain can respond to** *specific* **words used in a metaphor.** For example, Lacey, Stilla and Sathian (2012) demonstrated that certain words can activate the parts of the brain that are most closely associated with the other (non-visual) senses. Get this (!): If the metaphor has a textural component ("I've really had a *rough* day"), the *touch* center of the brain "lights up." Same thing goes for "I *rang* him like a *bell*"—*hearing* center; "I wanted to win so badly, I could *taste* it"—*taste* center; and thanks to the band, Nirvana, "*Smells* like teen spirit" activates the *smell* center. **In general, however, good metaphors (without specific mention of an emotional-center-based word or words) are more likely to elicit** *positive* **emotional responses in comparison with the same, but metaphor-less, content.**[2]

Now, Let's Take a Look at Stories

If a good metaphor is like a visual image (or photograph), a good story is like a movie.

In "Speed of Darkness," the late poet, Muriel Rukeyser (1968), penned a line that would become renowned: "The universe is made of stories, not of atoms." If we consider how our brains perceive and record our experiences in the world, Ms. Rukseyer was dead on.

Think about how we get to know other people. It's usually the result of stories we tell each other about ourselves:

Q. "Are you from this area originally?"
A. "No. I was born in upstate New York. But, when I was a freshman in high school, my parents got divorced and my mother took the kids and moved back to St. Louis . . ."

Q. "How did you get involved with this Task Force?"
A. "Well, when I got transferred out of consumer products, I . . ."

Q. "How do you feel about Maddie's proposal?"
A. "At first I thought it was great. But, then I did some of my own research and . . ."

Even if you are asked to explain something very complicated—like one of your major belief systems—chances are that you'll respond in story form. Why?

Perhaps the analogy probably isn't 100 percent accurate. But it's believed that the **human brain files its experiences in something like story form** (with a beginning, characters, a sequence of events, etc.). Then, when the brain must recall and convey information that has been filed, the information returns in story form and, in the interest of energy conservation, the brain conveys it in the same way. However, the stories our brains file and later convey aren't always true to the original stories. And, for certain, we know that if we learn most—but not all—of a story, our brains (while operating below the level of our awareness) will over time begin to "fill in" some of the information that we *don't have* based only on what we *assume* is: a) *likely* to have happened and b) a *good fit* with the information that we *do have* (Gots, 2012; Medina, 2008). (Recall that our brains don't like ambiguity. They'd rather guess about any missing information than "leave holes in" a story.)

Why do stories have greater impact and memorability? There are many reasons. For one thing, good stories "draw us in" as we identify with a character or characters. **The brain literally creates a neural reproduction or representation of the story**—adding details or embellishments as they are imagined. These reproductions change or are "edited" as new information or insights become known (Speer, Reynolds, Swallow & Zacks, 2009). For example, while listening to a story, someone might be imagining the protagonist ("Chris") as a man. If it comes to light that Chris is a woman, listeners' brains would take that into account and adapt the reproduction accordingly. That doesn't happen without story-form.[3]

Furthermore, preliminary evidence (Zak, 2014) indicates that another response to stories is the secretion of oxytocin, a hormone sometimes referred to as the "love drug" because one of its effects is a greatly enhanced sense of empathy (Choi, 2011). In the brain, oxytocin acts similarly to many opiates and the highly addictive drug, Oxycontin (Vuong, Van Uum, O'Dell, Lutfy & Friedman, 2010).

Stories and Sense-Making

"Anyone leading a major organizational change program must take the time to think through its **story** – what makes it worth the undertaking – and explain this story to all of the people involved in making change happen, so that their contributions make sense to them as individuals."

(Lawson & Price, 2003)

BRAIN CONNECTION!

Good stories told by high-level and/or prestigious individuals become very deeply encoded in our brains and they "spread like wild fire" (metaphorically speaking).

Consider this excerpt from an English translation of a Miroslav Holub (1977) poem:

> The young lieutenant of a small Hungarian detachment in the Alps
> sent a reconnaissance unit out into the icy wasteland.
> It began to snow immediately, snowed for two days and the unit
> did not return.
>
> The lieutenant suffered: he had dispatched his own people to death.
> But the third day the unit came back.
>
> Where had they been? How had they made their way?
> Yes, they said, we considered ourselves lost and waited for the end.
> And then one of us found a map in his pocket. That calmed us down.
> We pitched camp, lasted out the snowstorm and then with the map
> we discovered our bearings.
> And here we are.
>
> The lieutenant borrowed this remarkable map
> and had a good look at it. It was not a map of the Alps
> but of the Pyrenees.

According to Basboll and Graham (2006), a famous management professor appropriated this poem and used it as a story of his own, supposedly a true one. The professor told the story at some conferences and incorporated it in six of his publications. He also conveyed it to CEOs and other executives, as well as to members of the media. Subsequently, the story was retold as true in the writings of other, very famous management professors, in speeches by numerous executives and in the media—all using the initial management professor as the source. Basboll and Graham say that this original professor created many and quite different learnings that could be inferred from the story, for example: "Plans, even when they are wrong, are useful because they serve as a pretext to start acting. What managers keep forgetting is that it is the action, not the plan, that explains their success" (Weick, 1983, p. 49). Basboll and Graham (2006, p. 197) marveled at the "tenacity with which [this 'borrowed' anecdote] has lodged itself in the imagination of organization theory for better or for worse."

In her book *Influence*, Jenny Nabben (2014) provides the summary shown in Table 5.1 of how the human brain responds to *stories* as opposed to how it responds to *information* presented in anything other than story form.

TABLE 5.1 Messages that Stick and Messages that Slip

The neuroscience of storytelling	The neuroscience of information
Stories activate multi-sensory cortices: motor, auditory, olfactory, somatosensory and visual.	Information mainly activates Broca's and Wernicke's area. Stories use sensory-specific words which are easier for the brain to imagine and then elaborate on.
Each person will have their own unique imaginative experience generated from these associations.	Information uses abstract, conceptual language that is more difficult for the brain to find associated sensory images.
Great stories are easily recalled due to the power of their sensory associations.	Information is difficult for the brain to record and remember (which is why we use acronyms and other recall devices to help us remember).
Characters in stories generate emotional associations and we can identify with the character.	We don't identify with information. Great stories are always emotional. Information is devoid of emotion.
Stories have recognizable structure: beginning, middle and end, which is familiar to the brain.	Information is more linear.
Stories motivate us to move away from or toward something. These responses are deeply embedded in the brain as motivational drives.	Information is not inherently motivational unless knowing about something has an additional benefit to us in terms of our ability to survive or thrive.

Source: Nabben (2014)

Thanks, Jenny. That's Storytelling 6, Information 0 right there!

Could anything be better than that? Yup. Good stories with good metaphors. But, better still is "visual-storytelling"!

Visual-storytelling (VST) as a concept is quite simple. It involves using images (still or moving) or other types of graphics to—as much as possible—*tell* the story. (**Stories with images are more engaging** (i.e., more deeply encoded in the brain and, thus, more easily recalled), as any author of children's books knows.) While there is extensive SCN research that demonstrates the brain's dynamic responses to visuals, their effect is understandable from simpler and more traditional points of view such as basic physics (e.g., the overwhelming number of stimuli to which humans are exposed are visual (Schifferstein, 2006)[4]), physiology (e.g., the brain processes visuals much faster than words (Potter, Wyble, Hagman & McCort, 2014)) and culture (e.g., decreasing attention spans, increasing need to filter out more irrelevant and inaccurate information, wide exposure to special effects in many mediums, even the emergence of "Visual Culture Studies" as a college major).

So, what's new about VST? Enthusiastic proponents of VST would have you believe that an entirely new medium has been created. In my view, the medium isn't new. What's new is that the functionality of graphics technology has advanced to such an extent that there are virtually no limits to how creatively visual images can be digitized, synthesized and manipulated—with eye-popping results. Yet, the effectiveness of visual images in communication campaigns about large-scale organizational changes doesn't have to be dependent on such high-level technologies.

For example: All too frequently, major organizational change efforts fail because the logic of the need for change is of such a scale or level of complexity that people can't get their "brains around it." That is, they lack an appropriate, existing "cognitive map" (cf., discussion about cognitive maps in Chapter 2) or mental model of the "big picture," the dynamic interaction of the forces that has created the need to change. In hundreds of organizations undergoing large-scale changes, it's been demonstrated successfully that **a highly complex cognitive map can be created for people by bringing together (and integrating) common existing cognitive maps in a new way—one in which a *story* emerges**. Then we can count on the brains of the employees involved to make them feel like they are "in" the story (Denning, 2011).

That's exactly what several innovative consulting companies (including TiER1) are able to do quite effectively—using "Learning Maps." A Learning Map is a large (perhaps 3′ × 5′–6′), colorful and dense-packed poster that depicts visually several relationships or story lines that reflect whatever particular and often unique challenges with which the client organization must deal. (Many maps cleverly include metaphors.) Usually, there are four to seven Learning Maps created for each client to—in the case of organizational change—depict the big picture of the need for the change and to enumerate the arduous tasks that lie ahead during implementation. **These maps don't describe the issues** in the big picture or the trade-offs that will have to be made while the changes are being implemented. **Instead, seven to ten participants are led to draw their own conclusions about problems and how they might be solved** by a facilitator working with a manual that includes dialogue-generating questions, several different types of scenarios that can be worked through and often something akin to a game in which subgroups might be asked to devise and try different ways to solve a specific problem.

I first worked with Learning Maps on a project for one of my clients, a Fortune 500 financial services firm. This company, with a truly outstanding performance record over many decades, was dealing with a problem that could put them out of business. It was the same crucial problem that many of their competitors—who also earned most of their revenues from the sale of life (and related) insurance policies—were facing. Through a wide variety of forces (including decreasing willingness of employers to pay for employees' life insurance, changes in government regulations and a cultural adaptation to the economy—especially very high interest rates), the populace became much more interested in immediate investment gains as opposed to protection against an event that could lie decades away

(Negley, 2013). The relief valve for life insurance companies was the Financial Services Modernization Act (Public Law 106-102, 113 Stat. 1338 enacted on November 12, 1999 by the 106th Congress). Its passage opened the door for insurance companies to also provide investment bank services. The client company with which I was working had created what appeared to be an outstanding strategic plan to become a multi-focused financial services firm. But, senior managers were stunned when they received strong, emotional push-back from long-time and highly valued employees who personally identified themselves with the insurance business.

About a week before my initial meeting with the client on this particular push-back problem, I had read a newspaper article about how The Prudential had solved this very same change-of-business communication problem—using Learning Maps. I made a referral to the consulting company[5] that was helping The Prudential and the client engaged them to create a Learning Map-based communication campaign for a second strategy roll-out. Luckily, the client retained me to help them (i.e., the client's change team) with that process and some related matters. That provided a great opportunity for me to experience the "magic" of Learning Maps from a first row seat. By the end of the project for this client, I was "sold" on the potential impact of Learning Maps.

Recall that Learning Maps can include metaphors, story lines and tons of visuals *and* the focus is on getting the learners involved to actively draw their own conclusions about the validity of the need for change and the likely effectiveness of the change that is being proposed.[6] Today, Learning Maps are an extremely important "weapon" in TiER1's organizational change methodologies "arsenal." With good reason, they play an integral role in most of the organizational change communication campaigns that TiER1 creates and manages.

Culture

I like to say that organizational culture is what people describe when they are asked, "What's it like to work here?" I've heard others say that it's the *personality* of the organization . . . or its *DNA* . . . or its *character* . . . or it's *"just how we do things around here."*

Employees infer their organization's culture primarily from:

- what they are **told** (e.g., in socialization/orientation programs; by senior managers through stories and ceremonies; through enterprise-wide communication campaigns, etc.);
- what they **observe** (e.g., how people interact with and talk about other employees; what behaviors are rewarded—and, especially—what behaviors are ignored; whether the organization's expressed values are consistently practiced; what kinds of information is shared with employees, etc.); and

- **collective observations** (e.g., results of internal "culture surveys," coverage of the organization in the media, especially if the coverage involves unethical behaviors, attitudes of customers, vendors, suppliers, etc.).

Organizational culture has long been demonstrated to have a direct and independent impact on individual and organizational performance. In recent times, the strength of this relationship has continued to be validated, now *across industries* (e.g., Jacobs, Mannion, Davies, Harrison, Konteh & Walshe, 2013; Navaresse, Yauch, Goff & Fonseca, 2014; Nold, 2012; Yazici, 2011) and **across national cultures** (e.g., Aksoy, Apak, Eren & Korkmaz, 2014; Neagu & Nicula, 2012; Zhou, Bundorf, Chang, Huang & Xue, 2011) *by researchers in many different academic and professional disciplines.* **The very same thing can be said about organizational communication** (i.e., hundreds of studies have shown that its overall quality has a direct and independent impact on individual and organizational performance, across industries and national cultures (Berger, 2014)).

Over the last 30 years, there has been endless debate among researchers about which of the two (culture, communication) is more powerful, about how the two are related, about how the two interact, etc. My view is that these questions aren't worth asking, much less answering. The facts are: Every organization has a culture and every organization must produce organizational-level communication. **Organizational culture can most assuredly have an impact on organizational communication and the reverse is also true.** What's important about culture and communication with regard to large-scale organizational change is that they (again, culture and communication) **must be aligned** (i.e., supportive of each other and both must support the proposed change) **or the status quo will win hands-down**.

In Chapter 1, I wrote:

> It has been well-established that change initiatives (and performance improvement processes in general) are dramatically more likely to succeed when the following conditions are created and maintained:
>
> - Everyone involved respects and works for the benefit of *all* organizational stakeholders.
> - Trust is built through honest, open communication and debate.
> - Input is broadly based; civil, principled dissent is welcome and respected.
> - People are given the information, and the time, that they need to adjust to change, as well as the skills that they need to implement it.
> - Contributions of individuals and groups to the success of the change effort are appropriately recognized.

If you look carefully at this bulleted list, you'll see that each of these "conditions" (or what I also called "change-facilitative values") has a cultural element *and* a communication element. How much of one vs. how much of the other doesn't matter. What matters is the **alignment, the harmonizing of the two**.

EXPERTS' INSIGHTS: ORGANIZATIONAL ALIGNMENT

When I was eight or nine years old, I had a large, wooden, ball-shaped puzzle that had, perhaps, 30–35 parts, no two of which were alike. The only way you could put the pieces together to "build" the final product was to start with the smallest pieces that would become the middle of the final (ball) form. Each of the pieces would only fit one (correct) way into the other pieces. That is, each one of the 30+ pieces had to fit perfectly with all the other pieces. So, if you were able to put the puzzle together completely what you would have is a ball-shaped thing in which every single piece was perfectly aligned with every other piece to which it had any bearing or relationship. "Solving" the puzzle was very, very challenging.

That puzzle is the metaphorical or pictorial way that I think about "the challenge" of organizational alignment. Every part of an organization has to fit perfectly with and support every other part of the organization to which it has any bearing or relationship. However, if you map that metaphor or picture onto a global organization with a couple hundred thousand employees and a couple dozen products or services—and all that comes with those two characteristics of the organization alone—the enormity and complexity of the organizational alignment challenge is incomprehensible. You literally can't see the picture for the pixels.

As a result of its complexity, this much is certain:

First of all, organizational alignment isn't an all or nothing phenomenon. No large organization is perfectly aligned. It's a matter of degree. At the same time, it is clear that some organizations are more (or better) aligned overall than others.

Second, alignment is a "systems" characteristic or dynamic. As such, if you change Variable A in the system to line it up better with Variable B, there's a chance that you'll be moving Variable A farther out of line with Variable C. Sticking with puzzle metaphors: Think Rubik's Cube.

Third, organizational alignment is really tough to measure because it is usually defined by subordinate concepts that are themselves very difficult to measure; organizational culture, for example.

Most formal alignment models used or referenced in consultant-driven, large-scale organizational changes (e.g., The Five Star Model (Galbraith, 2005); Elements of Design (Kilman, Shanahan, Toma & Zielinski, 2010); The Congruence Model (Nadler, Pasmore & Torres, 2006)) "work around" the issue of complexity by choosing to focus on a handful of macro-level categories (e.g., strategy, capabilities/competencies, process, rewards and people in The Five Star Model) and look for ways of aligning them—and whatever might fall within those categories.

My approach is the opposite. I try to identify as many sources of disharmony (misalignments) as I can and work on harmonizing (aligning) them. There's no recipe for exactly how to go about this. But, here's a list of key questions that should be asked of the focal organization's personnel. The answers to these questions will get you going in the right direction.

1. Are obstacles to performance regularly identified and removed?
2. Are changes in goals and procedures, etc., communicated clearly and promptly—especially to the groups that will be affected by the changes?
3. Do the people who support and enable change obtain greater rewards, recognition and/or opportunities for learning and advancement?
4. Do people know what is expected of them and why? Do people know what is expected of people in other departments and why?
5. Are espoused organizational values and enacted values identical on a day-to-day basis? (Another way of asking this: Are everyday behaviors tightly aligned with the organization's stated values?)
6. Do people have access to the information they need to make great decisions?
7. Do decision-makers have the resources and the control they need to operate dynamically?
8. Is performance accurately and adequately assessed?
9. Is performance feedback used to take corrective action?
10. Are management practices evidence-based?

Effective, Strategic Communication Campaigns: As Seen from the Front Line

by Stephanie Savely, TiER1 Principal Consultant, Solution Architect[7]

Author's note: Stephanie Savely has been on the forefront of highly successful communication campaigns that have been created for dozens of TiER1's clients. Over the years, I've come to greatly admire Stephanie's ability to efficiently extract important nuggets of information about a client's organization and the particular project at hand and turn them into the building blocks of campaigns that deeply resonate with the various and highly varying audiences in her client organizations. So, I've asked Stephanie to step up to the keyboard and share with you and me some of the creative infrastructure that serves as the foundation of her work.

Where to Start?

Effective strategic communication campaigns (hereafter, "campaigns") aren't quantum physics, but they do take thought in preparation and diligence in execution. Those two things are sometimes in short supply due to time pressures that our clients have imposed upon themselves or that were thrust upon them by other forces from inside or outside of the organization—or both.

Time pressures aside, new clients are invariably eager to see what we can do for them and they are chomping at the bit to get the campaign underway. That's ironic because the very first step in strategic campaigns is to look backward before we go forward. Understanding the organization's history and culture is critical to meeting audiences "where they are" in terms of their ability to receive your messages.

One of our first questions of clients is "how much organizational 'baggage' is there?" That is, what's the organization's experience with the execution of change initiatives? Is it pretty good at change and finishing what it starts, or is there a history of frustration and failed attempts? An examination of an organization's past change management performance is the starting point for the creation of an effective change-supportive campaign.

Depending upon the nature and amount of baggage, the ability (and willingness) of the various audiences to hear and understand your messages—much less embrace them—can be severely limited. As was pointed out in the Prologue, this diminished capacity is quite often a function of various anxiety-inducing neurotransmitters being secreted in the brain. But for my purposes, I'll just call it a mental block. If that block is present, we have to focus on finding a means of eliminating (or at least lessening) it before we can do anything else. There is a bit of art and a bit of science to doing that.

After two decades of working in the trenches trying to get people to do things differently, you'd think that I'd be cynical. But the opposite is true. Time and time again I've seen people, who initially were dead-set against the change, slowly become supportive once they are given enough information to enable them to understand the need for it and the tools necessary to execute it. I believe sincerely that most people want organizational changes to be successful (as long as they make sense and the pain/cost to the employees themselves isn't too great). Despite some requisite grumbling, I think that deep down most people (not all) are consciously or unconsciously looking for reasons to get onboard with the change.

To make that happen in organizations that haven't had successful experiences with change, you first have to acknowledge that history and how it can make the implementation of future changes more difficult—but not impossible—to implement successfully. I'm not talking about "burning platform" types of approaches. I'm talking about putting historical issues on the table but hopefully in a more mentally palatable way than they were initially *experienced*.

There are many ways to do that and I find that inserting a little humor is often very effective, sometimes necessary. The messages shouldn't criticize past efforts or embarrass anyone—but a chagrined acknowledgement—and perhaps an amusingly presented, fatalistic acceptance of the past—goes a long way toward developing more positive mindsets.

For one client, we created a video to help diffuse frustration with a program that had developed a bad reputation and ended up being quite different from how it was initially described. Interviews with viewers showed that two very short clips "stuck" in their minds and were recalled positively. In one, an actor talked about the program's history as it was intended to be while key employees provided less positive, but more historically accurate, color commentary. Another clip went like this: "We launched our first site for agents and called it 'WebGen,' (*name appears on screen, then is crossed out*) no, 'Next Gen,' (*second name appears on screen, then is crossed out*) no, 'Modern Link,' (third name appears on screen) yes, that's it!" [Big smile.]

A little tongue-in-cheek honesty—and a great delivery—can provide a release valve for pent-up frustrations and current fears.

What Are the Most Critical Objectives?

Understanding where you are starting is critical to being able to set appropriate objectives for communication strategy or change management strategy as a whole. The importance of setting effective objectives is quite possibly the most under-appreciated task in much of corporate America. For the overall performance of individuals, objectives-setting is often a tortuous experience relegated to once or twice a year, with hardly a glance at the result in between. That doesn't work for complex campaigns. You *must* set clear objectives and keep them *front and center* or you won't be able to manage expectations or keep the focus on the target. Otherwise, objectives will mutate and become diluted over time as multiple stake-holders impose their own perspectives on them. Trust me. Too many cooks in the communication kitchen is almost always a serious potential problem.

Objectives should be used to direct your time and resources decisions *throughout* any change initiative. If I only need to nudge one team a few steps, but completely change the entire work process and perspective of another, where should I make the bigger investment? What will result in the greatest ROI? No campaign is given unlimited resources. You have to plan carefully where limited resources will be spent and you can't do that without effective objectives.

In allocating resources, I favor the elements of a change initiative that will have big—rather than incremental—impacts. At the same time, it's important to recognize that some more modest-sounding objectives, if attained, **are necessary to enable the attainment of more ambitious objectives**. For example, an objective of experiencing no increase in the loss rate of key talent during the course of a major initiative might be of vital importance. You can't hit a three-run home run if nobody has gotten on base. Yes, I go for big innings. But, I still play "small ball."

Campaign objectives differ in many ways other than potential impact. Less complex initiatives will have a shorter time frame and, usually, more specific measurement of whether objectives have been attained. Yet, whether it's a discrete program with a "go live" date or a long-term culture-change initiative, **objectives-setting follows the same process**. That process involves the answering of a number of key questions. At each important milestone, what do I need each audience to think? What do I need them to feel? What do I need them to do and why?

These "what do I need" questions raise the question of measuring audience reaction. The importance of measurement and its role in large-scale change efforts have been covered in other parts of this Guide. Nonetheless, I'd like to chip in two additional perspectives:

1. Change management, and communications in particular, have a hard time getting respect in many organizations. Being able to demonstrate how you took your audiences from point A to point B goes a long way in building credibility. So, the sooner that demonstration, the better. For the initial assessment of whether a campaign is working, don't be thinking in terms of months. Often, audience reaction to a campaign can go up, down and up again in a two- or three-month period. You don't want to allow the possibility that the only measurement of effectiveness is during that down period. More frequent measurement results in more accuracy of *trends*. More importantly, that down period might have been caused by a specific, non-communication event. Frequent measurements allow you to capture co-incidental effects.

2. When talking about your objectives and measurement tactics with leadership and key stakeholders, make sure you talk about when and how you'll adjust your approach based on the feedback that's received. They need to understand upfront that adjustments are part of the process, so they aren't surprised or feel like something is wrong when adjustments are needed.

Think like a Marketer

Once we know where the organization has been and where it wants to be, it's time to—as we say at TiER1—"think like a marketer." At the risk of offending great communications professionals everywhere, there is typically a difference between how marketing teams and internal communications teams approach problems. There are good reasons for that, and the first one starts with a B and ends with UDGET. Having the ability to show the business how a "spend" drives buying—as marketers do—is pretty good leverage to drive a budget. Internal communications units have a harder row to hoe in that regard.

So how do you "think like a marketer"?

Get a Plan

First you have to put your objectives to work. (You didn't think we created them to "check a box" then let them gather dust, did you?) You need to give very serious thought to your program, timelines, audiences and objectives and put your pencil to work. What are the best ways to reach each audience, what are the components to the story you need to tell and how do they build upon each other? What are key events or dates that you can leverage or create to get your message across? In other words, WHAT are you going to do and HOW are you going to do it?

As I indicated earlier, resources to support a campaign (and thereby the plan to execute it) are almost always limited. So, you need to decide—based on objectives that have been set—how and where you will allocate resources with the most crucial objectives receiving the lion's share.

However, even if a theoretical campaign has little or no resources constraints, you should never deliver all of your messages with maximum power. Here's a metaphorical story from the opera world to help you remember this important point: Experts have often chosen Puccini's "Nessun Dorma" as the most powerful aria ever written. It was popularized (actually reaching No. 2 on the pop charts in the U.K.) (Tri, 2013) by one of the world's most powerful singers, Luciano Pavarotti. When Pavarotti completes the aria, concert attendees have a deep, visceral response characterized by cheering and crying and hugging—*almost* jumping up and down with joy—and many exit the hall happily humming it. Yet, imagine how differently audiences would respond if the entire opera was sung at full-blast-Pavarotti? It's certain that their reaction to Nessun Dorma specifically would not be as emotional nor its performance as memorable. Same with campaigns in organizations.

Go OmniChannel

If you've been hanging around the marketing water cooler, you might have heard this term. When thinking about your plan, it essentially means getting messages to each audience whenever and wherever they want to receive them while allowing individual audience members choices in how they want to interact with those messages. While we can't go quite that far with internal communications, it's important to reach your audience in a way that is *useful and meaningful to them*. More importantly, you must *ensure you are actually reaching your audiences*.

Many of our clients LOVE trickle down communications. That is, the President tells the VPs, the VPs tell the directors, and information eventually makes its way to the guy on the floor who actually does the work. Great (theoretical) way to show leadership support, but if they're your try or die communication tactics, they are only as good as their weakest link (possibly the link that's sitting on the beach when the big announcements are being made).

For one project, our transportation client was adamant about using the leadership chain as the primary form of information distribution. After the first few communications had taken place, we did a survey to see if we were moving the needle on awareness and desire among our audiences. Much to the client's pleasure, we were—for those that received the communications. Unfortunately, 25 percent of our end users reported never receiving a communication about the program. Those pesky weak links.

Don't get me wrong—trickle down has its place, and it can be a good way to show leadership support. But to be effective in campaigns supporting enterprise-wide organizational change, you have to supplement it with other forms of communication. Have it come from their manager, and then reinforce it with communications directly to them. One of the best supplements is a "pull" or "self-service" option in which all important information about the change is stored and easy to find place—and put that URL on every communication.

Get "Tailored"

One size does *not* fit all. Making sure you are tailoring your message to different audiences is another key component of thinking like a marketer. An ERP implementation looks very different to someone in Finance than it does to someone in Distribution. "Living the culture" when you are in Field Sales is a world away from doing it in HR. You can't have a unique campaign for every conceivable audience. But you can bring messages a little closer to home for many of the audiences.

By "home," three words: Context. Is. King. Knowing how a project applies to their everyday lives moves people closer to where we need them to be than giving them an abstract idea of what the change is supposed to accomplish in general. I want to know where the change fits into my processes. I want to know how my current systems will be impacted. I want to know how it will affect me, Jane Smith in Accounting, and whether I'll still be able to pick up my kid at daycare by 6 p.m.

I can hear you now—"Are you crazy? I can't talk to everyone individually!" Nope, but you can talk to four to six (or so) different groups in a tailored fashion. Look at all of your different audiences and blend together those that are largely similar. It doesn't have to be perfect. But it does get you A LOT further if you try.

We often create what we call Level 1, Level 2 and Level 3 messaging. It's not a completely clean taxonomy, but it's a good framework for a team to use as a reference.

Level 1—The Universal Story. This is the part that applies to everyone. What are we trying to accomplish, why is it important, what are the major parts and pieces. This is the elevator speech, those first few slides in the master deck.

Level 2—The Translation Layer. This next layer of information adds meat to the story, but often this level of detail is where things become different for different audiences. Here are the specifics and here's what it means to your group(s).

Level 3—The Details. These communications typically contain logistics or directions. We need you to do this at this time. Attend training. Log-in to something. That sort of thing. Depending on how you break up actual launch and sustainment, the groups you use for Level 2 may need different Level 3 communications. If you are talking to Finance as a group in Level 2, Finance in the US and Europe may have different training instructions or need to be in different places at different times. Make sense?

Multi-tiered messaging helps you tell parts of the story when they need to be told which helps your audiences remember them better (as opposed to what is often the case: A dense-packed, information dump).

Get Visual

Creating a visual identity can make getting your message heard infinitely easier. It helps you cut through the "noise" and helps your audiences instantly recognize and prepare themselves to think about your topic. Some people may call this "branding" but I don't for a couple of very specific reasons. When many people hear "branding" they automatically think logo and tagline. And while that may be a logical part of some programs, it's not necessarily the right answer for all programs, and might not be a hit with your corporate brand standards crew.

Creating a *somewhat* distinct look and feel is important though. I say somewhat because any identity should fall within your brand standards. If your colors are shades of blue, rolling out a Mardi Gras themed identity isn't going to work. Good visual identity is distinct but supports the organization's overall communication milieu.

That said, you need to choose the appropriate level at which to create the common visual identity. If you have a portfolio of programs, and those programs have multiple projects all working together toward one goal, it's best to create visual identity at the portfolio level, then use other elements—sublogos, colors, etc.—to help the individual programs and projects differentiate themselves. At the receiving end, there are few things worse than audience members getting multiple communications from multiple projects that all look different, but are actually interrelated. You don't want to make people "work" at figuring out those relationships on their own.

Get Emotional

Now we know the parts and pieces of a communication plan as well as its general look and feel. Next we need to make very important decisions about the words, phrases and tone that will resound with your audiences.

The most powerful messages are *tangible* to the focal audience and elicit an *emotional* reaction. In business today, not much is more tangible and emotion-arousing than wasting money directly or by having a disconnect between your project's priorities and where money is allocated. People understand intellectually that those things happen in most organizations. But, they seldom experience that knowledge *emotionally*. Change campaign messages need to induce that emotional experience. We've found that making a clear business case for the acceptance of our primary messages can create just the type of emotional reaction that we need. That can be as simple as identifying tangible, potential cost savings (or productivity increases) *in terms that are meaningful to the audience at hand*. For example:

- In a project designed to help hospitals get reimbursed more by Medicare based on their Patient Satisfaction scores, we talked about how many additional nurse salaries the higher reimbursements could cover. What nurse doesn't want more help on the floor?
- In another project designed to make a school transportation company's supply chain more efficient, we talked about how many new buses the saving could buy. Location managers salivate at the idea of new buses.

In the book *Made to stick* (Heath & Heath, 2008) mentioned earlier in this chapter, the authors provide a really powerful example of an intern who illustrated how the company was wasting money by not consolidating and leveraging their glove purchases. The intern got a sample of every glove ordered by every department, then labeled each glove with the price paid by that department. When executives walked in and saw the sheer number of types of gloves, then realized that they were paying drastically different prices for identical gloves and not taking advantage of volume purchasing, they were standing in line to sign up for the changes the intern recommended. That's the kind of emotional spark we try to create.

While emphasizing the importance of emotion, the Heaths are careful to credit two other key components of powerful messages:

1. They *engage the intellect*. For example, they make sense from a business perspective.
2. They *provide a clear path for the audience to do what we need them to do*. You have to help them help you. Often a lot of what is perceived as resistance is really lack of clarity. If I'm not exactly sure what to do, I'll just do nothing (or, more likely, do what I've been doing previously).

Messages that effectively combine emotion, intellectual engagement and clear direction are remembered, shared and, most importantly, trigger action.

Rinse and Repeat and Repeat

A marketing adage used to be that someone had to hear a message eight times before the light bulb goes on. With the incredibly high number of daily communications in current workplaces, I'm guessing that's probably doubled by now.

We often get a lot of push-back on the number of message repetitions we recommend. Executives (and even communication professionals) often tire of core messages long before most audience members become truly aware of them. You can sometimes reduce the push-back (or delay its onset) by message variation (e.g., new spins, different media, new stories as illustrations, etc.). But, no matter how creative you are in this regard, there *will be* a point at which people who control the project purse strings will accuse you of overkill. At that point, you have to reach deep down inside yourself, Red-Bull your resolution and just say no to their bored brains. There is no overkill communication-wise in large-scale changes.

Audiences need to hear the same message over and over for it to work its magic. Nike's message is always "Just do it." Every time. All day long. They don't get bored and say "Just try it" or "Give it a shot" or "Win." Just do it. For years. For decades even. And you know what, it works.

I tell client leaders that when they overhear a conversation and notice their own words being used by someone to describe the program, then *it's just beginning to work*. So keep plugging away.

Messages that are consistent, sustained and repeated become part of our beliefs and drive our behavior (i.e., lead us to action).

Work the Plan

When launching a change initiative, you have only one chance to make a positive first impression and engage your audiences' attention at the outset. Reversing a negative first impression is many, many times more difficult than creating a good impression from the start.

We often begin strategic campaigns, "baggage" or no, by talking about the Past, Present and Future. *People crave context to understand what is happening.* People want to know why the change is necessary. If we're successful as a company, why is the status quo no longer working? And if we've stumbled while implementing this type of solution in the past, how is this attempt going to be different? The Past and Present conversations give us the opportunity to address any baggage that's out there, level-set and lay the foundational context for moving forward.

The appropriate forum for the Past, Present and Future conversation depends greatly on the company size, how geographically dispersed it is, size/length of the initiative and amount of baggage there is to address. Learning Maps (or "Roadmaps") and videos provide longevity and consistency of message when working with large organizations and long programs. Presentations at organizational meetings can be effective in smaller, less geographically dispersed groups with less baggage. Again, no matter the specific circumstances, you'll need a multi-layered approach to ensure the message is heard multiple times in multiple ways.

Maintain Awareness and Escalate Buy-In with FUN

The daily grind (i.e., day-to-day work assignments) and institutionalized incentives and rewards are powerful distractions from a focus on the "work" of making the change happen. The common disruptions of a normal work day have the same effect and they occur approximately every three minutes (Silverman, 2012). Want to get really focused and stay that way for a while? It's easy. Have fun.

Having fun, especially the experience of laughing, has a powerful focusing effect. It also results in the secretion of neurochemicals (like endorphins) that make you feel good physically and put you in a state of "positive anticipation" (Rock, 2009) that helps maximize your ability to learn, accept and retain information (Davachi, Kiefer, Rock & Rock, 2010). If you can get people to associate your campaign with having fun, they'll work the plan *for you*. That is, they'll be likely to more deeply encode your message in their brains and more likely to share with coworkers any positive insights they have or conclusions they draw.

How can you "make" people have fun? As indicated at the outset of this section, there's the use of *campaign-related* humor (e.g., Top ten reasons why you should NOT attend the XYZ training, "No. 10: Our customers really love us and are super loyal, so they don't care if our products are late and don't work"); *campaign-related* contests (e.g., first department with 100 percent of employees completing and returning feedback surveys might be given money—that the organization had already set aside for charitable donations—that the department can re-allocate to its favorite causes); funny campaign slogans (I'm reminded of the Hanes Underwear print advertising campaign: "Wait till we get our Hanes on you"; the creation of funny campaign avatars or mascots; and whatever else you can create that fits both the campaign and the culture. (BTW: I'm sure you know that many campaigns include provision of little gifts—coffee mugs, tension-reducing squeez-ies and so on. You'll be doing your campaign's identity a disservice if you choose gifts that have no relation to the campaign's content.)

The effects of fun are a main reason why many organizations are now using gamification in their internal campaigns. Among others, Accenture (Lumbreras, 2012), British Gypsum (Powell, 2015) and Yahoo (Finkel, 2010) have experienced great success with "serious games." In addition to turning work into play (i.e., fun), games can be used to convey information, to test whether communications have been understood and to provide feedback on how the campaign and the change it represents is being received/evaluated. As indicated earlier, understanding what's working and what's not working is vital to your program's success. (Additional information on the uses and impact of gaming will be provided later in the chapter on planning and designing training.)

Align Communications and Training

In a subsequent chapter, you will learn why it is important that training content and training methods (or media) must be aligned. Well, it's just as important that training be aligned with a campaign. But, aligned how? It's more than a matter of consistency.

One way to look at this is that training needs to *reinforce* the content in the campaign. So that, if a major element of a campaign is faster customer service, then there should be training that is clearly related to faster customer service. Preferably, there will also be a symbolic connection. If you use a running greyhound in the campaign to symbolize faster customer service, then any training on that con-cept should also include that symbol. You don't have to mention the greyhound in training. The connection between the campaign greyhound and the training greyhound will occur automatically (below the level of awareness) in the brains of the trainees.

These conscious or unconscious connections are important. They help people see how the different elements of a complex change process are related. It's a sense-making thing. And the establishment of these connections can't be left to chance.

Communications people need to work with training designers to plan exactly where and how these connections will be made. That is, training designers need to clearly understand campaign objectives and work with the communications people to assure that key messages in the campaign and in training are purposely and overtly tied together. Campaign avatars or mascots, mentioned just above, can also assist in helping people make connections.

Coda and a Purposefully Repeated Sentence

Communication campaigns don't have to be fancy or crazy expensive. **But, they do take thought in preparation and diligence in execution.** Done right, they can be a very high-payback investment in the success of any large-scale organizational change.

Great *job, Stephanie! Thanks for sharing your expertise with us.*

DOUBLE DIP!

"Experts' Insights" and "Brain Connection" join forces for a powerful, insightful connection!

EXPERTS' INSIGHTS: WHEN COMMUNICATION CAMPAIGNS INVOLVE STAFF REDUCTIONS

plus

BRAIN CONNECTION! WHEN COMMUNICATION CAMPAIGNS INVOLVE STAFF REDUCTIONS

Many large-scale organizational changes end up sooner or later resulting in an elimination of jobs. With mergers and acquisitions and ERP system implementations, it's almost guaranteed. In fact, it's usually an expressed goal. That's not to say that the goal is always reached, at least as it is originally intended. Often, some jobs are eliminated and different types of jobs are added over time, creating a net increase. **But, Change Leaders and consultants need to be prepared to handle small to possibly very large reductions in staff.**

The principles of effective communication and communication campaigns don't actually change during the planning and implementation of staff reductions. **But, employee sensitivity to communications is increased, often dramatically so.** So, I like to remind people who are involved with staff reductions—even tangentially—to attend particularly to two very critical communication challenges:

1. **It is extremely important that you convey your <u>respect</u> for the other person(s) in <u>every</u> communication.** This isn't just a courtesy to people who might or will lose their jobs. **It can have a gigantic effect on how the people who remain with the organization absorb and react to the loss of**

colleagues and coworkers. *Think* of it as one of your signature behaviors. *Think* of it as one of your most important challenges. *Don't think* that signs of disrespect, whether intentional or un-, will be readily forgotten.

(Yes. Yes, this respect principle applies all the time. But, here we're looking at circumstances in which formal communications and casual, everyday conversations are subject to much greater scrutiny, not all of it logical or rational: Emotions *will* be involved.)

In the main, respect is most directly demonstrated through the four Ps.

Patience. Know in advance that you are going to be asked the same questions about possible reductions and possible targets of reductions over and over again. In fact, you may be asked the same question over and over again by the same person. **Remember that when people expect to (or actually do) hear bad news, hormones are secreted in their brains that can literally make it impossible for them to comprehend much if not most of what is being said to them.** Sometimes people will be "certain" that they "remember" something that you didn't say because they either hoped to hear it (or dreaded hearing it). Demonstrating impatience (by, for example, telling a person that you have already answered that question three times) never leads to positive outcomes. It only increases the probability that the other person will experience more anxiety or become more even more emotionally sensitive to what you have to say or convey in writing.

Promptness. People might have no difficulty waiting a day or two to get an answer about some things. **However, when their livelihoods are on the line, every hour can seem like a week.** Again, there is a neuro-physiological response involved here. Psychologists have likened ambiguity during stress as equivalent to a hard punch in the stomach or an excruciating headache. Yes, business has to continue to be conducted, so you can't always immediately drop whatever you are doing to respond to an email or to take a phone call. But, keep in mind an analogous situation that you might have experienced in the past. Have you ever been in a position where you were anxiously waiting to receive word from a doctor or nurse about the seriousness of a problem being experienced by a loved one? That's what it's like. Put yourself in those shoes and try your best to be conscientious about responding to requests for information as promptly as you reasonably can.

Professionalism. First, watch your language; watch your tone. No jokes. They can, and likely will, be interpreted emotionally. For example, let's say that the local college or professional football team has lost three or four games in a row. You might come in on Monday morning and say that "they ought to cut the whole team and start over." How would you guess that people who are fearing loss of their jobs would interpret what for you is an only "off-hand," non-work-related comment? Second, at all times, make sure that you MODEL the behavior that you would expect of employees. Times might be very tough in your life as well. But, depressive or angry behaviors are astonishingly contagious. Don't be a carrier.

Politeness. Attend to eye contact. People tend to make more eye contact when they are being honest. On the other side of the coin, people become more distrustful when they don't receive a "look in the eye." Don't walk away while answering someone's question. Listen to each question in its entirety; don't start to answer based on the first three words in the statement of the question. Use your organization's espoused values to guide and enable your communications.

2. Study and understand all organizational communications about possible staff reductions and consider those communications to be "masters" from which you need to make (exact) copies.

- Stick to the known facts. Sure, just like everyone else, you might be wondering about how everything is going to work out in the end. But, speculating about that is no help to people who may believe that your guess is better than others'—e.g., that what is a wild guess on your part is actually based on "insider information" that hasn't been shared with them.
- Neither minimize the nature of the challenge ("Hey. Don't worry. It's all going to work out") nor exaggerate its difficulty ("This is going to throw a giant monkey wrench into our entire project . . .").
- **Don't fill in any gaps or provide "missing" information by making assumptions**—no matter how logical the assumptions appear to be.
- Know in advance that people will be looking for assurances. In fact, some people will be desperate for them. So avoid ANYTHING that might be considered a promise or a guarantee—even if only implied—like, "I can't imagine that this is going to affect our department very much." It doesn't matter that your only intention may be to provide solace. These kinds of statements can create serious legal liabilities for your organization.
- When possible, provide information/answer questions by referring to—and even physically pointing to—previously distributed "official" information.
- Keep in mind that "I don't know" is a perfectly acceptable answer (unless it's used to blow someone off). Yet, if you are unsure how to answer a question, know in advance to whom or to what the questioner should be referred. **Do not promise that you will get the information and get back to the questioner. Your credibility will be diminished if you have to come back with, "I wasn't able to find out," or something similar.**
- If you hear information being provided that you <u>know</u> to be false, politely, casually intervene into the conversation. However,

    - you should avoid absolute statements like, "I'm absolutely certain that . . ." You might be absolutely incorrect.
    - you should avoid "you-statements" like, "You don't understand what Todd was trying to say." You-statements lead to arguments, not to resolution or clarity. Try leading with, "What I think that Todd was trying to say . . ." or "Perhaps Todd was trying to say . . ."
    - when possible, talk to "mis-informers" in private.

Notes

1 My all-time favorite business metaphor (for which I can't find an original source) is: "Best Buy has become the showroom for people who buy their electronics online." There are several messages packed into that one.

2 In working with a client, I created a "metaphor competition" among Sponsorship Team members randomly assigned to groups of five or six. The task was to create a (preferably multi-faceted) metaphor that would represent the kind of culture that senior management wanted to adopt—to overcome the fact the organization wasn't *fighting hard enough against its competitors* in maintaining or gaining market share. The "winning metaphor" was a battleship characterized as follows:

   a. There is a Ship's Code (*values are clearly communicated, defined, understood and practiced*)
   b. Everyone knows where the ship is headed (*the vision is clear*)
   c. Crew members are regularly apprised of the ship's location and status (*performance and progress are regularly measured and frequently communicated*)
   d. Crew members are made aware of the possibility of rough seas ahead (*economic and competitive challenges are not hidden*)
   e. The mission/purpose is seen as noble (*the business or some other major purpose extends beyond profitability*)
   f. Performance levels among crew members are addressed immediately and appropriately (*good performers are recognized and rewarded; poor performers walk the plank*)
   g. The helm is never abandoned (*people step up to the wheel when the need arises*)
   h. The engine and props are respected and cared for (*people are seen as the organization's source of energy and power and are treated and valued accordingly*).

3 Yang (2007) described how Yum Brands' CEO, David Novak, "does his own talking":

> Several times a year Novak runs a three-day training seminar for Yum managers in which he shares stories from his own career. It is an intimate way of spreading values among employees and gives them a chance to learn what's happening at Yum. "They see their CEO, and it makes a big company small," says Novak. "They learn how we're looking at our strategy. So they walk away with more knowledge. If you have more knowledge, you care more about the company, and you're more committed."

4 In most cases, perception is multi-modality. That is, it involves more than one of our senses working together. However, our visual sense is involved in perception more than any of our others.

5 The company was Root Learning, now called Root Inc.

6 You can learn a lot more about Learning Maps and see many examples of them in Haudan (2008).

7 Stephanie is currently Director, Provider Relations at EyeMed.

References

All web site URLs accessed on December 12, 2015.

Aksoy, M., Apak, S., Eren, E. & Korkmaz, M. (2014). Analysis of the effect of organizational learning-based culture on performance, job satisfaction and efficiency: A field study in the banking sector. *International Journal of Academic Research, 6(1)*, 301–313.

Basboll, T. & Graham, H. (2006). Substitutes for strategy research: Notes on the source of Karl Weick's anecdote on the young lieutenant and the map of the Pyrenees. *ephemera, 6(2)*, 195–204.

Berger, B. (2014). Read my lips: Leaders, supervisors, and culture are the foundations of strategic employee communications. *Institute for Public Relations.* Retrieved from www.instituteforpr.org/read-lips-leaders-supervisors-culture-foundations-strategic-employee-communications/.

Choi, C. (2011). A love-hate relationship? "Feel-good" oxytocin may have a dark side. *Scientific American,* January 12. Retrieved from www.scientificamerican.com/article/a-love-hate-relationship/.

Davachi, L., Kiefer, T., Rock, D. & Rock, L. (2010). Learning that lasts through AGES: Maximizing the effects of learning initiatives. *NeuroLeadership Journal, 3,* 53–63.

Denning, S. (2011). *The leader's guide to storytelling: Mastering the art and discipline of business narrative.* San Francisco, CA: Jossey-Bass.

Finkel, E. (2010). Yahoo takes new 'Road' on ethics training. *Workforce Management, 89(7),* 7.

Galbraith, J. (2005). *Designing organizations: An executive briefing on strategy, structure, and process.* San Francisco, CA: Jossey-Bass.

Geary, J. (2009). *Metaphorically thinking.* Presentation at TedGlobal, July, Oxford, United Kingdom. Retrieved from www.ted.com/talks/james_geary_metaphorically_speaking?language=en.

Gots, J. (2012). *Your storytelling brain.* BigThink Blog. Retrieved from http://bigthink.com/think-tank/your-storytelling-brain.

Haudan, J. (2008). *The art of engagement: Bridging the gap between people and possibilities.* New York, NY: McGraw-Hill.

Heath, C. & Heath, D. (2008). *Made to stick.* New York, NY: Random House.

Heath, D. & Heath, C. (2011). *The myth of the garage.* New York, NY: Crown Publishing Group.

Holub, M. (1977). Brief thoughts on maps. *The Times Literary Supplement,* February 4, 118.

Jacobs, R., Mannion, R., Davies, H. T. O., Harrison, S., Konteh, F. & Walshe, K. (2013). The relationship between organizational culture and performance in acute hospitals. *Social Science & Medicine, 76,* 115–125.

Kilman, J., Shanahan, M., Toma, A. & Zielinski, K. (2010). Demystifying organizational design. *Boston Consulting Group White Paper.* Retrieved from www.bcgperspectives.com/content/articles/organization_design_organization_demystifying_organization_design/.

Lacey, S., Stilla, R. & Sathian, K. (2012). Metaphorically feeling: Comprehending textual metaphors activates somatosensory cortex. *Brain and Language, 120(3),* 416–421.

Lakoff, G. (2003). *Metaphors we live by.* Chicago, IL: The University of Chicago Press.

Lawson, E. & Price, C. (2003). The psychology of change management. *McKinsey Quarterly,* June. Retrieved from www.mckinsey.com/insights/organization/the_psychology_of_change_management.

Lumbreras, S. (2012). Accenture – engaging through gamification. *Simple-communicate.com posting.* Retrieved from www.simply-communicate.com/case-studies/enterprise-2-0/accenture-engaging-through-gamification.

Medina, J. (2008). *Brain rules: 12 principles for surviving and thriving at work, home, and school.* Seattle, WA: Pear Press.

Nabben, J. (2014). *Influence: What it is and how to make it work for you.* Upper Saddle River, NJ: Pearson Education, FT Press.

Nadler, D., Passmore, W. & Torres, R. (2006). Organizing for growth: Architecting the organization to support enterprise growth. *Marsh & McLennan Companies' Viewpoint.* Retrieved from www.mmc.com/knowledgecenter/viewpoint/archive/nadler2006.php.

Navaresse, D., Yauch, C., Goff, K. & Fonseca, D. (2014). Assessing the effects of organizational culture, rewards, and individual creativity on technical workgroup performance. *Creativity Research Journal, 26(4),* 439–455.

Neagu, E. & Nicula, V. (2012). Influence of organizational culture on company performance. *Revista Academiei Fortelor Terestre, 17(4)*, 420–424.

Negley, E. (2013). Investors not dying to buy so-called "death bonds." *Business Weekly*, November 26. Retrieved from http://businessweekly.readingeagle.com/investors-not-dying-to-buy-so-called-death-bonds/.

Nold, H. (2012). Linking knowledge processes with firm performance: Organizational culture. *Journal of Intellectual Capital, 13(1)*, 16–38.

Potter, M., Wyble, B., Hagman, C. & McCort, E. (2014). Detecting meaning in RSVP at 13 ms per picture. *Attention, Perception & Psychophysics, 76(2)*, 270–279.

Powell, S. (2015). The secret to a successful internal communications campaign. *3seven9 Blog*, May 15. Retrieved from http://3seven9.com/insight/in/2015/05/the-secret-to-a-successful-internal-communications-campaign/.

Ritchie, L. (2013). *Metaphor*, Cambridge, UK: Cambridge University Press.

Roberto, M. & Levesque, L. (2005). The art of making change initiatives stick. *MIT Sloan Management Review, Summer*, 53–60.

Rock, D. (2009). *Your brain at work*. New York, NY: Harper Business.

Rukeyser, M. (1968). *The speed of darkness*. New York, NY: Random House.

Schifferstein, H. (2006). The perceived importance of sensory modalities in product usage: A study of self-reports. *Acta Psychologica, 121*, 41–46.

Schmidt, G. & Augart Seger, C. (2009). Neural correlates of metaphor processing: The roles of figurativeness, familiarity and difficulty. *Brain and Cognition, 71(3)*, 375–386.

Silverman, R. (2012). Workforce distraction: Here's why you won't finish this article. *Wall Street Journal*, December 11. Retrieved from www.wsj.com/articles/SB100014241278 87324339204578173252223022388.

Speer, N., Reynolds, J., Swallow, K. & Zacks, J. (2009). Reading stories activates representations of visual and motor experiences. *Psychological Science, 20(8)*, 989–999.

Tri, K. (2013). Cross-overs. In J. Edmondson (Ed.), *Music in American life: An encyclopedia of the songs, styles, stars and stories that shaped our culture* (pp. 317–322). Santa Barbara, CA: ABC-CLIO.

Vuong, C., Van Uum, S., O'Dell, L., Lutfy, K. & Friedman, T. (2010). The effects of opioids and opioid analogs on animal and human endocrine systems. *Endocrine Review, 31(1)*, 98–132.

Weick, K. (1983). Misconceptions about managerial productivity. *Business Horizons, 26(4)*, 47–52.

Yang, J. (2007). A recipe for consistency. *Fortune*, October 29. Retrieved from http://archive. fortune.com/magazines/fortune/fortune_archive/2007/10/29/100792956/index.htm.

Yazici, H. (2011). Significance of organizational culture in perceived project and business performance. *Engineering Management Journal, 23(2)*, 20–29.

Zak, P. (2014). Why your brain loves good storytelling. *Harvard Business Review Online*, October 28. Retrieved from https://hbr.org/2014/10/why-your-brain-loves-good-storytelling.

Zhou, P., Bundorf, K., Chang, J., Huang, J. & Xue, D. (2011). Organizational culture and its relationship with hospital performance in public hospitals in China. *Health Services Research, 46(6)*, 2139–2160.

PART II

Implementation Issues and Challenges: How to "Do" Change Leadership

.

6

UNDERSTANDING AND OVERCOMING RESISTANCE TO CHANGE; BUILDING BUY-IN

A Brain-Based Understanding of Resistance to Change

What if your boss came to you and said: "I'm going to ask you to take on a very challenging large-scale change project:

- it will require a ton of extra work over a long period of time;
- it will most likely be emotionally draining, if not outright exhausting;
- for years, you won't be sure how the project will turn out;
- you'll be on call seven days a week and 24 hours per day; being called to work in the middle of the night is virtually unavoidable;
- there will be many unknowns but it's certain that you'll have to acquire new skills that may be difficult for you to master;
- scheduling will be complex and increased short-distance travel is involved;
- you'll have to complete tasks repeatedly that many people find unsavory;
- your patience may be tested on a nearly daily basis;
- your pay won't increase; in fact, your discretionary income will be reduced substantially."

Would you willingly take on a project under these conditions?

Unlikely? **Well, then, isn't it amazing that so many people are absolutely delighted to take on a large-scale change project like having children!** Please read the bulleted statements above one more time with childrearing in mind.

The material on human behavior presented earlier is the basis for understanding and overcoming resistance to change. "Resistance" is just the name given to a specific category of behaviors that I'm going to cover in more depth in this section.

The "Inevitability" Issue

I'd like to start with the issue of whether resistance is inevitable. Unfortunately, if you work as a Change Leader or change management consultant for any reasonable length of time, you will undoubtedly encounter some managers who have the attitude that resistance to change is just one of **many negative characteristics of human nature that have to be plowed through or run around**. I'll call these people "Change Enforcers." Such managers tend to see workers as lazy and dishonest—if left to their own devices. In union shops, you might deal with managers who believe that union members resist change on principle and in every shape and form. **The ironic thing is that managers who have these beliefs tend to behave toward their employees in ways that bring out the employees' worst (and most resistant) behaviors.** The good news is that the percentage of managers who feel this way has decreased dramatically in the last decade plus. Nonetheless, **it's good to have some "talking points" at the ready to counteract the thinking of Change Enforcers** (in real time). So . . .

> Do people naturally resist change? Yes.
> Do people naturally embrace change? Yes.
> Do people differ in their predisposition to change? Yes.

Explanation of yes, yes and yes: **Acceptance or resistance to change is a learned behavior.** That means that it's based on each individual's experience with change in the past. Let's take the example of people who, as kids, had to move from city to city several times as they were growing up. Does the act of moving a lot predict future acceptance or resistance to change? Nope. Some kids have a better experience in School B than they had in School A, and a better still overall experience in School C. These kids, as adults, tend to have a predisposition toward being accepting of major life changes. On the down side, the vast majority of kids who move a lot don't have progressively more positive experiences (Oishi & Schimmack, 2010). So, their attitudes about change are likely to be quite different.

Think about this in the context of work. If you really, really like your job and someone wants to change it by taking away the things that you like best about it, you're pretty likely to resist making that sort of change. However, if your boss came to you one day and said that you're in for a sizable pay raise and guess what, a company car(!), you probably wouldn't have too much difficulty embracing that change. In fact, sometimes people are motivated to seek out changes on their own—whether it's a new job, or trying a new restaurant or doing something on vacation that they've never done previously.

So, it's not change *per se* that people resist or embrace. It's the type of change and its (personal) effects that can lead to fierce opposition or grateful acceptance.

Managers who tend to see employees in a negative light across the board have very strong brain circuits/connections between "change" and "resistance." During relatively short-term projects, you might not have any real chance to help these people make new connections of equal strength. But, dealing with such managers and "winning them over" can be critical to the success of many changes. In part, that's because managers with this view of human nature are typically VERY resistant to doing the things (e.g., being empathetic, sending out supportive communications, etc.) that you need project team leaders to do. (Again: Ironic, isn't it?)

EXPERTS' INSIGHTS: WINNING OVER CHANGE ENFORCERS

1. Earlier, I made the argument that **people are most likely to change their behaviors when they reach conclusions about the desirability of the new behaviors on their own** (Pulakos, Hanson, Arad & Moye, Forthcoming; Rock, 2006). **For this reason, it's often useful to ask Change Enforcers to help you understand the history of changes in the client organization.** There are two things to shoot for here. One is the possibility of identifying a change that was well-accepted and one that wasn't—and having the focal manager describe the differences between the two scenarios. With luck, the manager will "discover" some factors that can have an impact on acceptance. The second is to have the manager think about the employees who have been most affected by major changes in the past and list out the effects on them. Sometimes you can facilitate a micro-epiphany when people come to the realization (on their own) of how employees have historically been "burned" by changes.

2. If Change Enforcers don't see the light on their own, sometimes their behavior can be moderated by the use of stories—or parables, if you will. Effective Change Leaders and consultants don't just bring their own thoughts and experiences to each new project; they bring the thoughts and experiences of the people with whom they've worked on previous change efforts as well. If you're relatively new to change management, team leadership or consulting in general, **you might find it helpful to keep a journal of key or particularly effective behaviors that you've witnessed**, along with a bit of the circumstances. (As I've argued in another context earlier in this Guide, the act of writing these vignettes down, and occasionally looking over the lot, can help strengthen your memory of them.) **Having your own, personal collection of parables can be very useful in dealing with Change Enforcers**. I have a somewhat standard opening for the telling of these parables. (No, it's not "Once upon a time," but you're not too far off.) It might begin with something like this: "You know, I worked with a guy in another manufacturing company whom I really admired. He was usually able to turn [the current problem] to his advantage by just. . . ." Despite appearances on the outside, you will likely be surprised by how many of the gruffest Change Enforcers wouldn't mind being admired by you either.

Okay. Parables about what, you ask?

Well, for just one example, with Change Enforcers, it's useful to have a parable or two at the ready for each of these ways that resistance/resisters can be a good thing:

- Resisters can raise tough questions that can improve the change itself (or its implementation).
- Resisters can slow down the pace of change to keep people from feeling/being overwhelmed.
- Every manager has a truly bone-headed idea at one time or another. Resisters can stop your bone-headed ideas from becoming reality.
- Resisters can often be co-opted and become effective Change Leaders (Have you ever heard the saying that "prisoners sometimes make the best jailors"?).

When People DO Resist Change, WHY Do They?

There are as many reasons for resisting change as there are employees in any focal organization. However, the most common reasons for resistance across organization types have been identified reliably[1] ("Elan," 2014; Kantor, 2012; Prosci, 2014a; Quast, 2012). They are listed below. But, a true frequency count or rating for each is not available. So, they are <u>not</u> presented in the order of expected likelihood of occurrence:

Concern about potential (or certain) loss of something important
>Most often power, status, autonomy, control, coworkers and/or boss, etc., even loss of the job itself.

The change presents a threat to the employee's need to maintain or enhance her self-image
>For example, "I'll make a fool of myself if I try that," or "I'll never be able to learn to make those calculations as quickly as I'll need to."

Concern about the extra effort required
>Particularly if the person is already stressed from too much work or pressure—or just mentally and emotionally exhausted from having to deal with many other recent changes (i.e., "Change Fatigue"; more on this concept forthcoming).

Failure to truly understand the need for change
>Change-focused communication campaigns often use terms and phrases that have no meaning for many members of the organization. Thus, the need for change isn't necessarily communicated effectively. This comes as no surprise, as a recent Florida State study shows that <u>less than 20 percent of corporate office employees (managers and non-) know accurately what's expected of them in their current jobs</u> and the vast majority experience varying levels of ambiguity—a key source of mistrust (Ash, 2013).

Inertia, habit
>Cf., "strong, well-established brain circuitry" or "automatic behaviors." (Note that ignoring or taking no action at all in response to a stimulus in the environment (e.g., ignoring or failing to respond to requested help on a project) is considered an "automatic behavior.")

Disagreement with the solution (or means-to-solution) chosen
> If the people affected by the change get to choose and/or create the solution, this usually isn't a problem as people typically don't disagree with themselves. The problem is that anything but trivial self-determination during enterprise-wide changes today is becoming rare.

Low tolerance for change in general
> This one is still important but is less frequently a major stumbling block as older workers leave the workforce.

Lack of trust in management
> I've witnessed a few successful changes when trust was at a low point. But, in most cases, no-trust means no-go.

Involvement/investment in past change projects led to personally undesirable outcomes
> Fool me once, shame on me . . .

Inadequate time to accept and adjust
> **This is such an important reason for resistance that it will be handled in detail in a following section.** (See also TiER1's Change Leadership Model in Chapter 12.)

These reasons why people might resist change share four important characteristics:

1. The primary <u>reasons for resisting change are not independent</u>. That is, **people might resist a particular change for several of these reasons simultaneously**. In fact, more than one reason per person is the norm.
2. Not everyone in a team or group will have the same reasons for resisting change. Some reasons might be shared, but **typically the particular combination of reasons will be <u>different for different individuals</u> in the same work unit**. So, Lee from Group A might be resistant because of potential loss of status and low trust in management, while Alex from the same work group might be resistant because of low trust in management, disagreement with the solution chosen and a unique reason that isn't on the list of most common reasons. (More on this in the next section.)
3. **The role performed by individuals (e.g., manager vs. non-manager) has a strong effect on the likelihood that particular reasons for resisting change will come to the fore.** In my experience, these are most common.

For **managers the most common reasons are**:

*   fear of losing power, resources, responsibilities and/or opportunities (such as the opportunity for promotion);
*   already stretched and stressed by the workload and/or responsibilities;
*   don't want to deal with the employees who will resist the change, or fear that they won't be able to manage the changeover effectively;

- don't really understand the need;
- generalized anxiety.

For **non-managers, the most common reasons for resistance are notably more likely to be**:

- fear of job loss;
- fear of having to do more with less, or for less, or with less support;
- fear of not having the skills necessary to perform well with the new system or software;
- enjoy the current way of doing things or current coworkers themselves;
- don't trust management or certain managers to do the right thing in the right way.

4. **Look again at the two lists in No. 3 above. Note how many of these sources of resistance can be fixed by better communication.** This is yet another reason why communication effectiveness is such an important component of the likely success of large-scale change.

Inadequate Time to Accept and Adjust to the Change: A Key Component of Resistance

During large-scale organizational transitions, employees can feel like their world is crumbling down. That's especially true for employees who have worked a long time for a particular company doing pretty much the same type of job for several years. In mergers and acquisitions (M&As), for example, employees can be bombarded with dozens of "unintended" or "unanticipated" changes:

- after coming out on top of a contentious battle with their counterparts to secure control of a merged entity, "winning" executives will often hypocritically expect their non-executive-level employees to establish equal partnerships with employees from the other organization—leading to employee indignation and perceptions of unfairness (Wagner & Muller, 2009);
- it's highly likely that a substantial number of jobs will be eliminated, at all levels of the organization (Wagner & Muller, 2009), but identification (i.e., knowledge) of the specific positions that will be cut can be a painfully long time in coming;
- attempts to standardize policies and procedures can result in serious arguments with regard to which organization has the better way of doing any number of things—large and small (Wagner & Muller, 2009);
- if the organizations have been using different ERP systems, that can cause the need for an enterprise-wide organizational change within an enterprise-wide change for one of the organizations;

- while fielding questions and trying to allay employee concerns about the organizational marriage, many company reps will make honest (and often dishonest) misstatements—which, when exposed, greatly reduce trust in future communications and trust in general (Galpin & Herndon, 2014);
- tensions might increase as a result of fear of losing benefits (or in-network health providers) as well as vacation time or sick days; in fact, in the case of organizations from different national cultures being merged, the entire human resources system for one of the organizations might be turned completely on its head;[2]
- people that have been "downsized" might be offered other jobs—but in another state or country;
- one of the cultures is highly likely to change (or become at odds with the "other" culture) (Marks, Mirvis & Ashkenas, 2014; Rusli, Ovide, Fleisher & Grundberg, 2014);
- bosses, work groups and coworkers can be re-organized; and
- greatly elevated stress levels can be responsible for gastrointestinal and cardiovascular problems as well as an increase in on-and-off-the-job accidents and injuries.

Collectively, the psychological adjustments that people have to make to major organizational changes can be daunting, if not quite painful. And, people are usually expected to make these adjustments "on their own time," i.e., there's typically not very much direct support provided for individual concerns and stresses.

In an influential 1991 book (revised in 2003 and 2009) entitled *Managing transitions: Making the most of change*, William Bridges argued that **most managers view major organizational changes as occurring in a very discrete period of time and whatever that planned length of that time is, it is almost always much shorter than the amount of time that it takes people to accept and adjust to the change psychologically**. (Again, I'm talking about the typical complex enterprise-wide change project here—not raises or promotions, etc., that are easily absorbed psychologically.)

Like many other experts, Bridges argues that adjustment to change occurs in stages. However, in comparison with other experts, his model proposes the largest number of possible stages (over 20!). The norm, in contrast, is three to five stages. Bridges' model is also unusual in that it is "curvilinear" or "U-shaped," meaning that employees' adjustment levels go down-down-down, through about half of his 20+ stages, until they bottom-out and start the long, hard climb back up the other side of the U.

In comparison, TiER1's model (presented in Chapter 12) anticipates that individual performance is likely to be dampened due to psychological adjustments being made at two to four key, largely predictable points during the change process. TiER1's model also differs from Bridges' model in shape. Rather than a U-shape, the shape of TiER1's has no descent into a bottoming out. Rather, it modulates—

something like a radio wave—but its direction, while non-linear, is always along an upward path. (Graphic representations of the TiER1 model are provided in Chapter 12.)

So, which model is right? Well, in fairness, *neither* is right in terms of being able to "fit" or perfectly predict every possible psychological need for adjustment during large-scale changes. That's because all such models attempt to mirror a dynamic process of acceptance and adjustment that is different in different organizations, for different people and for different kinds of changes. And, that simply can't be done with a static, one-dimensional diagram. Nonetheless, both models are useful and here is what I hope that you will "take away" from them—or any other model of the adjustment to, and acceptance of, change:

1. **The amount of time that it takes to physically make a major change in an organization and the amount of time that it takes for the people who are affected by the change to accept and adjust to it are usually going to be different.** And, the second amount of time (accept and adjust) is almost always: a) substantially longer than the first, and b) greatly underestimated by management.

2. With a big change, people inevitably react to it by progressing (or "degressing") through a number of stages. **The exact number of stages and the "linearity" of the stages differ from project to project and both are influenced GREATLY by how well the change is managed.**

3. When any fairly large number of people is involved with a major change, you will find that **people start out from different positions (stages) of acceptance and progress at different rates through the various stages. And, some people can get stuck in a particular stage (taking a long time to get through that stage, or even never getting through that stage) while others will move quickly through various stages, even jumping ahead by skipping some of the stages that others have to work through.** As an illustration, let's focus on five people who attend a meeting in which it is announced that their employer is going to implement an ERP system that has been chosen by an internal task force. On the day of the announcement, the reactions of the five focal people could be something like this:

Chris—naïve optimism
Lee—apprehension
Jan—severe apprehension
Jody—indifference
Reese—anger

Why would their reactions vary so greatly? Here's a purely theoretical rationale:

Chris—naïve optimism due to high level of trust in boss
Lee—apprehension due to participation in past projects that were unsuccessful

Jan—severe apprehension due to job function being in jeopardy with new system

Jody—indifference due to status as a part-timer who plans to move on after impending college graduation

Reese—anger due to expectation of being chosen for project leadership but was not

So, let's see how these people might react over time in Table 6.1.

TABLE 6.1 Example of Possible, Different Paths for Individuals While Adjusting to Change Over Time

Chris	Optimism		Skepticism	Testing		Acceptance
Lee	Apprehension	Testing	Acceptance	Providing Support		
Jan	Severe Apprehension			Anger, Acting Out		Departure
Jody	Indifference			Acceptance		
Reese	Anger	Acceptance	Providing Support	Champion		

Announcement of change   Go live

Time >>>>>>>

While this is a "made up" example, Table 6.1 reflects some of the variety of movements through stages that you are likely to encounter. For example, check out Reese. It's not at all uncommon that a group member who has the strongest negative initial reaction might end up as a Champion (strong supporter) of the change. Chris and Lee are an interesting contrast because they started out with different reactions but after seeing how the ERP system would actually work (i.e., testing), they both came to accept it. In fact, even prior to the date of "go live," Lee was working to improve the system. Note that these are just examples of possible, not guaranteed, reactions that you might encounter. For example, not all groups will include people like Jan who "never come around" and, as a result, leave the organization. That certainly happens; just not as often as the other reactions in this example.

EXPERTS' INSIGHTS: USING A METAPHOR TO EXPLAIN THE STAGES OF ACCEPTANCE

The concept of individual progression patterns through stages of acceptance is sometimes hard for employees implementing a change project to understand in the abstract. It's also sometimes difficult for Change Leaders/consultants to explain, particularly if you find yourself in a meeting that doesn't lend itself to using any of the visual examples above. Under these circumstances, you may wish to use "grieving" as a metaphor for the acceptance process.

Fair warning: Some people with whom you deal might recently have had a death in the family or they fear that one is coming (e.g., family member in Hospice). Likewise, someone might be going through a divorce and grieving the "death" of a marriage, etc. So, while "grief" can be a powerful metaphor, it can also be a very sensitive topic. With this in mind, it's usually best to play it straight with this particular metaphor. That is, this is not a time to inject humor into the conversation.

I'm going to point out a few of the ways in which the grief metaphor "works." Perhaps you'll be able to add some further dimensions on your own.

Two factors (centrality and vulnerability) have major impacts on how grief will be experienced for most people. <u>Centrality</u> essentially refers to how close the focal person is to the person who dies or is lost (for example, as a spouse or as a close friend). It's almost always much more difficult to deal with the death of a spouse than with the death of a 98-year-old, great, great aunt. In the same way, a person would be expected to have more difficulty dealing with the death of a family dog than with a child's pet goldfish.

<u>Vulnerability</u> focuses on the outcomes that result from the death. Let's look at death of a spouse, which is almost always very high in centrality. What about vulnerability? It depends on whether the survivor is well-covered by insurance, has to deal with a heavy debt structure, whether provision was made previously for children's education, how health care would be paid thereafter, etc. The more obstacles to survival you have to face after the death (i.e., metaphorically after the change), the more vulnerable you are.

What's the relation of centrality and vulnerability to an enterprise-wide change? Well, the more central to your job and to your job satisfaction the change is, the more your emotions are likely to be involved. Same way with vulnerability. If the focal change could cause you to lose your job, you're more likely to be emotionally involved in the changeover than if it was clearly not going to affect your life or your livelihood in any way. **The point being that you can often predict in advance "how much grief" a change project is going to cause particular people by looking at how central the changeover is to their jobs (and to their concepts of self, of course) and how likely the project is to affect their security with the organization. The greater the centrality and vulnerability, the greater the potential grief.**

The people who study grief professionally believe that all people who are grieving go through predictable stages of acceptance and adjustment. One leading expert, Elisabeth Kübler-Ross (2005), posits five stages:

- Denial—"No! This can't be happening!"
- Anger—with the person who died or with the world for letting the death occur or with one's self for not being able to prevent the death.
- Bargaining—survivors who are religious might try bargaining with God on the order of "If I do X or Y, will you let me wake up tomorrow and this will all have just been a horrible dream?"

- Depression—fatigue, listlessness, everything requires a greater effort, etc.
- Acceptance—different "terms of acceptance" for different people.

Kübler-Ross believes that you just can't get to acceptance without experiencing the other stages if only very briefly.
  What do you think?

Identifying in Advance the Likely Reasons for, and Causes of, Resistance in a Particular Setting

To effectively deal with (i.e., overcome) resistance, you can't wait for it to happen and then decide what to do. You need to anticipate, understand and plan for it. An extremely valuable tool at your disposal here is **Force Field Analysis (FFA)** (Lewin, 1951). Given the great utility and wide applicability of this tool, I'm going to provide a general and broad background for it. Then, I'll apply it to a specific enterprise-wide organizational change.

General Background on and Effective Use of FFA

Kurt Lewin was one of the most influential psychologists of all time. His primary contributions came during the 1940s when he headed the Research Center for Group Dynamics at MIT.

  Dr. Lewin had a tremendous impact on our **understanding of change and the forces that influence it**. He created FFA to help people, **usually working in groups**, gain his insights into the number and complexity of factors that influence how change is perceived and why behavior does change (or doesn't) as managers hope that it will (Burnes & Cooke, 2013). Imagine this: As we go for an afternoon stroll, a number of *physical* forces bombard our bodies and influence exactly where, how long and how far we will walk. These forces include gravity, wind or rain, the pull of our dog on a leash, music coming from a nearby bandstand, the sudden appearance of a "shady character" or even the smell of bread baking at a restaurant down the street.

  In the same way, social behaviors (such as joining a club or voting for a presidential candidate) are affected by many *psychological* forces acting together. Lewin believed that these forces are <u>dynamic</u> and <u>conflicting</u>. So, they can change over time (dynamic) and push our thinking and our behaviors in more than one way at the same time (conflicting) (Burnes & Cooke, 2013). Consider another physical example: Body weight. In part, weight is determined by good forces (getting enough exercise) and bad forces (eating ice cream by the gallon) simultaneously. Obviously, exercise and eating habits can change over time. But, most people, in the relatively short term, reach a point of equilibrium (or steady-state or balance point) between the forces that push our weight up and those which would lower it. So, for most of us, our weight tends to vary in only a small range during a short period of time, such as a week. However, when vacation time or the holidays roll around, many people exercise less and eat more, so the equilibrium is broken, weight is gained and a new (hopefully only temporary) equilibrium is reached.

At work, most people maintain a steady-state of effort and performance. That is, they typically don't work at 90 percent of capacity one day, 10 percent the next and 60 percent the next, although in certain jobs (e.g., firefighter) dramatic swings in effort might be required. Even then, there is a <u>typical</u> steady-state (e.g., on the days when there are no fires to fight).

Of course, managers want to influence the amount of effort (and the level of performance) that their employees manifest. **I'm going to use a Call Center example as an illustration of how this might work in FFA.** Let's say that Casey effectively handles 40 customer service calls per day and Jody usually covers only about 30. Jody's manager's goal might then be to get Jody's average closer to 40, perhaps 35. FFA can be used to **help Jody's manager think of ways to move the 30 calls/day equilibrium to 35 calls/day** (as a first step).

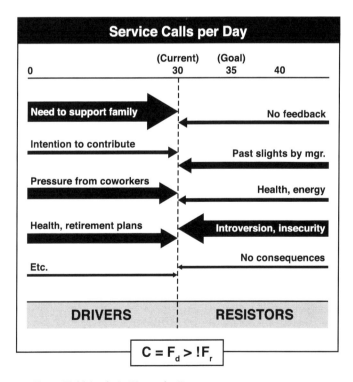

FIGURE 6.1 Force Field Analysis (Example 1)

In FFA, 30 calls would be considered the "current state" or "current performance" and 35 as "future state" or "goal"—or something along those lines. (FFA has been used so much by so many types of people and organizations that the jargon changes from user to user and place to place.) You would then try to think of all the positive and negative factors that are creating a point of balance at 30 calls. **The positive forces are labeled as "driving forces" or "drivers" and negative forces are labeled as "restraining forces" or "resistors."** It's important to think of as many of these as possible. In the example given in Figure 6.1, only a few such factors have been listed. Note that the perpendicular line represents the current state or balance point.

Jody's performance has been holding at an average of 30 calls per day because the drivers and resistors have reached a balance point or equilibrium at that rate. **A positive change (C) will occur only if the force of the drivers (F_d) becomes stronger than the force of the resistors (F_r).**

Once a steady-state or equilibrium has been in place for a while, it takes a substantially (noted by "!" in the diagram) stronger force of the drivers, in comparison to the overall strength of the resistors, to create movement or change. You could think of this extra resistance as the power of habit or repetition or a well-established cognitive map as was presented previously; Lewin, operating without any of the current insights into brain circuitry, compared it to the physical phenomenon, inertia.

In Figure 6.1, **the strength of the drivers and resistors is represented by the thickness of the arrows**. (The wider the arrow, the greater the force.) Sometimes, the length of arrows is used to portray strength. Many other options exist. For example, some people prefer to use numbers in place of arrows. With numbers, a force assigned the weight of 8 would be thought to be about twice as strong as a force assigned the weight of 4, and so on.

Once as many drivers and resistors as possible are identified (and their relative strengths estimated), <u>attention</u> (of the individual or, preferably the group, using FFA) <u>shifts to brain-storming ideas for how the strength of drivers can be increased (or additional drivers introduced) and how the strength of resistors can be reduced or eliminated.</u>

Sometimes FFA users will also allocate weights to the possible actions that could be taken to affect drivers and resistors. That is, they try to predict which courses of action are likely to be feasible and most effective and so on. Five factors are important to note here:

1. <u>The most powerful or effective changes in behavior usually occur when drivers are strengthened **AND** resistors are weakened</u>. Occasionally, strengthening a single driver or weakening a resistor will have an impact. But most behavior patterns that have been in existence for some time are more robust (i.e., less susceptible to easy change) than that.

2. <u>Many times, the strongest resistors are really difficult to weaken</u>. When that is so, **you might have to create lots of changes in relatively less strong**

resistors to impact the overall effect of the restraining forces collectively. But, it should be obvious that the biggest impact can come from weakening the strongest resistors and either making current drivers stronger or introducing powerful new drivers. This combination is often referred to as working in the "impact zone" or concentrating on the "big levers" or other similar jargon.

3. If positive change occurs, it will not be sustained unless systems and management behaviors are in place to support the change, that is, to maintain the new equilibrium. For example, an organization-wide audit of expense account reimbursement requests might lead to a reduction in the number of false or exaggerated claims. But, if no further audits occur, claim behavior will (often fairly quickly) return to its previous level of inaccuracy. However, it is important to note that harshly punitive actions—even if consistently manifested/enforced for long periods of time—tend to "lose their control" of behavior over time and bring about unintended consequences including, especially, lower levels of customer service. In fact, it is extremely difficult to maintain high levels of customer service in organizations which allow threats of repercussions for not adhering very closely to rules and regulations to predominate.

4. Many drivers lose their steam over time. A key human survival trait is a high level of adaptability. For example, while there are people who completely "lose it" when tragedy or hardship occurs—think loss of spouse or loss of job here—most people adapt to these kinds of major changes as time goes by. If we lacked this adaptability, the majority of us would be miserable all the time, if not suicidal. However, there's a downside to that adaptability. We also readily adapt to good things. So, as an illustration, the prospect of a long-sought-after promotion might act as a strong driver—at least until it's obtained. Then we quickly adapt to the new status level and it soon becomes the norm or status quo rather than anything special. If there is no eminent prospect of yet another promotion, the force of this driver can completely dissipate.

5. Resistors are often based on what are called false or invalid scenarios (or cognitive maps in the minds of the focal employees). For example, an employee might not do what the organization desires (let's say, train direct reports well and keep them fully informed) because of an unfounded fear that this would lead to a loss of the employee's status as a "go-to" expert. This is one of many reasons why a high level of trust in management (supported in large part by open and accurate communication) is an essential precursor of effective behavior change. **When trust is high, and honest communication is the norm, employees construct fewer alternative scenarios on their own.**

Summary: FFA is a powerful means of analyzing situations and creating plans for organizational change (such as a structural reorganization or the elimination of a department or product or service or a major IT product implementation) as well as changing the behavior of specific employees. Likewise, it is extremely useful for: a) estimating the likely success of many kinds of proposed initiatives and programs and b) retrospectively evaluating the effectiveness of existing initiatives and programs that have subsequently been implemented. <u>**Its strength lies not only in helping people recognize the complexity of the forces affecting the focal situation, but in obtaining "buy-in" through the wider involvement of employees in planning, decision-making and evaluation.**</u>

Okay. Now, let's use FFA to analyze the resistance to the installation of a major, enterprise-wide software system with the following conditions: At the time that the mythical IT project is announced, about 30 percent of the affected employees look favorably upon it. Our goal is to increase that percentage to 90 percent! Under these conditions, what might a completed FFA look like? Perhaps something like that shown in Figure 6.2.

WHOA! This doesn't look good! There might be a 30 percent current acceptance rate at the outset (i.e., at the time of the project announcement), but the odds are certainly against it staying there. The biggest driver of acceptance so far is the quality of the people who have been chosen for the Sponsorship Team. If the team stays together for the duration, chances are that this might continue to be a

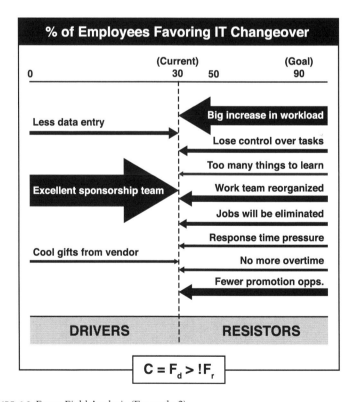

FIGURE 6.2 Force Field Analysis (Example 2)

strong driver at many times during the implementation. However, right now, the big resistors are only in the "worry" (i.e., theoretical) stage. Once more is known (e.g., when the actual number of jobs that is going to be eliminated becomes clear) some of these resistors are going to become a LOT more powerful and the percentage of employees who favor the change will drop as a result. Something (namely, increasing the number and strength of drivers, and eliminating or decreasing the strength of the resistors) is going to need to be done well and done quickly or the Sponsorship Team will have a major problem on its hands.

I'm going to take a wild guess that you're wondering whether this completed analysis (in Figure 6.2) is anything even close to being realistic. Am I just overloading the resistor side of the chart to press a point? Not at all. In fact, some of the sources of resistance I could have added (or repeated from previous sections) are:

- Fear of not being able to understand or "keep up with" the new system
- Comfort with the current system
- Ingrained behaviors
- Disagreement with the need for the new system—or the choice of a particular new system
- Lack of trust in management
- Low tolerance for change in general
- And more!

Perhaps you're thinking about the impressive, potential benefits of the new software. **Don't those benefits drive acceptance?**

Well, benefits—like what? Like these?

- Streamline processes and eliminate busy work
- Reduce labor costs
- Improve information sharing
- Create new performance metrics
- Improve management reports
- Easier and broader access to data
- "How-to" knowledge doesn't leave the organization via turnover or retirement
- More people can see the bigger picture
- Processes are standardized.

These are certainly important benefits. But, take a second look at them. They largely benefit the *organization* rather than the end-users or the worker-bees who have to "do" the implementation.

This is a point that I made earlier. In many enterprise-wide changes (especially those involving IT/ERP systems), **the benefits of the change accrue almost exclusively to the organization** (e.g., streamlined processes, reduced labor costs) while possible negative outcomes (e.g., job elimination, dramatic short-term increases in workload) accrue to the employees. **The result: The goal of getting employees to accept (much less embrace) and adjust to these kinds of changes is EXTREMELY CHALLENGING.**

Overcoming Resistance

I hope that the previous section helped you better *understand* the causes and manifestations of resistance to change. Although I tried to provide some tactics for dealing with resistance in that section as well, I'm now going to shift the focus **primarily to means of** *overcoming* **resistance**.

Earlier, I listed the most common reasons why change in work organizations is resisted (if it is). I repeat that list here (and I can hear your brain circuitry firing up and reinforcing the connection between the neurons that house "resistance to change" and the ones that house the following possible reasons for resistance):

- Concern about potential (or certain) loss of something important
- The change presents a threat to the employee's need to maintain or enhance her self-image
- Concern about the extra effort required
- Inadequate time to accept and adjust
- Failure to truly understand the need for change
- Inertia, habit
- Disagreement with the solution (or means-to-solution) chosen
- Low tolerance for change in general
- Lack of trust in management
- Involvement/investment in past change projects led to personally undesirable outcomes.

It would be nice if, in each major change project, we could simply look for any occurrences of these reasons for resistance and somehow counteract them. That, in fact, is possible for a few of the sources of resistance. For example, "failure to truly understand the need for change," might be overcome largely by the implementation of a masterful communication plan. However, other reasons for resisting change can't simply be counteracted. An example here: Often people <u>will</u> lose power or status or control as a result of the change. It's not just paranoia or misunderstanding. Better communication isn't going to fix this concern.

We STINK at AF!

A number of top researchers (including David Gilbert at Harvard, Tim Wilson at the University of Virginia, George Lowenstein at Carnegie Mellon and Daniel Kahneman at Princeton) have spent several years studying the phenomenon that they call affective forecasting or AF. ("Affect" is emotion or feelings, "forecasting," of course, is prediction of the future. So, put'em together and you're dealing with how well people can predict the way that they will feel if X, or Y or Z happens somewhere down the road.) Turns out that we're really good at predicting whether something will make us happy or unhappy. But, we stink at guessing the extent of our eventual happiness or unhappiness. More specifically, good things (on average) don't make us feel as good as we think that they are going to and bad things don't make us feel as badly as we think they will. Now, when bad things happen, that's good—because the "bad-ness" is less than we anticipate and so we can "shake off" the associated unhappiness more easily than expected. But, when good things happen, that's bad. And, it's the basis for the fact that many (some would argue, most) people are never REALLY satisfied with what they have. Think bigger TV screen, cooler phone, nicer car, younger, richer or more attractive spouse.

So What?

What can Change Leaders or consultants conclude from the AF research? First, you should be cautious in estimating the initial impact and/or the shelf-life of even highly desired rewards given to the employees or team members with whom you are working. Second, be thinking Self-Image: All the available evidence indicates that the hard-wired enhancement function (about which I've "talked" in previous sections of this Guide) never loses steam. So long as you're smart enough to identify the ways in which specific individuals come to feel good about themselves, you can keep laying it on and they won't get tired of it.

EXPERTS' INSIGHTS: OVERCOMING RESISTANCE TO CHANGE

Bob Mager (e.g., Mager & Pipe, 1984) and Ferdinand Fournies (1999) are two well-known "masters" of overcoming resistance to change who have separately created taxonomies to help the not-so-masterly among us understand why people aren't doing what we want them to do and what we can do about that. I'm going to combine some of Bob's and Ferdinand's ideas here and present a checklist of sorts that you should find helpful when you need to generate ideas about how to change someone's behavior. This list will also be useful to you in talking with managers, Sponsorship Team members and Implementation Team members about what they need to do (or stop doing) to affect changes in others' behavior.

Okay. Somebody (or some group) isn't doing what we want them to do. We can ask ourselves . . .

1. Does the person know what she is supposed to do and is she capable of doing it? (Does the person have the knowledge and the ability to do what is supposed to be done?)

   - Example (knowledge): An employee is directed to "greet each and every customer" and, as a result, gives each and every customer a hearty, "Yo, Dude! Que' pasa?" Probably not what the manager had in mind.
   - Example (ability): Employees who have been successful at a given task are often asked to train others when they have little or no idea on how best to go about that.

2. <u>Is performance punishing</u>? (Does a negative outcome result from doing what is supposed to be done?)

    •   Example: A College class runs from 10 a.m. until 10:50 a.m. The profes-
        sor lectures until 10:48 and then asks the class, "Does anyone have any
        questions?" In this scenario, the professor—no matter how earnest she
        might be in her desire to solicit questions—usually receives no response.
        There might be a whole bunch of students in the class who would like
        to ask a question—and a couple who really need to ask a question—but
        they don't. Why? Because doing what the professor wants, no matter how
        reasonable the request, will make a student who asks a question "look
        bad" among his peers who want to get out of class a.s.a.p., as evidenced
        by several students craning their heads around the room and sending
        out a clear non-verbal sign of "no questions, if you know what's good for
        you!" This "performance punishing" scenario can be easily reversed. What
        the professor can do is stop lecturing at 10:40 and say, "As soon as I am
        asked—and get to answer—three good questions, I'll dismiss the class."
        Now, the students (at least three of them) can ask away and they'll receive
        nothing but "love vibes" from other members of the class.

3. <u>Is non-performance rewarding</u>? (Does a positive outcome result from <u>not</u> doing
    what is supposed to be done?)

    •   Example: Bob Mager provides what may be the very best example of this
        phenomenon, in recounting some consulting work he did in Africa back
        in the day. Managers of a mineral exploration company told Bob about
        a problem that they were having with their drill rig operators. The noise
        from the drill rigs was literally deafening and there was a strict rule that
        operators had to wear ear protectors whenever they were near a work-
        ing rig. White operators wore the protectors as required. Black operators
        would covertly work without ear protectors and would eventually become
        completely deaf as a result. The company had tried many approaches to
        solving this problem—at least with regard to new hires. But, manage-
        ment was completely stumped. It was only when Bob (using a self-image
        enhancement framework) interviewed people in the black drill rig opera-
        tors' villages that he found out how failure to wear ear protectors was
        "rewarding"—even though it led to a severe physical disability. As it
        turns out, being a drill rig operator was the highest status job available
        at that time to black Africans in the region. Deafness, despite its obvious
        downside, performed a self-enhancement function among the operators
        because it identified them as occupants of these highly desired positions!
    •   Deaf drill rig operators are NOT a good thing. Being deaf is a safety hazard.
        For example: Despite the overall high level of noise on the job, operators

can sometimes avoid accidents because they may hear a piece of equipment beginning to malfunction or hear the shouts of coworkers that something is going wrong. So, the managers sought Bob's advice on how they could "turn this situation around." In Bob's lingo, this would mean removing the reward that results from non-performance. In his particular case, however, Bob didn't need to remove the reward. He simply made it meaningless. From that point forward, the company provided drill rig operators with elaborate "permanent" metal bracelets that identified them as operators and uniform shirts with a drill rig logo.

Note that some types of "non-performance is rewarding" are very difficult to counteract. Take the case of <u>absenteeism</u> (i.e., getting rewarded for not going to work). If you have a physically demanding job, what's more "rewarding," digging another ditch or laying around on the couch all day and drinking beer or eating muffins?

4. <u>Does performance matter</u>? (Is there a negative consequence that results from <u>not</u> doing what is supposed to be done?)

   • Example: For decades, the majority of large corporations had in place affirmative action plans that establish a policy committing all managers to making special efforts to hire and develop women and minorities. While those policies might look good on paper, managers who ignore them usually faced no consequences for doing so. It's been demonstrated repeatedly that policies like these have no impact, unless managers are individually held accountable for behaviors and outcomes in support of the policy. **Consequences for (continued) undesired behaviors are crucial.**

5. <u>Are there obstacles to performing as desired</u>? (Is it simply more difficult than it has to be to do what is supposed to be done—or to do it the way it's supposed to be done?)

   • Example: Sometimes, people don't do what you want them to do—even if they know how to do it and really want to do it well. They may simply be thwarted by

Working Around Obstacles Rather Than Eliminating Them

Anita Tucker coined the term "work-around cultures" to characterize organizations in which employees continually/repeatedly expend unnecessary effort and time to overcome (or work-around) physical or policy-based (etc.) obstacles to performance and—in the process—come to see themselves as "heroes" for doing so. These organizationally abusive (<u>but self-image enhancing</u>) practices exact a heavy toll on productivity and profitability and constitute what I call states of "continuous process tolerance" rather than "continuous process improvement" (Tucker, Edmondson & Spear, 2002, emphasis added).

unnecessary barriers. It might be that they can't get the information or supplies that they need—or at least they can't without going through a painful, often dysfunctional bureaucratic process. Ideally, these obstacles will be identified prior to a change implementation and steps will have been taken to counteract them. However, usually that is simply wishful thinking. Even with the best of intentions and effort on the front end, barriers to performance will most often crop up during the implementation itself, perhaps even quite far into it. Change Leaders are always on the alert, looking for ways that doing the right thing can be made easier for those who have to do it.

6. <u>Are emotional or medical problems involved</u>? (Are people distracted psychologically or physically from doing their best?)

- Example: Here's another "roll forward" from previous coverage so that you can strengthen yet another neural circuit: In larger organizations, anywhere from 6 percent to 13 percent of the workforce seeks help through the companies' Employee Assistance Programs. However, studies have shown that only one in three or four of the employees who should seek help actually do. Assuming that these troubled people are distributed somewhat evenly throughout the organization, this means that at any given point in time, a significant number of people with whom you'll be working on a major organizational change project are simply incapable of their best performances at that particular point in time.

There's no real fix at the ready for the Change Leader or consultant on this one (No. 6). However, I strongly encourage you to be sensitive to the fact that there may be more than "meets the eye" in certain cases in which employees don't comply performance-wise. You should also be aware that, if you are an outsider to the organization or to the department(s) involved, people with emotional or medical problems might look to you for the solace and empathy that they haven't received from their manager or colleagues. I'm not suggesting that you play therapist or excuse people from delivering good and on-time performance because of their personal problems. At the same time, we know that making yourself available for an off-agenda conversation here or there may provide just the bit of support that these people need—and to which they might respond well.

BRAIN CONNECTION! LETTING PEOPLE TALK ABOUT THEMSELVES CAN BE A USEFUL TOOL

Over the course of my professional life, I've had the opportunity to observe and evaluate (and sometimes coach) perhaps as many as 200 trainers or teachers. Often an evaluation of the programs themselves was involved. While my formal focus was never on the trainees per se, I've had ample opportunity to draw the following, subjective conclusions about them:

1. Trainees often seem to derive substantial gratification from the occasion to "share" their opinions with others—even when those opinions are: a) virtual repetitions of opinions that other trainees had shared only moments previously and/or b) unrelated to the topic at hand.
2. Trainees frequently appear to make a strong but unconscious link between "how much I talked about myself" and "how much I learned." That is to say that they apparently experience (below the level of awareness) a positive correlation between the two, and they attribute the cause of their experience to the skills of the trainer!

Recently, researchers at the Harvard University Social Cognitive and Affective Neuroscience Lab have documented why some of these effects occur: Using brain-scanning technology they found that when people talk about themselves, it triggers the same chemical reaction (i.e., a dopamine secretion) they experience during sex and this "motivates" them to share personal information frequently (and get a nice buzz from doing so) (Ward, 2013).

Notes

1 By "reliably," I mean that most proposed common reasons for resisting change appear on many of the lists provided by credible organizations and experts. Of course, the lists aren't exactly alike and some lists contain reasons that don't appear on others while some reasons that appear on a list or two aren't found on any of the other lists. The list based on research by Prosci (2014b) is based on the largest recent sample of practicing managers world-wide and, therefore, is likely to be the most reliable overall.

2 For a few years, I regularly convened a Roundtable for CEOs and CFOs of companies operating in the Cincinnati region whose parent companies were headquartered in Germany (i.e., German businesses). Most of the companies had been relatively recently acquired.

Acclimating to the German business culture was extremely stressful for most of these 15 or so executives. The early meetings of the Roundtable can be summarized by, "Thank God I have someone to talk to about this." There were, of course, a large number of different business customs that had to be learned (e.g., being early for a meeting is a no-no because it can inconvenience German executives whose schedules are tight and rigid; breakfast meetings were rarely held; dress is much more formal; first names are rarely used; short emails might be found insulting, etc.). However, by far the most difficult transitional challenges centered on cost accounting procedures. For example, in

German business culture there is a strong drive toward mapping out and costing each of the steps in almost any process which results in a much higher number of cost centers, an extreme-emphasis on the accuracy of any metric and the use of specific costing practices that are far less common in the U.S. such as computing the cost of idle capacity and use of replacement cost depreciation. As you might imagine given the high level of social support provided by the German government, differences in human resource cost accounting (e.g., employer contributions health/dental/vision care and retirement) are extreme.

Many other differences are detailed in Krumwiede and Suessmair (2007).

References

All web site URLs accessed on December 12, 2015.

Ash, B. (2013). What happens when employees are left in the dark? *Florida State 24/7*, February 20. Retrieved from http://news.fsu.edu/More-FSU-News/24-7-News-Archive/2013/February/A-question-of-accountability-What-happens-when-employees-are-left-in-the-dark.

Bridges, W. (1991, 2003, 2009). *Managing transitions: Making the most of change*. Philadelphia, PA: Da Capo Press.

Burnes, B. & Cooke, B. (2013). Kurt Lewin's Field Theory: A review and re-evaluation. *International Journal of Management Reviews, 15*, 408–425. DOI: 10.1111/j.1468-2370.2012.00348.x

"Elan" (HRZone). (2014). *Know organizational change & know how to break employee resistance*. HRZone. Retrieved from www.hrzone.com/community-voice/blogs/elan/know-organizational-change-know-how-to-break-employee-resistance.

Fournies, F. (1999). *Why employees don't do what they're supposed to do and what to do about it*. New York, NY: McGraw-Hill.

Galpin, T. & Herndon, M. (2014). *The complete guide to mergers and acquisitions*. San Francisco, CA: Jossey-Bass.

Kantor, R. (2012). Ten reasons why people resist change. *Harvard Business Review Blog*. Retrieved from http://blogs.hbr.org/2012/09/ten-reasons-people-resist-chang/.

Krumwiede, K. & Suessmair, A. (2007). Comparing U.S. and German cost accounting practices. *Management Accounting Quarterly, 8(3)*, 1–9.

Kübler-Ross, E. (2005). *On grief and grieving: Finding the meaning of grief through the five stages of loss*. New York, NY: Simon & Schuster.

Lewin, K. (1951). *Field theory in social science*. New York, NY: Harper and Row.

Mager, R. & Pipe, P. (1984). *Analyzing performance problems*. Belmont, CA: Lake Publishing.

Marks, L., Mirvis, P. & Ashkenas, R. (2014). Making the most of culture clash in M&A. *Leader to Leader, (71)*, 45–53.

Oishi, S. & Schimmack, U. (2010). Residential mobility, well-being, and mortality. *Journal of Personality and Social Psychology, 98(6)*, 980–994.

Prosci. (2014a). *Proactively manage resistance to change*. Retrieved from www.change-management-coach.com/resistance_to_change.html.

Prosci. (2014b). *Best practices in change management 2014*. Loveland, CO: Prosci Research.

Pulakos, E., Hanson, R., Arad, S. & Moye, N. (Forthcoming). Performance management can be fixes: An on-the-job experiential learning approach for complex behavior change. *Industrial and Organizational Psychology: Perspectives on Science and Practice, 8(1)*. Retrieved from Member web site (Society of Industrial and Organizational Psychology).

Quast, L. (2012). Overcome the 5 main reasons people resist change. *Forbes.* Retrieved from www.forbes.com/sites/lisaquast/2012/11/26/overcome-the-5-main-reasons-people-resist-change/.

Rock, D. (2006). *Quiet leadership: Six steps to transforming performance at work.* New York, NY: Collins.

Rusli, E., Ovide, S., Fleisher, L. & Grundberg, S. (2014). Culture clash: Minecraft fans fear Microsoft. *Wall Street Journal (Eastern Edition), 264(61),* B1–B4.

Tucker, A., Edmondson, A. & Spear, S. (2002). When problem solving prevents organizational learning. *Journal of Organizational Change Management, 15(2),* 122–137.

Wagner, R. & Muller, G. (2009). *Power of 2: How to make the most of your partnerships at work and in life.* Washington, D.C.: Gallup Press.

Ward, A. (2013). The neuroscience of everybody's favorite topic. *Scientific American,* July 16. Retrieved from www.scientificamerican.com/article/the-neuroscience-of-everybody-favorite-topic-themselves/.

7

ASSURING MEETING EFFECTIVENESS

Just about 15 years ago, Tom Krattenmaker, writing in a Harvard Business Review Newsletter, quipped that meetings are the Kudzu of corporate life: They keep growing until they cover everything and virtually nothing can kill them.

Guess what? In those 15 years between the publication of Krattenmaker's (2000) column and today, meeting frequency has increased substantially. A commonly expressed frustration in large organizations today is, "I don't do anything anymore. I just go to meetings." It's often a legitimate complaint. And, of course, while people are in meetings they're not able to "do" their jobs or complete the work that is their responsibility. Across time, that means that work backloads keep increasing, as does employees' self- and boss-imposed performance pressure. In my experience, more work and more pressure can easily reach a point where performance quality decreases and conflict or incivility increases nebulously (i.e., below a level at which the source of the increases can be easily recognized).

When enterprise-wide organizational changes are being planned and implemented, there is a palpable increase in meeting frequency and that increase results in more and *competing* pressures as employees involved with the change will be "torn" between the demands of the projects and the demands of their "regular jobs."[1] So, knowledge of effective meeting planning, design and management can be a great asset.

Begin at the True Beginning

An important thing to consider about meetings is that they don't begin when the physical gathering of people (i.e., the actual meeting) commences. Meetings really begin in the conceptual stage, when they are planned. And, the No. 1 planning issue is to interrogate the very need for the meeting in the first place. If you can't convince yourself beyond doubt that a meeting is truly needed and that important outcomes will result, others are highly unlikely to find value in the time that they are being asked to invest. If a relatively small group is involved, try to imagine what each possible attendee would find to be of value before you finalize your decision to hold the meeting.

If you are helping to plan a meeting, but not running it, don't hesitate to politely raise this value-by-individual issue with the person who is. Bear in mind that some people find the act of being in charge of a meeting rewarding in itself. They might enjoy being in control or being able to "share" (read, "pontificate") their views. I say that some people use meetings to "establish competence," that is, to show others what they know. So, don't assume that because someone is exuberant about leading a forthcoming meeting that it will be a good one in the eyes of attendees.

View Each Meeting as a Project

I recommend that you think of each meeting as a (mini) project. That is, it will involve:

- input from people who attend;
- objectives-setting;
- an action plan (agenda plus procedural guidelines plus "wrap-up");
- evaluation;
- follow up;
- follow through/assessment of progress.

People

A key factor in the success of any meeting is having the right people, and the right number of people, in attendance. Large meetings have their purposes. But, for action-oriented meetings, the general rule is smaller is better—traded off against the need to represent people or units that will be affected by any action to be taken, having people there (if possible) who can approve proposed actions, and having the appropriate subject matter experts on hand to keep the meeting from being bogged down with unknowns.

After the objectives (cf., next section) are finalized for a specific meeting, it's always a good idea to re-evaluate the list of invitees. Look at the list from two perspectives: Whether people are missing who should be included and whether people on the list will serve no real purpose.

If the number of attendees at a particular meeting is large or unwieldy, look for ways of increasing participation and idea-generation. For example, small group discussions, real-time online input, and so on. Audience response/polling systems can be of great value here.

Objectives

Meetings that lack clear objectives usually end up being memorable. That is, the attendees will almost certainly remember how you wasted their time. **So, specifying in advance what you want to achieve from each and every meeting is a must.** And, this is not a decision that is made best in isolation. There should be input on the objectives from a reasonable number of people and perspectives. The process of gathering this input not only results in better, sharper objectives. It also typically generates advance support for what you want to accomplish among those who have been consulted.

Take a real *hard* look at any meeting objectives that involve information transmittal only. Conveying information orally that could have been sent out prior to the meeting and read at individually convenient times by the participants is a guaranteed way to train people to arrive late or fail to attend.

Action Plan

If you've done a good job on objectives-setting, the agenda should flow easily from them. **Be sure to consider the objectives in setting the *order* of the items on the agenda.** Key discussion items, for example, should generally not be scheduled at the very end of a meeting, when important participants might have been called away or when time can run out. Likewise, agenda items that require a complex set-up (explanation) should generally not be scheduled first—as people who unavoidably show up late might have difficulty contributing effectively (if they missed some or all of the explanation).

With rare exceptions (e.g., if confidentiality is an issue), agendas should be sent out in advance. A nice touch is to ask whether anyone wants to add an agenda item. This is a good way to find out what is on people's minds that might otherwise not be "exposed" at the meeting. However, it does require skillful handling of the emotions of people who suggest irrelevant, inappropriate or just plain stupid topics for discussion.

Procedures or "ground rules" for recurring meetings can be established by agreement at the initial meeting or by email prior to the first meeting. If discussion of ground rules is going to be "live," it's best to indicate on the advance agenda what particular rules will be considered. That might look something like this:

1. Introductions
2. Establishment of procedures/ground rules (how we'll handle off-agenda items, whether votes can decide issues of disagreement, whether discussion time for each item will be limited, whether representatives are responsible for finding substitutes when they cannot attend, etc.).

One important ground rule should be that meetings will begin and end on time. Discussing the value of this rule is usually a waste of everyone's time. Alternatively, it can be handled as follows: "Unless someone wishes to disagree, we'll assume that one ground rule that we don't have to discuss is that meetings should begin and end at the scheduled times."

If meetings do *not* begin as scheduled, attendees who arrive at the appointed hour are essentially wasting their time waiting for others to show up. This is yet another way to "train" people to arrive late. Meanwhile, people who don't do what you want (i.e., they don't arrive on time) are rewarded for coming late—by not having to waste *their* time. Starting on time "fixes" both sides of this problem.

Other ground rules may cover whether a Recorder will be appointed, whether minutes will be distributed and to whom, and how off-agenda topics/discussions will be handled (e.g., whether they will be assigned to a "parking lot" for attention only if time is available at the end of the meeting or for attention at a subsequent meeting), etc.

Every meeting should end with a wrap-up, that is, a summary of what has transpired and what people have agreed to accomplish prior to the next meeting—with immediate corrections or additions from the floor. This task can fall to the person who has led the meeting, the Recorder or a person who has previously been assigned this specific role.

Evaluation

There is a tendency for people who lead meetings to believe that those meetings are effective unless someone complains or registers concern. On the other side of the coin, in many organizations, there is a tendency for disaffected meeting participants to suffer in silence (i.e., not complain no matter how ridiculous a meeting turns out to be). **However, the effectiveness of meetings should not be assumed nor ineffective meetings tolerated.** There should be frequent opportunities for participants to offer suggestions for increasing meeting effectiveness—either during meetings or via email follow-ups. **(Note that people are much more comfortable suggesting improvements than they are offering criticisms of the status quo.)**

Follow-Up

It's a long-established truism that the greater the length of time that elapses between the end of a meeting and the receipt of a meeting summary, the less likely meeting participants are to read that summary. So, for this reason and others, it's important to send out summaries promptly. What's promptly? Receipt within three working days should be the target.

The summary should include a very clear specification of who-has-agreed-to-do-what-by-what-specific-date. Those who have agreed to take on a particular task may be asked to confirm by return email that their assignments and target dates are accurate. People who were supposed to attend the meeting but were unable to do so should be asked to respond if they see any problems or have any concerns about what others had agreed to undertake during their absence. They may also be encouraged to volunteer for any tasks not yet assigned to others.

Follow Through/Assessment of Progress

If there is not another meeting scheduled prior to the due date for the completion of some of the tasks assigned, **about half way between the receipt of the meeting summary and the task completion date, it's a good idea to email or call or go to see each person responsible for a task.** You should ask them if things are going well and if there is any way that you can help or find help for them. This serves as a reminder to those who might have forgotten their responsibilities and as an indication that the expectation of task completion in a timely manner is fully expected. It also enables you to anticipate any trouble spots and institute proactive measures to keep things on schedule.

You need to start meeting like this!

EXPERTS' INSIGHTS: MEETING EFFECTIVENESS

1. It's commonly recognized that some people are uncomfortable speaking up in meetings. The larger the number of people in the room, and the more "big shots" who are in attendance, the greater is the hesitancy of such people to express their concerns or to offer their potentially very helpful ideas. However, this phenomenon, which psychologists refer to as "reticence," can occur frequently even in groups with as few as three–five participants (Sluis & Boschen, 2014).

Studies have shown that the longer reticent people go without speaking to the group as a whole, the harder that it is for them to do so. If they manage to get through two or three meetings without chiming in, the probability that they will speak out—unless required to—drops to nearly zero. On the other hand, reticent people who speak out two (or even better, three or more) times during the initial meeting of a particular group are generally freed of their reticence (at least during discussion of non-threatening topics and/or ones in which they have at least a bit of experience/understanding). So, unless the number of attendees at an initial group meeting makes it infeasible, it's a good idea to "manufacture" circumstances that will require each person to speak at least a couple of times. This might involve a round of self-introductions, followed by other rounds in which individuals report why they were assigned to this group, how many people at the meeting they've worked with before, whom they are representing, etc.

Of course, occasionally breaking the group down into discussion teams followed with group-by-group report-outs by people who are comfortable "in front of the room" is another way of insuring that reticence doesn't preclude obtaining input from all parties. **But, I recommend this technique as an addition to, not a substitution for, the contrived speak-outs in the initial meeting.**

2. Some meeting facilitators would never think of reading long-ish documents aloud during a meeting. **Yet, it never occurs to many of those same people that an introduction prepared by a speaker very often IS a long-ish document.** The pain of listening to such introductions being read is exacerbated when there are more than one or two speakers or panel members or experts (or whatever) who are going to participate. These long-form introductions can be sent out in advance with the agenda and copies distributed at the meeting. This allows you the option of honoring your guests with only a sentence or two punctuated by a few well-chosen superlatives. Perhaps something like this:

> We are really pleased and honored that such admired and respected specialists [or whatever] are here today to share their expertise with us. I'm sure that we are all very eager to hear what our guests have to say, so I will dispense with covering the biographical information that you received in advance and that you also have before you. So, let me please introduce to you Chris Jones of ABC, Marty Smith from XYZ, and our own, Lee Kramer from the DEF Division. You will note that—beyond the great overall experiences each of our guests brings here today—they have been asked in advance to tailor their remarks to their current, unique perspectives: Chris on design issues, Marty on implementation, and Lee on evaluation. So, let's get to it.

At this point, you've gotten through the introductions quickly and you've even unobtrusively reminded the speakers to stick to their assignments. The final bonus is that you've established yourself as someone who really knows how to manage a meeting.

3. If the group decides that it's best to target in advance how much time should be devoted to each item on the agenda, it might be wise to appoint a time-keeper. The time-keeper's role isn't to cut people off in mid-comment. Rather, it is to politely alert people when planned time for discussion is running out. And, draw their attention to it again if it is necessary. In a group of any size, there will undoubtedly be participants who simply can't perform this task tactfully and pleasantly. Rather than getting stuck with a poor, perhaps irritating, performer over the long-term, it may be best to rotate this assignment. **As meetings go by, you should see time-keepers adopting the best behaviors of the more effective time-keepers in previous meetings.**

4. When the same group members meet weekly or even more often, the easiest—but not necessarily the best—thing to do is to schedule the meeting in the same room every time. That way, everyone knows where to go. However, meeting in the same room over and over and over again can leave people with the feeling that they have been participating in one, endless meeting. If it's possible to change the venue occasionally (perhaps over fresh-baked cookies in the cafeteria—or a

similar variation), that can go a small way toward clearing out some of the déjà-vu-fog that might be hovering over the meetings. Of course, any time that the venue is changed from the standard meeting place, you'll want to send out a reminder of the new location a couple of days in advance. (Sending out a reminder the day of the meeting is usually a wasted effort as many people today are more than 24 hours behind on their email.)

In novel settings, it is very important to get things started promptly and similarly to the way you would in the regular setting. You want to give people the subtle message that this alternate setting is simply a change of place, not a substitute for the actual meeting (nor is it an opportunity to exchange cookie recipes).

Note

1   "Project vs. regular job?" That's usually how people involved see/describe things. One of the big challenges of leading enterprise-wide change is to get people to feel that working diligently on the success of the change is, in fact, a central part of their *regular* (i.e., real) job.

It's also worthy of note that there is strong evidence that chronic stress lessens and, in some extreme cases, eliminates the brain's ability to fend off depression and the body's ability to produce antibodies that are necessary to fight infection. People who are "stress-sick" will end up with even greater work-backlogs and compounded by less ability to catch up.

References

Krattenmaker, T. (2000). Before and after the meeting. *Harvard Business Publishing Newsletters*, October 1.

Sluis, R. & Boschen, M. (2014). Fear of evaluation in social anxiety: Mediation of attention bias to human faces. *Journal of Behavior Therapy and Experimental Psychiatry, 45(4)*, 475–483.

8

PLANNING AND DESIGNING TRAINING WITH THE BRAIN IN MIND

Enterprise-wide change projects typically involve a substantial amount of training (and, presumably, learning). Yet, for most types of large-scale changes (such as culture change, strategy reformulation/redeployment and mergers/acquisitions) the structure, content and even the delivery methods for training will vary with the situation, the goals of the project and the culture of the focal organization. So, once again, I'm going to turn on the IT/ERP-installation-as-perfect-example switch. It will provide me with the structure and content that I need to be able to write pointedly and "example-laden-ly" about the kinds of training planning and design issues that are inherent in most super-complex organizational improvement programs.

So, let's take a look at some of the things that Change Leaders and consultants are up against training-wise when it comes to an ERP implementation or some other type of enterprise-wide IT transformation:

Major Challenge No. 1a: The Amount and Complexity of What Needs to be Learned

The intricacy of enterprise software (and other major IT products) today has grown to a point of literal incomprehensiveness for all but a few technical geniuses. **Unfortunately, that doesn't stop many trainers from jamming as much information as possible into the programs they conduct. It's no surprise (to anyone but those trainers) that exposure to too much information is overwhelming and feeds both misunderstanding and resistance.**

Clearly identifying what it is that trainees need to learn is *always important*—regardless of the scale of the project. But, in ERP implementations, when we're dealing with an enormous amount of extremely dense content that must be learned quickly, **it is *crucial* that we identify what people** <u>**really**</u> **need to learn and what they** <u>**DON'T**</u> **need to learn (i.e., at least what they don't need to learn right now).** Be assured that what people need to learn is LESS than what most software-product purveyors will tell you. Yet, it's usually <u>not</u> the case that there should be less training.

In a nutshell, this is what people typically need to learn about a new IT system:

a)   how the overall system works at a <u>conceptual level</u>—with that information presented in ways that are tailored to the level of sophistication and to the specific job functions of various groups of learners and

b)   how individual employees should <u>use</u> or operate the software/hardware/ system to do their jobs effectively and efficiently.

No more and no less. This is the wheat, all else is chaff.

Major Challenge No. 1b: The Variety and Flashiness of Training Media and Methods that are Available

There are lots of very smart and aggressive marketing people out there who are involved in large-scale IT changeovers and the provision of the requisite training that goes along with them. In fact, ERP software training alone has become a *big* business in its own right. Think of any training method/medium that you can (from user-group blogs to knowledge warehouses to context-sensitive help-screens to function key memory cards) and it's available from a variety of vendors.

<u>Okay, so let's put major challenges 1a and 1b together.</u> What we get is:

•   an enormous amount of extremely dense content; and
•   tons of different ways to deliver that content.

People who do a lot of work in the training field often refer to these two issues as "the what" (1a) and "the how" (1b). Typically, far too little careful attention is paid to either one. Yet, usually "the what" gets even less attention than "the how."

Think about it. And, be honest! If you had a choice of scrubbing and filtering an overwhelming amount of extremely dense content for training or getting to decide which of several cool ways of delivering the content would be used, what would you choose? If you said scrubbing and filtering the content, you're in for extra laps after practice. You *know* that that wouldn't really be your choice.

Training methods/delivery: This is what most members of project/implemen-tation teams choose as their focus. They tend to involve themselves more in the selection of training methods and leave most of the training content decisions to the product purveyors. **That's not only a bad choice; it's a choice that shouldn't be made at all. Content and methods aren't independent.** They

FIGURE 8.1 When Learning Content is Not Closely Aligned with Training Methods, Disaster Can Result

are parts of the same whole. Choice of training methods MUST be made in light of the training content involved and vice versa.

Hey! You practically skipped right over that last sentence and it's very important. So, now you have to read it again: **Choice of training methods MUST be made in light of the training content involved and vice versa**.

BRAIN CONNECTION! THE AMOUNT OF INFORMATION PROVIDED

Social critics have worried for decades about U.S. students' continually falling science test scores when compared to the scores of students in other countries (Martin & Mullis, 2008; O'Brien, 2010). Many experts now believe that the primary reason behind the decline is that approaches to teaching sciences in the U.S. tend to focus on breadth of learning, rather than on depth (Fenichel & Schweingruber, 2010; Howard, 2006). That is, the emphasis is on presenting as many scientific facts or fields of scientific study as possible. The idea is not dissimilar to the old "melting pot" notion of what makes the U.S. strong: Pour enough different things (diverse peoples) into the container (the U.S.) and somehow things will mix and meld together resulting in a better, stronger product (the nation). Analogously, in teaching science, it has long been asserted domestically that we need to pour many different things (scientific ideas across many fields and all of history—*including ideas now known to be invalid*) into the container (students' brains) and somehow things will mix and meld together resulting in a better product (greater understanding of science as reflected in higher scores on standardized tests). Sounds good, except for one thing. It doesn't work; things don't automatically mix and meld together in our brains.

As covered previously: When we learn, our brains make a weak, physiological connection between two things (e.g., one idea and another) (Rock, 2006). Barring repetition and/or practice, our brains send those weak connections from active consideration (working memory) to storage (in long-term memory) as soon as possible. If we don't repeatedly make that connection again and again, we won't be able to access the information (i.e., retrieve it from long-term memory) when we need it. That's because the brain buries (or "prunes") connections (neural circuits) that aren't used frequently (Willis, 2008). That is, of course, the physiological basis of what we call "forgetting." **Brain circuits only become faster, stronger and more durable when they are reactivated many times.**

Neuroscience studies of brain functioning have shown that people develop a deeper understanding of complicated subject matter when **they study relatively few key ideas in progressively more sophisticated ways**. As a result, the National Research Council (Fenichel & Schweingruber, 2010) now recommends that science teaching should focus on a small number of core ideas such as atomic-molecular theory, evolution theory, cell theory and force and motion. Learning about these core topics should then be "scaffolded" from grade to grade by adding progressively deeper "doing science" experiences **with the same topics** (Caine, Caine, McClintic & Klimek, 2008). And, that is exactly how science and math have been taught in China (No. 1 in national test scores) and Singapore (No. 2) and Japan (No. 3) for over 50 years (Delaney, 2008; Howard, 2006).

Major Challenge No. 2: Training for IT Changeovers Typically Suffers From Many Egregious Planning and Design Flaws

A. Training at the <u>conceptual level</u> is usually based on the sales presentations or marketing materials of vendors. Dense harangues about the wondrous complexity and Nirvana-inducing capabilities of the software is *not* best presented at the outset when learners are perhaps at their most anxious about the forthcoming changes and their roles in them. As a result of heightened anxiety, what is presented is often perceived as threatening (e.g., "standardization of procedures" being interpreted as "loss of individual discretion and authority," etc.) and/or unlikely to be remembered (e.g., because it is generic, thereby lacking the context of participants' jobs or job functions).

B. Training in support of actual <u>use</u> typically lacks "fidelity." **Fidelity refers to the amount of similarity between the key learning elements in the training situation and those same elements in the trained-for situation.** Feature learning to drive in a car with an automatic transmission and then being expected to drive a car with a manual transmission. There are thousands of similarities between the two cars. But, one critical element that is different can cause dysfunctional performance "on the job" of driving the second car.

Possibly the most common example of a lack of fidelity in large-scale IT projects is the difference between the specific stimuli on computer screens in training and on the job. Many IT training initiatives are begun before the new software is fully adapted to the current customer. So, the software that is used in training is a version that was set up as a generic simulation or that was developed for a previous customer. The result? People learn to do things one way in training (with help) and then have to learn to do them a different way on the job (working alone, or with others who were trained with the same low-fidelity materials). This makes an already complicated situation even more complicated for the trainees. They have to: 1) stop using the brain circuits that they were beginning to establish and 2) create and strengthen still newer ones—all by their lonesomes.

C. For training at the <u>conceptual level</u> *and* for actual <u>use</u>, there is usually too long a delay between when something is learned and when it can be applied. So, the recently activated neural connections fall into disuse and can no longer be retrieved when they are needed. That is, they are forgotten. (As you know, because it's been repeated several times already: <u>Brain circuits only become faster, stronger and more durable when they are reactivated many times!</u>)

In both conceptual-level and use-level training, it is important for trainees to understand system dynamics. That is, they need to understand (and appreciate, i.e., be sensitive to) the effects of their actions on the performance, stress levels and workloads of others in different units.

Major Challenge No. 3

The importance of training in major IT projects is typically underestimated at the outset and when projects expand in scope, run over budget and/or get behind schedule, training is the first thing to be cut or minimized (Bolman & Deal, 2008).

How much training is really needed? The target percentage of the overall project budget that should be devoted to training is in dispute. Estimates range from 5 percent to 50 percent—giving a clear sign that *somebody* is crazy. In any case, percentage-of-budget is definitely not the place to start.

Training planning and design usually begins with task analyses. However, with IT projects—at least those involving reputable vendors—you can usually depend (for a start) on the task specifications that are provided with the software/hardware or system. The initial step, then, is to create a matrix of what needs to be learned x (i.e., by) the groups and individuals who need to learn it. Table 8.1 gives a generic example.

Let's shift from challenges/problems to solutions. Here's what you need to do to meet the three daunting challenges delineated above:

1. Focus on what people really need to learn; eliminate dense-packing.
2. Tailor conceptual level training to the specific job functions of the current client; **eliminate threatening concepts and materials (or anything else) that is only relevant to the software purchase decision**.
3. Maximize the fidelity of all training materials and stimuli.

TABLE 8.1 Planning Template: What Needs to be Learned for the Groups and Individuals Who Need to Learn It

Type of Training	Role A, Jobs a–n	Role B, Jobs a–n	Role n, Jobs a–n	Etc., etc.
1. Conceptual model				
Level 1				
Level 2				
Level 3				
Level n				
2. Use/operational skills				
Segment A				
Type a-1				
Type a-2				
Type a-n				
Segment B				
Type b-1				
Type b-2				
Type b-n				
Segment n				

4. Minimize the amount of time that transpires between what is learned and when it is applied or used (preferably on the job).
5. Carefully lay out the "what needs to be learned" by "who needs to learn it" matrix; review/re-evaluate it, have others from different perspectives do so as well.
6. Focus on what people really need to learn. (This one bears repeating, so I did.)

Okay—so what about that training-costs-as-a-percentage-of-budget-for-the-total project-thing? As indicated previously, there is no magic number. But, it's likely to come up in discussion. If the vendor provides training, it will come up as part of their sales pitch. But, the time it's most likely to come up is when financial people take a look at what the project is going to cost overall, collectively drop their jaws and as-one shout, "Do we really have to spend that much on training!?!?!"

No matter when or how the issue is raised, I try to postpone the "percentage" discussion for a point in time <u>after</u> the what-needs-to-be-learned-by-who-needs-to-learn-it matrix is in final form and an estimate of the cost of doing the training effectively for the entire matrix has been derived. Then, look at that estimated cost number and give it a "reasonability test" against the projected cost of the entire project. **Just keep in mind that cutting corners on training has been the downfall (or a major contributor to the downfall) of many an enterprise-wide change.**

EXPERTS' INSIGHTS: PLANNING AND DESIGNING TRAINING

1. Expectations, leveling and accountability. In enterprise software training (and most other forms of complex IT-based training), what psychologists refer to as the "perceptual set" (i.e., the learning readiness) of trainees changes dramatically from the initial training session to the second or third. At the first session, people usually arrive in an anxious frame of mind. They don't know what to expect and some fear that they will not be able to understand the material, that they will not be able to master the skills required or that in some other way they will look foolish. (Earlier, I provided another way of saying this: They fear that they will not be able to maintain (much less, enhance) their self-images.)

By the second or third session, that initial anxiety is typically replaced by stone-cold boredom. It's not just that the content itself is boring, although it usually is. **Rather, boredom sets in because trainers usually spend so much time in the second or third meeting making up for what went wrong in the first session and getting everyone (especially those who were unable to attend the first session) "up to speed" or "on the same page."** In other words, valuable training time is devoted to wasting time.

You can greatly reduce the amount of anxiety that trainees experience in the initial session **by providing—in advance—complete information about what will be covered during the session and what the performance expectations**

for trainees (if any) will be. (This also supports "accountability," to which I'll return shortly.) When possible, you may wish to include an agenda as well. (These same practices should be replicated for subsequent training sessions. That is, advance materials or pre-work for later sessions should include an agenda, an explanation of how the forthcoming session(s) fit with or support what has already transpired, etc.) Keep in mind: Attendance might be far from perfect; you need to keep the people who aren't there for Session D or Session H informed about how what they missed fits into the overall logic of the training.

In general, whether it's an early-occurring session or one that comes much later, you can reduce wasted time (and boredom) by providing background or self-study materials that explain the context for the training along with readings or assignments designed to "level" employees prior to each session. **("Leveling" refers to any process designed to assure that all trainees have at least a certain minimum understanding or exposure to the forthcoming content.)** It's best if this pre-work is accompanied by a clear explanation of each trainee's responsibilities. That is, each participant will be accountable for completing the pre-work, actively participating in the training and applying what is learned as soon as possible back on the job.

Of course, managers and work group leaders need to be trained or coached to support full participation by trainees (and, if necessary, to "enforce" accountability). A major part of that support can be provided via brief "importance-of/report-out" meetings. **That is, it is very helpful if managers or group leaders meet with their people prior to training sessions to show that they (the managers and leaders) know what is going to transpire during training and that they believe that it is <u>important</u>. After training sessions, managers and team leaders can again meet with the trainees and have them <u>report out</u> what they have learned, what questions or concerns they might have, and so on.** The "report-out" sessions reinforce (through repetition) what is learned and they validate the managers' and supervisors' previous expressions of "importance-of."

When planning "full participation" by trainees, keep in mind that the two types of participation that have the strongest impact on learning are: 1) application/practice on the job as soon as possible after initial learning takes place and 2) requiring trainees to provide training to others as soon after the on-the-job practice as possible. Of course, not every employee can be an effective trainer. But, for those who can do it well, their understanding of the system is likely to take a giant leap forward when they have to prepare to train others and then actually do the training. What's that? You ask if self-image is involved here? It most certainly is; you are absolutely correct! Those employees who do well at training their colleagues also have a great chance to experience some good ole self-image enhancement in the process.

2. Trainer effects. You already know that individual trainers vary widely in their competence and effectiveness. The "right" trainer can have an ENORMOUS impact

on learning and on reduction of resistance. But, here's an additional level of complexity to the trainer effect: **The right trainer for conceptual level training is very seldom the right trainer for use/application training**. When it comes to complex software training, the kind of people who see the trees usually aren't the ones who see the forest and vice versa. **If the Technoids who provide the use/application training must also provide conceptual level training, it is usually a good idea to have co-trainers in the latter.** These co-trainers might be Sponsorship Team members, the manager of the group being trained or people from an internal training staff . . . or you.

A common affliction of technical trainers is what I call "Super-sophisticated User Syndrome." A lot of the people who become experts in (i.e., super-sophisticated users of) complex software systems (or, really, any complex system) often lose all sight of what it's like to be a novice user. No matter how well-intended such trainers are, they usually have great difficulty manifesting empathy for, and patience with, novices. <u>Often, they can't even recognize that technical jargon is technical jargon and not everyday language</u>. **And, as you were just about to guess, SCN research has found that <u>empathy and patience</u> are two of the very most important characteristics of trainer (and teacher) effectiveness.**

3. Bull's-eye, not Bull####, Training. An absolutely fantastic way to convince employees that training is not worth their time is to provide training that is too general or provide it to people who don't need it. For example, effective communication is undeniably a crucial component of successful large-scale change projects (IT or not). So, many client organizations will bring in communication trainers to conduct programs on general communication skills when what people really need is skill development in certain specific behaviors such as supportive communication or performance coaching or conflict resolution. **It is equally as mistaken and ineffective to provide skill training to people who won't use those skills during the course of the project.** Yes, meeting management skills are important. But, they are only important (now) for people who will actually manage meetings. Rest assured. There will be plenty for every employee involved to learn. **But, everyone does not need to learn everything right away**. If people will not need to apply knowledge or a skill shortly after training, don't do the training.

4. Job aids. Have you ever tried to think of the name of a movie (or whatever) and your friend says, "I think that it starts with a 'C'." And, bam! The name of the movie pops right into your head. **Sometimes we need just the tiniest hint to bring back a relatively complex association or connection.** (Once you remember the name of the movie, you'll remember a lot more about the movie itself.) **So keep in mind that simple connection-makers (diagrams, keyboard templates, checklists, trouble-shooting lists, etc.) can be extremely helpful to people who are trying to establish new brain circuitry.** (Hah! A great segue!)

5. Brain circuitry. Earlier in this Guide, I recounted some of the tactics learned from SCN research that can help us overcome resistance to change. **Many of**

<u>**those tactics are equally relevant to the planning and design of training programs as well**</u>.

Do you remember the example of cardiac re-hab patients? They "learned" that they could dramatically reduce the likelihood of a second, serious heart attack simply by making some changes in their eating habits. **Yet, because that learning was <u>passive</u>—they were simply told about the relationship between heart healthiness and diet—only one in eight patients made the desired change.**

In the same way, a "telling" approach to software skills training is likely to be ineffective. So, should we eliminate all telling/selling/lecturing? No. That simply wouldn't be practical in most IT conversions. **However, to whatever extent possible, we need to design training programs that are interrogative (organized around questions) rather than declarative (here are the answers).** That is, the trainer creates the general framework of what is to be learned—but doesn't fill in all the gaps for people. The trainees must—as often as possible—actively consider information and draw their own conclusions.

Laundry List Time

Here's a laundry list of other factors that SCN research has clearly demonstrated to have a very positive impact on learning effectiveness. The more of these that you can build into training programs, the better:

- Priming for positive outcomes; avoid discussion of negatives; lots of positive reinforcement/recognition of correct answers or actions or ideas;
- Chunking; short bursts of learning with lots of repeated practice; more depth, less breadth;
- Repeated focus and attention—or what's called "directed mental effort"; trainees must actively choose to focus on positive/desired results;
- Anything that increases trainee perceptions of being in control;
- Visualization; visual imaging of processes and task series/effects;
- Use testing as a learning opportunity; people are more likely to remember something if they got the related question wrong on a test; going over a test after it's been taken and explaining or having the trainees explain why right answers were right and wrong answers were wrong is usually also very helpful. Here, people can learn from how others understood or thought they understood specific test items.
- Use movement and exercise to increase heart rate; make people think while they walk or stretch;
- Fresh, clean, cool air; environmental richness; high protein/complex carbohydrates in snacks; and
- In subsequent sessions, remind trainees of their insights in previous sessions and have them describe the behaviors they manifested as a result of those insights.

Finally, here's a tip that requires a bit more explanation that just a bullet:

- Don't ask people to describe things for which they have not yet acquired the appropriate descriptive language.

If you do, they'll make up (erroneous) "connections" that they will subsequently have to be trained to "disconnect" or disregard. As an illustration, let's say that we stage a wine tasting in which people (who lack expertise in wines) are asked to sample an unlabeled selection of red wines and to rate their preferences. They do so and we record the ratings. Subsequently, the same people are asked to describe the difference between an excellent Merlot and an equally excellent Pinot Noir. Once they have verbalized their descriptions, they will unwittingly change their preferences among the original (blind) selection of wines to get those preferences in line with descriptive adjectives they had apparently only made up on the spot (as they were asked to do). For example, if someone happens to use the word "hearty" or the word "full-bodied" to describe the ideal Merlot, they will likely choose the heaviest wine from a selection (of bottles labeled as Merlots) as their preference—even if they had previously rated the lightest (Merlot) wine in the (blind) sample as the best, i.e., their clear preference.

A Reflection on Technology, Accelerated Learning and The Buddha (Mindfulness Meditation)

If you talk about training to managers in any large organization today, they're likely to tell you that getting employees' knowledge and skills up to speed as *quickly* as possible and then maintaining their knowledge and skills over time as *efficiently* as possible is essential to the performance, perhaps ultimately even to the survival, of their organizations. If you talk to *training managers* (or their bosses) in any large organization today, they're likely to tell you that they are feeling continually increasing pressure on their departments to train employees both faster and better in order to reduce "time to value" (Hoffman, Ward, Feltovich, Fiore & Andrews, 2014, p. 5) and increase ROIT (return on investment in training). The exclamation point on the need-for-speed issue is that CEOs have come around to the point (Galagan, 2013) that they are far less concerned with the direct costs of training than with the amount of time that training takes. (CEOs in the same sample indicated that they not only want training of shorter duration, they want their employees to *stay productive while they're getting training*—a very tough order indeed.)

Educational and training technology appears to have the greatest, or the greatest potential, impact on learning speed—especially simulation and gaming. Research conducted by the U.S. Marine Corps, for example, found that simulation and "serious gaming" can reduce war fighter training time by as much as 50 percent (Berka, Johnson, Fidopiastis, Kruse & Skinner, 2014). Let's consider simulation[1] first.

I've had the exciting opportunity to view simulators in action for flight training, armor (tanks) and heavy equipment operation, bus driving safety during icy conditions, Use of Force decision-making (police), chemical processing and surgical procedures, including the use of new surgical equipment.[2] While you were reading the preceding, bulleted list of characteristics of maximally effective training programs (priming for positive outcomes, chunking, movement to increase heart rate, etc.), I'll bet that you were thinking something along the lines of, "Geezz. This is all pie-in-the-sky stuff." Well, it's not. The kind of simulators I'm referring to can reliably and repeatedly nail everyone of those bullets. For example, you get maximum fidelity to the point that brain activity and cardiovascular responses nearly mirror what you'd record if the trainees were actually doing the trained for task (Berka et al., 2014), extremely realistic visualizations, training chunks in whatever length or type best fit, immediate, comprehensive and objective feedback (with trainer effects eliminated) and much more.[3] **Yet, perhaps the most important of all simulator capabilities is provision of unlimited "deliberate practice"** (Ericsson, 2009).

It's now widely agreed that **practice does not make perfect, deliberate practice does** (Ericsson, 2009). To illustrate the differences between practice and deliberate practice, Ericsson, Prietula and Cokely (2007) point to the majority of the world's golfers. They argue that the learning or performance trajectory for beginners is typically high for the first several months of playing fairly regularly. At some point, however, that trajectory levels off for most golfers such that even playing (i.e., practicing) twice a week (a frequency all but out of reach for most still-employed duffers) typically leads to only very slow, marginal decreases (if any) in the average number of shots taken per round. They provide data to show that this occurs because when you play a game of golf, you only get one opportunity to take a swing from any particular spot on the course and that doesn't allow you to correct your mistakes or learn exactly what you did that led to a good shot. With deliberate practice, you would take many consecutive swings from the same spot. In so doing, you'd get much more extensive and useful neural- and muscle-based feedback on your performance and be able to adapt your game accordingly.

Again, simulators allow for unlimited deliberate practice, a huge advantage over other types of training methods.

On to gaming (which is actually a specific type of simulation). Most likely every kid who became addicted to playing video games was chastised on numerous occasions for doing so. "Why are you wasting your time doing that?" "Are you nuts?" "If you think that you're going to be able to get a job playing 'serious' games, you are seriously out of your mind!" Turns out, such gamers are far from crazy.

Given that gaming is a type of simulation, it has many of the benefits of training in a simulator plus some that are unique to gaming:

- In most cases, games are less expensive to create (and rapidly becoming more inexpensive) and are more portable than simulators (Beidel, 2011).

- Gaming can be presented online to many trainees simultaneously.
- High-frequency players often develop improved peripheral vision (Buckley, Codina, Bhardwaj & Pascalis, 2010), economy of movement and attentional weighting skills (the ability to focus on critical aspects of a situation and ignore less important things and purposeful attempts at distraction) (Giannotti et al., 2013).
- It's been demonstrated that making mistakes can accelerate learning. That is, making an error on a test or on the job can draw the brain's attention with sufficient focus that what has been done incorrectly will be remembered as an inappropriate choice or act (Castaneda-Mendez, 2014). Sometimes, such mistakes can operate below the level of conscious awareness to decrease desire/motivation to learn below the level of conscious awareness as threats to one's self-image. In gaming, however, mistakes are common *and inherent in the medium*. In games, that is, the brain expects to make many mistakes and to learn from them. Thus, in games, accelerated learning can occur because the brain records all of the player's mistakes—but the ubiquity of mistakes in games is such that they are usually not a threat to players' self-images.
- When Massively Multiplayer Online Role-Playing Games (MMORPGs) are involved, **participants have opportunities to work (well or poorly) in teams and to demonstrate "step-up leadership" (emergent, circumstantially determined, self-initiated, temporary leadership) that is much needed (and very difficult to propagate reliably) in major work organizations today** (e.g., Thomas & Vlacic, 2012).
- Metaphorically speaking, the control mechanisms of the entire universe of product manufacturing (e.g., designing 3-D printed parts for jet engines), transformation processing (operating chemical processing panels), service provision (e.g., manipulating laparoscopic surgery robots) and military operations (e.g., "piloting" unmanned aerial vehicles, i.e., "drones") are continually being re-designed to resemble and/or work like gaming consoles on which, of course, gamers have plenty of experience before they are trained for a particular job.
- Gamers can provide thousands of hours of their own pre-training and deliberate practice for free.

Let me return for a moment to the issue of gaming and *leadership*. Many research reviews (e.g., Balzert, Pannese, Walter & Loos, 2012; Boinodiris, 2014) have extolled the virtues of games/gamification in business settings and hundreds of major U.S. corporations (not only the "usual suspects"—like Microsoft, Apple and Google—but also more traditional organizations—for example, Deloitte, Canon, IBM, Marriott, Target and the World Bank) have made games a key component of their training methods. Common applications include customer service, opening/closing procedures, adhering to fair employment practice laws, machine operation, procurement and many, many others. But, leadership?

Yes, leadership. The U.S. Military, Deloitte and IBM are among the "leaders" when it comes to leadership training by games. Jim Spohrer, a senior IBM executive involved with leadership games, has been quoted as saying that:

> What we've found is that success as a business leader may depend on skills as a gamer . . . Smart organizations are recognizing valued employees who play online games and apply their skills and experiences as virtual leaders to the 'real world' jobs.
>
> (Seriosity, 2007)

At Deloitte's Leadership Academy, there was a serendipitous effect as a result of the introduction of gamification. Unexpectedly, it was found that *senior executives*—who in most organizations wouldn't be caught dead in a live training program (there's that self-image factor again)—became frequent "players" of leadership games, often during travel time (Bodnar, 2014).

Simulation and gaming = the future of learning, training and development. And, the future is now.

Notes

1 By simulation, I'm referring to training conducted with electronic, computer-managed simulators, not role-playing or board game simulations.
2 If you haven't the experience of seeing simulators in action, you can get a really good feel and exposure (though "second hand") by going to YouTube and searching for "using simulators for training" or any type of particular simulator (e.g., flight simulators, laparoscopic surgery simulators, etc.).
3 One other very important capability of simulators is the opportunity to practice dangerous tasks in a safe environment.

References

All web site URLs accessed on December 12, 2015.

Balzert, S., Pannese, L., Walter, M. & Loos, P. (2012). Serious games in business. In M. Cruz-Cunha (Ed.), *Handbook of research on serious games as educational, business and research tools* (pp. 539–558). Hershey, PA: Information Science Reference.

Beidel, E. (2011). Gaming technology puts soldiers boots on ground. *National Defense Technology Magazine*, December. Retrieved from www.nationaldefensemagazine.org/archive/2011/December/Pages/GamingTechnologyPutsSoldiers%E2%80%99Bootson Ground.aspx.

Berka, C., Johnson, R., Fidopiastis, C., Kruse, A. & Skinner, A. (2014). Exploring subjective experience during simulated reality training with psychophysiological metrics. *Marine Corps Warfighting Laboratory Workshop, Quantico, VA*. Retrieved from www.researchgate.net/publication/236587791_Exploring_Subjective_Experience_during_Simulated_Reality_Training_with_Psychophysiological_Metrics.

Bodnar, Z. (2014). Using game mechanics to enhance leadership education. *eLearn Magazine*, February. Retrieved from http://elearnmag.acm.org/archive.cfm?aid=2583703.

Boinodiris, P. (2014). *Serious games for business: Using gamification to fully engage customers, employees and partners.* Tampa, FL: Meghan-Kiffer Press.

Bolman, L. & Deal, T. (2008). *Reframing organizations: Artistry, choice and leadership.* San Francisco, CA: Jossey Bass.

Buckley, D., Codina, C., Bhardwaj, P. & Pascalis, O. (2010). Action video game players and deaf observers have larger Goldman visual fields. *Vision Research, 50(5)*, 548–556.

Caine, R., Caine, G., McClintic, C. & Klimek, K. (2008). *12 brain/mind learning principles in action: Developing executive functions of the human brain* (2nd ed.). Thousand Oaks, CA: Corwin Press.

Castaneda-Mendez, K. (2014). *What's your problem? Identifying and solving the five types of process problems.* Boca Raton, FL: Taylor & Francis Group.

Delaney, P. (2008). Asian students top latest global math, science study, report Boston College researchers. *EurekAlert*, December 10, Boston College. Public News Release. Retrieved from www.eurekalert.org/pub_releases/2008-12/bc-ast121008.php.

Ericsson, K. (2009). Enhancing the development of professional performance: Implications from the study of deliberate practice. In K. Ericsson (Ed.), *Development of professional expertise* (pp. 405–431). Cambridge, UK: Cambridge University Press.

Ericsson, K., Prietula, M. & Cokely, E. (2007). The making of an expert. *Harvard Business Review, 85(7–8)*, 114–121.

Fenichel, M. & Schweingruber, H. (2010). *Surrounded by science: Learning science in informal environments.* Washington, D.C.: National Academies Press.

Galagan, P. (2013). Greed for speed. *T & D, 67(5)*, 22–24.

Giannotti, D., Patrizi, G., Di Rocco, G., Vestri, A., Semproni, C., Fiengo, L., Pontone, S., Palazzini, G. & Redler, A. (2013). Play to become a surgeon: Impact of Nintendo WII training on laparoscopic skills. *PLoS One, 8(2)*, February 27. Retrieved from http://journals.plos.org/plosone/article?id=10.1371/journal.pone.0057372.

Hoffman, R., Ward, P., Feltovich, L., Fiore, S. & Andrews, D. (2014). *Accelerated expertise: Training for high proficiency in a complex world.* New York, NY: Psychology Press.

Howard, P. (2006). *The owner's manual for the brain: Everyday applications from mind-brain research* (3rd ed.). Austin, TX: Bard Books.

Martin, O. & Mullis, I. (2008). *Trends in international mathematics and science study.* Report released by the TIMSS & PIRLS International Study Center, Boston College, December 10.

O'Brien, K. (2010). What happened to studying? *The Boston Globe (Ideas)*, July 4.

Rock, D. (2006). *Quiet leadership: Six steps to transforming performance at work.* New York, NY: Collins.

Seriosity (2007). IBM and Seriosity Study: Online gaming is good for business. *Seriosity Press Release*, June 28. Retrieved from www.seriosity.com/downloads/IBM_GIO_Press_Release.pdf.

Thomas, D. & Vlacic, L. (2012). The business of collaborating: Designing and implementing a group decision-making scenario using the TeamMATE collaborative computer game. In M. Cruz-Cunha (Ed.), *Handbook of research on serious games as educational, business and research tools* (pp. 446–477). Hershey, PA: Information Science Reference.

Willis, J. (2008). Building a bridge from neuroscience to the classroom. *Phi Delta Kappa, 89*, 424–427.

9

MEASUREMENT AND METRICS WITH THE BRAIN IN MIND[1]

In my experience, "measurement" and "metrics" are used interchangeably and you can make a good case that they should be. However, I try to draw and maintain a distinction between them. **I think of measurement as the act of measuring and a metric as the result of the measurement.** So, if you use a ruler to determine the length of an envelope, that's measurement for me. When you find out that the envelope is 12.5 inches long, the 12.5 inches is the metric. If it would amuse you, you can check whether I'm consistent in the use of these terms. BTW: If you do check, that's measurement. The percentage of consistency is the metric.

The following are some precepts in regard to measurement and metrics across the board and how they are relevant to large-scale organizational change projects.

1. A long-standing and usually valid maxim is that "what gets measured gets done." The idea behind the saying is that the act of measuring something (usually) keeps a focus on whatever it is that is being measured and that focus (often) results in people taking actions necessary to correct any problems that occur. Think about the relatively new diagnostic systems in cars, like the ones that let you know when tire inflation is low. Many people don't take the initiative to manually assess the pressure in their tires. As a result, they often travel with pressures that are dangerously low. However, most people don't ignore the tire pressure warning light. The measurement provided by the car itself spurs people to take appropriate action.

With regard to large-scale change projects, it's probably better to look at this maxim in reverse. If you don't measure something, it might not get done. That says that all important outcomes (and the relative amount of progress toward those outcomes) should be measured and monitored. (This measurement and monitoring process helps inform and guide the implementers' *neural spam filters*.) **At the same time, the number of such measurements needs to be traded off against . . .**

2. The common tendency to measure too many things. Too much measurement can be worse than none at all. If you measure things that aren't all that important, people working on the project will tend to lose their focus on the things that really are. **Focus can also be lost if . . .**

3. Too many measures are monitored by too few people. In projects where there are lots of measures, the care and feeding of measurements needs to be divided. You don't want one person in charge of checking all the gauges in a nuclear power plant! That's particularly true when, as is likely in major changeovers, people assigned to measurement functions typically have many other responsibilities as well.

Dividing responsibility across measures is especially important when there are several *subjective* measures in play. Subjective judgments open the door to either unintentional (based on pre-existing cognitive maps) or intentional invalid measurement or misinterpretation of results (e.g., based on intentions to sandbag the project). **One very common misinterpretation is the failure to realize that . . .**

4. Not all metrics have the same value. If you encounter people who provide analyses on the order of, "78 percent of our metrics show that we're making appropriate progress toward . . .," there's usually a dead fish or two in a closet somewhere. Super-high performance on second-tier goals almost never compensates for less than desirable performance on the most important goals.

5. "Right" measures are to be preferred to "wrong" measures. As shown previously, the brains of most people have a bias toward optimism and thus respond more positively to "97 percent of the products on Line 2 had zero defects" than they do to "the defect rate for Line 2 is 3 percent." **Let's call it a quirk of human nature. But, it's a nice quirk—because it's so easy to use to your advantage!**

6. The most important metrics in any change project are the ones that bear directly upon key business outcomes for the organization as a whole. Given the complexity of enterprise-wide changes and their duration (remember that we can be talking three-four-five-six years here), this measurement principle is often violated for many reasons: People forget what the higher-level business outcomes are, new people aren't told what those outcomes are, and change implementers and monitors are waging daily battles in their "regular jobs" that demand their attention—and many more.

7. Simple, timely metrics are preferred to more complicated, infrequent metrics. Metrics that have to be explained at quarterly meetings do not drive performance on a daily basis. Ideally, people should be able to easily figure out for themselves where they stand. Likewise, reports of metrics should be as current as possible. Nothing is more crushing than a scenario like this: In Quarter 2, Chris' unit had

a problem making their milestones. Chris' staff got together at the end of the quarter and put forth a plan to do better from that point forward. By the middle of Quarter 3, all their milestones for Quarter 2 and the first half of Quarter 3 had been met. Then Chris and all his peer-managers are asked to attend a meeting in which the overall results, as they stood at the end of Quarter 2, were presented. NOT a highly motivating experience for Chris or his team.

BRAIN CONNECTION! MORE ON THE BRAIN'S LOVE AFFAIR WITH "THE VISUAL"

Simple and timely? Better still, simple, timely and VISUAL. I covered the brain's love of the visual in Chapter 5 (particularly in the section on visual story-telling). But, I'm adding it in here because it is most definitely relevant.

One of the best metrics I ever saw that met all three of these criteria was the "Thermometer" graph that United Way used to publicize the progress (i.e., accumulated donations) of each regional campaign. One quick glance at the "temperature reading" and you knew immediately how things stood at the moment—as United Way staffers updated the red line in the thermometer daily.

---

8. <u>Measurement systems that include internal and external customer satisfaction, before, during and after the change, are strongly preferred to those that do not</u>. The "customer" segment needs to be interpreted very broadly. That is, the segment needs to be highly inclusive.

9. <u>Metrics that drive cooperation are preferred to metrics that stimulate competition</u>. I hold this truth to be self-evident. However, there are some exceptions. In the right circumstances, where interdepartmental trust and respect are high, some "friendly" competition can lead to higher performance and be a source of fun for the troops.

10. <u>Metrics should drive the right behaviors</u>. There's a national sales training program that teaches inside sales people to figure out their phone-calls-to-completed-sales ratio and from that derive the theoretical number of calls they would need to make to achieve their sales quotas for the week. For example, if you've made 50 calls and sold five products, then your calls-sale ratio is 10–1. If your weekly sales goal is ten products sold, then to reach your goal, you need to make 100 calls per week or 20 per day. However, the program makes no mention of the quality of each call. So, most people who go through this program invariably focus on the *number* of calls they can make—where even leaving a voice message counts as a "call." You can imagine the ultimate effect on sales.

11. A close corollary to No. 5 above: <u>Measure outcomes, not effort</u>. The classic example here is the student who can't understand why he got a "C" on a project

because he "worked so hard on it." The same sort of conclusion is often drawn in enterprise-wide changes. A common source of the problem is measurements based on time-to-completion. Let's say that after a corporate merger or acquisition it's decided that there's a lot of fat in certain positions or levels in the two organizations that can be eliminated. So, a plan is put in place to evaluate the competence, past performance and "keep-ability" of the people in each of those jobs. It's okay to estimate how much time it's going to take to do that. For an illustration, let's say that the estimate is 5,000 hours. No problem so far. The problem evolves if the metric monitors report that after 2,500 hours, the work is half done. That's only true if the original time estimate is valid, meaning that after 2,500 hours of effort, half of the relevant employees have actually been evaluated. Even then, the time-to-completion (or effort) measure doesn't account for the fact that remaining (as yet unevaluated) people in the cohort might prove more challenging to assess or that other big projects (aka, distractions) may slow down the process in the second half of the allotted time period.

12. <u>People will often work harder toward, and put more credence in, metrics that they have suggested, chosen or created themselves</u>. Recall that people are usually more committed to an action if they were able to draw the conclusion themselves that the action is necessary. So, measurement systems are preferred that include at least a few of these bottom-up metrics.

13. <u>At least some metrics in use should "triangulate."</u> (That is, three independent pieces of data all pointing to the same conclusion.) As much as "objective" measures are valued, often each objective measure only gets at part of the concept or performance supposedly being measured. Let's say that you're trying to assess the quality of quarterbacks in a particular football league. Well, the number of passes each quarterback has completed is a nice objective measure. But, it certainly doesn't provide a complete picture of "quarterback quality." You would also want to know how many passes each quarterback has attempted, and how many interceptions each has thrown. Even with these three measures, you still lack a comprehensive assessment. But, together they provide a better assessment than any one does in isolation.

14. <u>Never recommend the adoption of measurements used by another organization without prosecuting their relevance to the focal or home organization</u>. No matter how admirable the other organization, no matter how similar it appears to be to the focal organization, each measurement that is adopted in your current project needs to be judged on its own, stand-alone value. While it's actually a very GOOD idea to find out how other organizations have measured success, that information must be critically evaluated. Use any good ideas that you find; just make sure that the "fit" is right for each.

15. Okay, this is the last measurement and metrics precept in the list; but it's No. 1 in my heart. If you feel that you have built a strong relationship with an implementation team, <u>it is often very helpful to let the team "in" on the metrics by which you are evaluated by your manager(s)</u>. This helps team members understand

why you do some of the things you do, why you emphasize certain things over others, and so on. If you play it just right, team members will start working toward higher performance on your personal metrics as well as on their own.

Okay. There you have my 15 favorite recommendations with regard to measurement and metrics during large-scale organizational changes. If you want an example of a company that sets the standard for measurement and metrics in an on-going, every-day management system, look no farther than Procter & Gamble and their "Decision Cockpits."

Many companies swamp themselves with hundreds of reports offering conflicting information that has to be vetted and integrated. Not P&G. It took them almost a decade. But, they came to agreement on a small number of crucial metrics that meant the same thing to managers in every part of the company. Then they (working with Tibco—a data visualization specialist company) figured out a way to present all of the metrics **in real time on a single computer screen**. It's really something to behold.

EXPERTS' INSIGHTS: "UNOBTRUSIVE MEASURES"

(The one for 76 cents will do nicely. Thank you.)

In the early 1960s, four smart (common enough) and fun-loving (not so common) social scientists at Northwestern University (Eugene Webb, Donald Campbell, Richard Schwartz and Lee Sechrest) got together periodically over their brown bag lunches to share anecdotes, research ideas, observations on life and whatever else was on their minds. Legend[2] has it that one day, one of the four came to lunch with a story about an article he had just read in which the researcher had used an "oddball" measure of behavior. From there on out, such oddball measures would catch the eye of one or more of the four and they would dutifully report on them at the next lunch time gathering. It ended up as something of a "Can you top this?" competition. Before long, the list of oddball measures was lengthy enough to turn into a book and they turned it. Published in 1966, appropriately by Rand-McNally—as this was a roadmap to an entirely different way of assessing behavior—the book (*Unobtrusive measures: Nonreactive research in the social sciences*—Webb, Campbell, Schwartz & Sechrest, 1966) pretty much stood the world of social science research on its head. Or, at least, it helped social science research to get its head out of its box.

At that particular point in time—and for several previous decades—the primary measures of human behavior used by social scientists were surveys, interviews and written records. (And the most common research participants were undergraduate students in introductory psychology or sociology courses. But, that's another story in itself.) In any case, the common measures of behavior were direct responses from a "subject" and therefore subject to each subject's perceptions or biases or whatever.

Webb and his associates didn't suggest that social scientists stop gathering the measures that they already were. Rather, they suggested that the usual measures of behavior be supplemented by additional (unobtrusive) measures that were not as susceptible to interpretation or bias. Among many, many more, their collection of unobtrusive measures included the following:

- measuring the popularity of exhibits in a museum by recording the amount of wear on the floor tiles in front of them;
- assessing the amount of alcohol consumption in a "dry" county, not just by asking people whether and/or how much they drank, but also by counting empty liquor, beer and wine bottles in trash cans;
- estimating the racial harmony of college students by tallying the number of verbal interactions between whites and blacks in the moments prior to and following lectures in different disciplines;
- gauging the growing excitement of young children as a holiday approaches by measuring the size of their drawings of Santa Claus at Christmas and witches at Halloween. (If you simply must know, the drawings got larger and larger as the holiday approached and then are the smallest immediately after the holiday.)

Today such unobtrusive measures are fairly common. (One of my favorites is one that the City of New Orleans uses to estimate the relative size of the crowds at Mardi Gras each year: Number of dump truck loads of garbage that have to be removed from the French Quarter.) But, at the time of the publication of Webb's (and colleagues') book, the "unobtrusive" concept was as fresh as it was enlightening.

Here are some unobtrusive measures found to be useful during large-scale organizational changes:

- Audience participation in informational meetings about a forthcoming change initiative are typically not recorded. Having cameras in the meeting can squelch question-asking. And, certainly surreptitious recording (whether video or audio) is completely out of the question ethically and practically speaking. However, you can have a few people in the room, preferably seated in the back, keep a list of all of the questions that are asked by members of the audience. I like to use two people so that their notes can validate or clarify each other. Think of the duplicate recorder as a second opinion about what exactly the questions were. In advance of a Q&A, it's best to alert the audience to the recorders and assure them that they are recording questions only—not the names of the questioners. In some cases where trust is an issue, an offer can be made to have the recorders directly observed or to "show around" their notes at the end of the session.

- The frequency with which the same questions are asked across different groups in different meetings might help you identify the issues of central importance to the employees. Having a record of the questions also provides an option to subsequently send out polished answers to them—especially (or only) the most common inquiries. Perhaps the better use of the list comes after the next round of informational meetings (assuming that the same question-recording system is used). If any of the same questions continue to be asked in subsequent meetings with the same audience, it can indicate that the answers that have been provided need to be reformulated to make them more understandable and/or more palatable.

- Narcissism has many definitions. For my purposes here, let's just say it's a really strong need to demonstrate one's superiority over others—on a consistently recurring basis. In a highly detailed and in-depth study of 111 CEOs, Chatterlee and Hambrick (2007) found that those with high scores in Narcissism were more likely to take on dauntingly complex organizational changes (e.g., acquisitions of highly troubled companies.) Highly narcissistic CEOs who tackled these big, attention-getting challenges typically had either "really big wins" (highly successful broad-scale changes) or big losses with not so much in between. How was Narcissism measured? Unobtrusively: Prominence of the CEO's picture in annual reports, the CEO's prominence in company press releases, the frequency of use of first-person, singular personal pronouns in interviews and the distance between the CEO's annual cash compensation and that of the second-highest paid person in the firm.

- In meetings in which people from different departments are required to attend, you might want to objectively note whether people sit only with others from their own department or how much social interaction (gossip, banter, friendly chatting) occurs between members of different units. If the project is dependent upon inter-department cooperation and communication (and they all are), this might give you a hint on whether the departments might be antagonistic/feuding or whether there simply needs to be more non-task-oriented interaction between units to get their members more comfortable with each other.

Experts' Insights Coda: By the way, Unobtrusive measures *is still in print and available on Amazon. When I checked, you could get a used, softbound copy for 76 cents, or you could buy a new, hardbound reprint from 1999 for $114. The ratio between the number of buyers of each of these editions would provide an excellent unobtrusive measure of consumer intelligence!!!*

Notes

1 This chapter is obviously "lite" when it comes to references and citations. Yet, I don't claim that any of these ideas originated with me. After 40+ years of management consulting in which measuring individual and organizational performance has been a central part, my approach to measurement and metrics seems more like common sense—or perhaps just "what I do"—rather than what I learned.

At the same time, I recognize that I've used many phrases and examples repeatedly over the years to a point where their origin has been "pruned" from my brain circuitry. For example, I must have said to clients and students a couple of hundred times over the years, "If you want to know the obstacles that are constraining performance and how to overcome them, ask the people who do the work." I happen to remember that I used these words (or a similar version of them) in the very first consulting job I handled on my own *while I was still in graduate school.* So, it's very likely that I learned this approach from professors or other students. However, the exact source (or sources) is beyond the limits of my memory.

In terms of giving credit, the best I can do here is list out the sources of learning (about <u>performance measurement</u> in general) that I know for sure influenced my thinking and consulting and teaching over the years:

* Work that I did and hundreds of conversations I had with Chuck Raben and Jim Morris, to each of whom I owe a very great deal—both professionally and personally;
* Classes that I took with Irv Goldstein;
* The writings of and various presentations by Ed Lawler and Karl Weick;
* Robinson and Robinson (1995), the best book on consulting that I ever read;
* Brown (1996), the best book on measurement of organizational performance that I ever read;
* The many fine articles in "Secondary analysis" edited by Boruch (1978); and the following books: Campbell and Stanley (1963); Fuller (1997); Webb, Campbell, Schwartz and Sechrest (1966).

2 Irv Goldstein told me this *__story__*, circa 1972. The story form must have helped me remember it.

References

Boruch, R. (1978). (Ed.) Secondary analysis. *New Directions for Program Evaluation*, Special issue, *4*, v–115.

Brown, M. (1996). *Keeping score.* New York, NY: AMACOM Books.

Campbell, D. & Stanley, J. (1963). *Experimental and quasi-experimental designs for research.* Chicago, IL: Rand-McNally.

Chatterlee, A. & Hambrick, D. (2007). It's all about me: Narcissistic chief executives officers and their effects on company strategy and performance. *Administrative Sciences Quarterly, 52(3)*, 351–386.

Fuller, J. (1997). *Managing performance improvement projects.* San Francisco, CA: Pfeiffer.

Robinson, D. & Robinson, J. (1995). *Performance consulting: Moving beyond training.* San Francisco, CA: Berrett-Koehler.

Webb, E., Campbell, D., Schwartz, R. & Sechrest, L. (1966). *Unobtrusive measures: Nonreactive research in the social sciences.* Chicago, IL: Rand-McNally.

10

PERFORMANCE ALIGNMENT AND IMPROVEMENT VIA FEEDBACK

"There is no more important indicator of satisfaction and willingness to stay on the job than whether or not [a manager] has talked with [employees] recently about how they're doing on the job." Yet, "the gap between the amount of feedback employees want and how much bosses deliver" has continued to widen steadily "over the past 25 years" (Carroll, 2014).

Only 34 percent of respondents reported having received any helpful feedback from their bosses in the last six months (Cornerstone on Demand, 2013).

"Sixty-seven percent of people want to have Performance Feedback conversations 'Often' or 'All the Time,' but only 29% actually do. Thirty-six percent say they 'Rarely' or 'Never' receive performance feedback" (Zigarmi, Diehl, Houson & Witt, 2013).

Some years ago, I was working on a structural re-organization for a large financial services firm. One day, the EVP of HR invited me for coffee in the company cafeteria. We caught each other up on the structural issues at hand. Subsequently, she asked if I would be willing to meet with a manager who had made a request through channels for the training unit in HR to provide or contract out "a two–three day training program on time management and priority setting." I readily agreed.

Within the first 15 minutes of my meeting with the manager who had made the request for training, it came to light that only one of his 22 direct reports was a "time-wasting machine" and one other direct report very often worked on what she liked to do rather than the most important task that needed doing at that moment (thus, time management and priority setting). The issues with these two reports were clearly ones that should be "fixed" (or at least addressed) by a combination of performance feedback and coaching. Yet, rather than dealing directly with the issues as he should, this manager was willing to take all 22 of his employees off of the job for 16–24 hours of work time, exposing 20 of them to training that they didn't need. I wish that I could say that this was a very unusual scenario. But, I'm afraid that that's far from being the case. (Recall from Chapter 1 that most people would rather lie than provide negative feedback.)

Performance Feedback and Coaching During Large-Scale Changes

Change Leaders (and particularly consultants) don't have the luxury of having formal authority over many of the people whose performances they need to influence. **Yet, the performance-related communication disconnect between leaders and followers during major change projects often closely parallels what is found in formal, normal boss-report relationships.**

Most boss-direct report relationships are nearly perfectly designed to create and maintain effective barriers to feedback (in either direction)— even among the hardest-working, most well-intended people. Think about the underlying dynamic of how you communicate with your boss. Your main goal is to illustrate the magnitude of each of your many flaws so that overall you are judged to be as incompetent as possible, right? Nope: Just the opposite is true, of course.

Virtually all of us strongly desire to be seen as competent *and to be recognized for good or high performance.* Furthermore, we have that powerful self-image maintenance or enhancement thing going on. **Which, in terms of feedback, means we want to avoid anything negative or self-image-damaging.** Some of these kinds of behaviors might result when we find ourselves in a situation where our less than desirable performance might be exposed:

- we might try to avoid the boss while the potential exposure exists;
- if the boss can't be avoided, we might try to divert conversations about the problem or perhaps a deadline that's likely to be missed (who knows, maybe a miracle will happen and everything will get done properly and on time);
- perhaps we might even fake some numbers to make things look better than they are; or
- we could point fingers at coworkers who are messing up or holding up our work; and
- any number of other creative ways of staying "out of the doghouse."

Now, let's consider the feedback barrier from the manager's side. According to experts on holding employees accountable for their performance (Connors & Smith, 2009), there are five most common reasons why "managers fail to provide corrective-constructive feedback":

- a fear of offending someone or jeopardizing a personal relationship;
- a feeling that they lack the time to follow-up effectively;
- the belief that their effort wouldn't make much of a difference;

- a concern that, while holding some-one else accountable, they might expose their own failures or limita-tions; and
- a fear of sparking conflict or retali-ation.[1]

Each of these has an emotional basis. To these, **I'd like to add a few that are also emotion-based, but** *behavior-ally visible* **(i.e., they involve specific things that managers** <u>do</u>**)**:

- Most managers don't like to give neg-ative feedback <u>*to*</u> their direct reports *AND* **they often unconsciously behave in ways that repress feedback** <u>*from*</u> **their reports**. For example, some managers react so strongly to poor performance that they dramatically magnify the exist-ing tendency to filter (or stop) the upward flow of bad news.
- At the other end of the continuum are managers who are super-kind and understanding. **This type of man-ager sometimes blocks an equal amount of upward information flow because reports don't want to "hurt" or "disappoint" such bosses.**
- As noted at the beginning of this section, less than half of workers in non-production settings report that they receive helpful feedback from their managers on a regular basis. To top that off, almost 40 percent of employees surveyed said that **their managers actively discouraged them (i.e., the employees) from talking about problems or per-formance weaknesses** (Fast, Burris & Bartel, 2014).

The Barriers to Feedback aren't only Vertical, they're also Horizontal (i.e., Peer to Peer)

In a study at Brigham Young University (Maxfield, 2006), participants were asked if they worked with someone who is abrasive, unreliable *and* dishonest. A stunning 93 per cent said, "YES!" The participants complained very *emotionally* to the researchers: The abrasive-unreliable-dishonest people are terrible for the organization; they lower morale and productiv-ity; they drive away valuable employees; they get away with anything and are accountable for nothing!

However, when the study participants were asked how they deal with such people and the problems they cause, the top five responses were:

- 77 percent = "Work around" the person
- 57 percent = Complain about the person to others
- 47 percent = Ignore the person
- 30 percent = Drop hints to the person
- 23 percent = Tell the person how you per-ceive their behavior

There is corroborating evidence from many additional studies that people who create prob-lems in the workplace (for whatever reason) almost never get the information they need to cease and desist—even if they ever wanted to (which is another issue altogether).

So, guess what? If you're going to be an effective Change Leader or consultant, you're going to have to face up to the fact that the burden of setting people straight is likely to fall to you. If not all of the time, then much of the time.

Bottom line: **The brains of managers *and* their reports can be counted on to restrict the information that is absolutely needed for performance improvement. The necessary information doesn't go "up" and it doesn't come "down."**

In contrast to these managerial emotions and behaviors, Branden (1994)[2] argued that it is the responsibility of managers–leaders to create what he calls a "Positive Communication Climate"[3] consisting primarily of establishing these conditions:

1. People feel safe; they know they will not be ridiculed, demeaned, humiliated or punished for openness and honesty or for admitting "I made a mistake" or for saying "I don't know but I'll find out."
2. People are treated with courtesy, listened to, invited to express thoughts and feelings, dealt with as individuals whose dignity is important.
3. People learn how they can improve performance in non-demeaning ways that stress positives rather than negatives.
4. People are given the information (and resources) they need to do their jobs properly; they are given information about the wider context in which they work—the company's goals and progress—so they can understand how their activities relate to the organization's overall mission.
5. People are given authority appropriate to their responsibilities; they are encouraged to take initiative, make decisions and exercise judgment.

This is another way of saying that (or specifying how) **the _cultural norm_ of the workgroup, the department, the organization or the entire supply chain has to support using feedback freely, frequently and consistently to assure performance alignment and improvement**.[4] As difficult as this is to establish, it's even more difficult to sustain.

Even if the culture is change-friendly and feedback-facilitative, you will still need to be more than passably good at providing constructive feedback. And, I've already provided a ton of information about how you can do that and I'm going to roll those recommendations forward right now, but with a twist. I've broken them up into two categories: Things that focus primarily on "You" (the Change Leader/consultant) (Table 10.1) and things that focus primarily on "Them" (everyone with whom you interact during change management or on your "real job") (Table 10.2). If you're tempted to skip these two tables because the information in them has been provided earlier in this Guide, I'd encourage you to exercise some "free won't" and squelch that temptation. Recall that reactivation/repetition of neural connections dramatically increases the likelihood that you'll retain information and be able to retrieve that information from long-term memory when you need to apply it. Giving a total of about three minutes reconsideration to the material in these two tables puts you one step closer to being better at the crucial skill of providing meaningful feedback effectively. Don't miss your chance.

TABLE 10.1 Reprise of Feedback Guidelines (You)

You

Act with integrity; focus on results; treat people with respect; maintain confidences; be your best self at all times

Great self-monitors are able to turn the clock ahead and evaluate what they say and what they do <u>as it is being said or done</u>. How do they do that? There are three commonly recommended means of self-monitoring:

- Establish a practice of mentally imagining that you are "looking down" on the room in which you are interacting with others thereby creating the ability to "watch yourself in action."
- Mentally play back a meeting and focus on "prosecuting" each of your statements for rudeness, lack of respectfulness, etc. You are much less likely to repeat such behaviors once they have been identified and "labeled" as undesirable.
- Become alert to passing expressions, shifting postures or "side-ways looks" that might be signs of irritation or discomfort and so on.

Asking for, graciously accepting and acting upon personal feedback has a wonderful side effect. People who solicit feedback about their <u>own</u> behaviors are also seen as being more caring and concerned about <u>others</u>.

[F]ocus on how you can help people feel better about themselves if they work hard to implement and adopt the new system. On the other hand, if people don't move in the direction in which you're trying to "herd" them, try to identify the possible threats to their self-image that might be involved and do whatever you can to reduce or eliminate those threats.

A big part of aligning positive self-referent attitudes and high performance involves the judicious use of feedback. Here are some things to keep in mind as you provide feedback to clients—whether a high level executive or the lowest paid person in the client organization.

1. One old maxim certainly holds true: "Praise in public, criticize in private." For most people, few things are more threatening to one's sense of self than being criticized in front of coworkers—or worse still—in front of the "boss." When you must provide corrective feedback, make sure that it is specific (e.g., ". . . when these kinds of invoices arrive in your system, the very first thing that needs doing is . . .") and focused entirely on performance, not the person. In addition to looking for a private way of providing corrective feedback, you have to be sure that you can provide it calmly. Sometimes, this might even mean waiting until the next day to address an issue. Although, when your emotions aren't involved, feedback (whether positive or negative) should be as close in time to the actual performance as possible.

2. If you want your praise to have the intended impact, watch out for "blanket recognition." Here's an example: Ann, Mark and Courtney work on delineating each of the steps in a complicated manual process that will soon be automated. Their report turns out to be excellent. However, you are aware that Mark and Courtney did almost all of the work and Ann, if anything, was more of an obstacle than an aid. In these circumstances, you should try to avoid situations where you need to praise the <u>group</u> for its work. This is likely to greatly decrease the impact of the praise on Mark and Courtney and it sends a clear message to other implementation team members that you don't have to contribute to the project to get by (with flying colors, even).

TABLE 10.1 continued

You

Praise given at the completion of a major task should be "automatic." However, task completion is sometimes a reward in itself. With difficult tasks, it is often the case that people more dearly need praise and encouragement while the effort is still underway. So, don't wait until end-points to "make people feel good about their performance."

Empathy with the doers [of the change project] and users [of what has been changed] must be shown, preferably in direct interactions.

[You must have] empathy for, and patience with, people who disagree.

TABLE 10.2 Reprise of Feedback Guidelines (Them)

Them

[W]e need to measure outcomes, not effort. The classic example here is the student who can't understand why he got a "C" on a project because he "worked so hard on it." IT projects are particularly susceptible to this confusion of effort and performance quality.

Graham emphasizes that people only change when they decide to change and they decide how to change. So if, for example, one of your reports doesn't make her sales quota, you could ask, "Why didn't you make your quota this month?" That only leads to defensive excuse making. Rather, he suggests "What would have to be different so that you could make your quota every month?" and then let the report "paint the picture" of how to change.

. . . threats to self-images often result in direct and powerful negative effects on general psychological well-being and on everyday behavior.

Even though a belief statement can be blatantly false, the more often people hear that statement, the more likely they are to come to believe it.

Once well-established (repeatedly activated, compressed and compacted), [neural connections] not only control our perceptions, beliefs and behavior, they are extremely resistant to change.

[I]nformation that is inconsistent with a strong belief is very likely to be discarded by [the] brain's spam filter.

[We] pay a lot more attention to, and selectively remember, our positive (e.g., honest, courteous, smart, etc.) behaviors than we would the exceptions.

Saying this in another, simpler way, people's brains are powerfully attracted to situations in which they believe they will "look good . . ." . . . and, they avoid situations—sometimes even at great cost—where they expect that they will "look bad."

People are more likely to admit to fear and dishonesty than they are to admit to being envious.

Once a belief system is established (repeatedly activated, compressed and compacted), it is self-validating and very difficult to change.

. . . people are most likely to change their behaviors when they reach conclusions about the desirability of the new behaviors on their own.

New Stuff

Now, for some new perspectives—starting off in the ever-popular (and perhaps ever-overused) "Do's and Don'ts" format. If you must provide constructive feedback:

Do

- Take time to plan. Make some notes on the order in which you will present information or cover various topics. Establish a clear objective for what you intend to accomplish in the interaction.
- Get to the point(s). You can completely blow the impact of the feedback by spending the first ten minutes of a 20-minute meeting discussing trivialities (i.e., social chatting).
- Place the forthcoming constructive feedback in the context of overall performance—especially if the overall performance is good.
- Provide clear, specific examples of ineffective behaviors and the corresponding effective behaviors. Steer away from clichés that have different meanings to different people (e.g., "be a team player," "be more professional," "be more customer-oriented").
- Get the other person's perspective on those ineffective and effective behaviors.
- Ask how you can help.
- Come to an agreement on the problem before discussing corrective actions. (More on this below.)
- Establish corrective actions. (And, more on this below.)
- Set a time frame for corrective actions to be implemented. (Also, more on this below.)
- Agree on when and how to follow-up. (Yep. More on this below.)

Don't

- Make assumptions about the causes of behavior (e.g., "I realize that you resent John because he received the promotion for which you were working so hard, but . . .") or about anticipated reactions (e.g., "I know that you're going to argue that the schedule was too tight to begin with . . .").
- Exaggerate or over-state to make a point (e.g., "never once on time" or "always makes the same mistake"). It only takes *one* occurrence of successful performance to counteract your argument. Likewise, don't inflate the number of occurrences of an undesirable behavior. If you say, "they made this mistake at least ten times," someone might challenge you to name all ten—or at least a very high percentage of the ten.
- Try to use "shame" as a motivator: "We're all adults here and we should act like it." This gets translated as "You're acting like a spoiled child, you idiot."

- Provide "negative" feedback on things that can't be changed. That's like telling someone to get taller.
- Bury the "negatives" in a swath of schmooze. Only the schmooze will be remembered.
- Provide your opinions. Stick to the facts.
- Patronize or condescend (e.g., "Surely, you should be able to . . .").
- Back away from your objective when confronted with an emotional response.

EXPERTS' INSIGHTS: OBTAINING SELF-GENERATED FEEDBACK FROM OTHERS

Insight No. 1. There are lots of reasons why we provide "constructive" feedback to others. **Many of them have nothing to do with wanting the focal person to improve his organizational performance.** Sometimes, we act out of anger, sometimes out of frustration. Sometimes, we just want the other person to know that we know that she is screwing up.

Here's a guarantee: You will never be maximally effective as a Change Leader, as a consultant, or even across-the-board as a leader, if you aren't able to eliminate ALL of those "sometimes" from your behavioral repertoire. **Every time, every single time, you prepare to give someone feedback, prosecute your intentions.** If you honestly aren't driven entirely by performance improvement (whether it be the organization's performance or the personal performance of the individual involved), then don't just bite your tongue. Glue it to the top of your mouth and staple it there as well.

Now, this doesn't mean that you can't experience feelings of anger or frustration or whatever. And, it doesn't mean that you can't share your feelings about the situation with whom you are providing feedback. But, if you allow your emotions to drive the conversation, you WILL say things that you will later regret. There is just no (good) place for emotional outpourings in conversations like these. If you show your anger or frustration, someone needs to provide some serious constructive feedback to you.

BRAIN CONNECTION! "REACTIVE AGGRESSION"

One of the reasons why we sometimes get so angry and frustrated with the performance or behavior of others is that we take too long before we deal with it.

Imagine that one of your direct reports, Avery, has developed a consistent habit of ending sales calls with "Catchyalater." You believe that this is unprofessional and you really want Avery to stop using that phrase. Your brain knows this; Avery's brain doesn't. At a level below conscious awareness, each time you are within earshot of one of Avery's calls, your brain is anticipating a reward (that Avery will stop being unprofessional). When that doesn't happen, your brain secretes X amount of a noxious neurochemical. The next time Avery's behavior doesn't fix itself, the noxious secretion is a bit stronger—and so on during the next 25 Catchyalaters. Eventually, the amount of the secretion is strong enough that you blow up and "let Avery have it." (In SCN, this reaction on your part is called "reactive aggression" (Blair, 2012). A metaphor for reactive aggression is a boil that festers and finally ruptures to relieve the pressure within it.)

Prior to the blow up, Avery's brain was consciously or unconsciously aware that you had heard many Catchyalaters and expressed no displeasure or concern.

The point? Don't nitpick; don't micro-manage. But, don't ignore substantive performance issues. **Always keep in mind that no feedback is actually a form of feedback. What you ignore, you condone.**

<u>Insight No. 2</u>. Several times previously, I mentioned brain/behavior expert David Rock. He's the guy who argues that if you want people to change their behavior (aka improve their performance, aka do what you want them to do) then you have to help them "re-wire their brains." **That is, you must get people to draw their own conclusions (make their own connections) about why and how they should change. If people are only told what they should do or not do—rather than being guided toward drawing their own conclusions—they will simply continue to follow established patterns, habits, etc**. (Pulakos, Hanson, Arad & Moye, Forthcoming; Rock, 2006).[5]

Surely you remember those cardio-therapy patients! (Whoops. That was a type of condescension that I just told you to avoid. Let's try that again.) You might recall the cardio-therapy patients who were told that they should change their diets because such a change would dramatically reduce the likelihood of a second serious heart attack. They got it. They learned and understood the relationship between diet and heart problems. They saw the light! They vowed to change their eating habits! But, only one in eight did so.

Okay, then. What if we buy Rock's argument that we have to get people to draw their own conclusions? How would we do that?

Well, the first step is to <u>stop</u> doing something. And, it's going to be painful to stop because we like doing it so very much. It makes us feel like an expert! It makes us feel like a real leader! What is it? Giving directive advice; telling other people exactly what we think that they should do. In general, we're way more than willing to pass along our preferred solutions to other people's problems than we are to help people solve their own problems.

Rock suggests that to become better (change) leaders, we need to become more "quiet," that is, talk less. And, we need to ask more questions (of a certain kind) and let the people with whom we're working come up with their own answers.

Okay. What's the "certain kind of questions" that we need to ask? Well, I really shouldn't tell you the answer to that question. I should let you come up with the answer yourself (ha, ha). But, just this once, I'll be directive . . . We should ask solution-oriented questions rather than ones that are problem-oriented. Table 10.3 gives some examples.

TABLE 10.3 Problem-Based vs. Solution-Based Questions

Avoid problem-oriented questions like . . .	Rather, ask solution-oriented questions like . . .
Why isn't this working?	What do we need to do to make this work?
Why did you hit only 90 percent of your goal?	What do you need to do to be able to hit your goal the next time?
Who was responsible for this?	Who can fix this?
Why did you do that?	What do you want to do next time?

Get the idea? Rock's "Quiet (change) Leaders" ask solution-oriented questions and let people (have the time to) think through their own problems without providing solutions for them. Then, once the people involved have begun enacting those solutions, Quiet Leaders provide the reminders and encouragement their people need to stay the course. In brain/behavior terms, the most successful Change Leaders are ones who are best at getting other people's brains to cut new paths through the corporate jungle, rather than relying on the pathways that are already mapped (i.e., the connections that are already made/established).

This is usually more challenging than it sounds. While some people jump right into formulation of their own possible solutions, many people do not. Remember, those old brains of ours want to conserve every bit of energy that they can. Rock puts it this way: People have a certain amount of inertia around thinking for themselves due to the energy required (by using working memory). And, this is compounded by the fact that—in the world today—many people's mental circuits are tired from overwork. Yet, if they can be herded into thinking for themselves and coming up with a good idea, the act of having an "ah-ha!" moment gives off an energy of its own (via neural secretions) and makes people more willing to take action. No Red Bull or kick-in-the-pants needed.

Sooo, **how can you improve the ways in which you provide feedback**?!!!! I suggest you take five minutes to make some notes to yourself right now.

Notes

1 Carroll (2014) argues insightfully that these so-called reasons are "bogus."
2 Branden's creation of the concept of a "Positive Communication Climate" was formulated mostly by his observations of people at work (and in therapy) long before

confirmatory SCN research was available. Time did tell. Branden was not only correct in his thinking, his ideas have been consistently validated by hard science.

3 Elsewhere these or similar conditions have been considered part of what has been called a "Spirit of Joint Inquiry" (Schein, 2010), "A Learning Organization" (Senge, 2006) and "Evidence-Based Management" (Pfeffer & Sutton, 2006), among others.

4 That cultural norm must also apply to the groups and teams (e.g., sponsorship, implementation, etc.) created as part of the focal change process itself.

5 I believe that the issues of <u>drawing your own conclusions</u> and Gordon Graham's perspective on it are so important that I am repeating this Note from Chapter 2. If you aren't familiar with the training programs developed by Gordon Graham, you should be. That is, I think that everyone can benefit from the insights on human behavior that he developed (long before the very same ideas were being validated by SCN). Graham was a (very) hardened criminal who served 19 years in prison, including 12 months of "bread and water only" in a tiny, isolated cell in Walla Walla Federal Prison. (That sounds medieval, but it occurred during the 1960s.) Graham was able to turn his thinking and his life around and he became a management trainer with many Fortune 500 firms as clients.

Videos of many of his programs are still available on YouTube. The one that provided the most valuable insight for me is called "Effective Feedback." Today, it would likely be called "Performance Management."

The means by which Graham was able to change his life is described in this six-minute, low-budget shoot. More importantly, Graham explains that if you want to change someone's behavior, never tell them what you don't want them to do—because of how the brain records and replays that directive over and over and that interferes with acceptance of the new, desired behavior.

Likewise, Graham emphasizes that people only change when *they decide* to change and *they decide how* to change. So if, for example, one of your reports doesn't make her sales quota, you could ask, "Why didn't you get your monthly report in on time?" That only leads to defensive excuse making. Rather, he suggests, "What would have to be different so that you could get your report in on time, every time?" and then let the report "paint the picture" of how to change.

References

All web site URLs accessed on December 12, 2015.

Blair, J. (2012). Considering anger from a cognitive neuroscience perspective. *Wiley Interdisciplinary Reviews: Cognitive Science, 3(1)*, 65–74.

Branden, N. (1994). Creating high-self-esteem/high performance organizations. In R. H. Kilmann, J. Kilmann & Associates (Eds.), *Managing ego energy: The transformation of personal meaning into organizational success* (pp. 27–48). San Francisco, CA: Jossey-Bass.

Carroll, A. (2014). Bogus excuses: The real reasons why bosses aren't giving feedback. *Fast Company online*, October 16. Retrieved from www.fastcompany.com/3037140/the-future-of-work/bogus-excuses-the-real-reasons-why-bosses-arent-giving-feedback.

Connors, R. & Smith, T. (2009). *How did that happen?* New York, NY: The Penguin Group.

Cornerstone on Demand. (2013). *2013 U.S. Employee Report.* White Paper. Retrieved from www.cornerstoneondemand.com/resources/research/survey-2013.

Fast, N., Burris, E. & Bartel, C. (2014). Research: Insecure managers don't want your suggestions. *Harvard Business Review Online*, November 24. Retrieved from https://hbr.org/2014/11/research-insecure-managers-dont-want-your-suggestions.

Maxfield, B. (2006). Corporate untouchables – New VitalSmarts poll reveals 93 percent work with an "untouchable" no one confronts. *Businesswire*, September 28. Retrieved from www.businesswire.com/news/home/20060928005215/en/Corporate-Untouchables-VitalSmarts-Poll-Reveals-93-Percent.

Pfeffer, J. & Sutton, R. (2006). *Hard facts, dangerous half-truths and total nonsense: Profiting from evidence-based management*. Cambridge, MA: Harvard Business School Press.

Pulakos, E., Hanson, R., Arad, S. & Moye, N. (Forthcoming). Performance management can be fixes: An on-the-job experiential learning approach for complex behavior change. *Industrial and Organizational Psychology: Perspectives on Science and Practice, 8(1)*. Retrieved from Member web site (Society of Industrial and Organizational Psychology).

Rock, D. (2006). *Quiet leadership: Six steps to transforming performance at work*. New York, NY: Collins.

Schein, E. (2010). *Organization culture and leadership* (4th ed.). San Francisco, CA: Jossey-Bass.

Senge, P. (2006). *The fifth discipline: The art & practice of the learning organization*. New York, NY: Currency/Doubleday.

Zigarmi, D., Diehl, J., Houson, D. & Witt, D. (2013). Are employees' needs being met with "one-on-ones?" *Employee Work Passion, Volume 6*. Retrieved from www.kenblanchard.com/getattachment/Leading-Research/Research/Employee-Passion-Volume-6/Blanchard-Employee-Passion-Vol-6.pdf.

11

SUSTAINING CHANGED BEHAVIOR: THE BEST AND SECOND-BEST WAYS TO LOOK AT THE ISSUE

If you Google "sustaining organizational change," the number of hits is 3,330,000 (plus or minus 4; ha, ha). Of course, "sustaining organizational change" is only one of perhaps ten or more relevant search terms, so the universe of available reports, articles and books is gigantic.

As I'm typing this, I can't think of any other business/organizational topic on which as much has been written with so little useful, reliable information that can be harvested. I'm only partly joking when I say that the main (and often only) conclusion from many of the fairly large number of those sources I've browsed or studied is that sustaining major organization changes is important, hard and unlikely. Not a lot to work with there.[1] (The "hard and unlikely" part was painfully confirmed in one of The Forum Corporation's periodic surveys of managers around the world (Atkinson, 2012). Respondents were asked to rate their own organization's overall effectiveness in sustaining behavior changes. Sixty-three percent of the organizations rated themselves as "Not at all effective" or "Somewhat effective" while only 14 percent labeled themselves as "Effective" (11 percent) or "Highly effective" (3 percent).)

On the plus side, there has been a lot of thoughtful "cataloging" of the apparent characteristics of actual organization change implementations that: 1) give evidence of being sustained successfully, at least to the point in time when they were studied and/or 2) were DOA by the time at which it was assumed that "sustaining the change" would begin. (In my experience, having such a *discrete phase for sustaining change* is itself likely a death knell.)

Positive and Negative Sustainability-Impact Factors Identified via Surveys and Interviews

Martin, Weaver, Currie, Finn and McDonald (2012) conducted one of the very few cataloging studies that a) focused specifically on sustainability and b) studied its endurance over the long term (seven years). Their in-depth case studies of large-scale implementations in four health care systems found that the factors shown in Table 11.1 had the strongest positive and negative effects on sustainability in their sample organizations.

TABLE 11.1 Positive and Negative Factors Impacting Sustainability for Large-Scale Implementations in Four Health Care Systems

Strong, positive influence on sustainability	*Strong, negative influence on sustainability*
Innovation(s) viewed as continuous process requiring continuous nurturing	Objective evidence of impact is weak/lacking
Leaders of the change are powerful	Greater dependency on external groups/conditions
Greater cultural fit ("embedability") of innovation(s)	Greater complexity of the innovation(s)
Active network of supporters across units/divisions	Greater number of simultaneous changes

McKinsey & Company (Pustkowski, Scott & Tesvic, 2014) came to different conclusions based on their interviews with "2,000 global executives" in organizations that were able to provide clear evidence of sustainability two or more years after the designated end of an implementation period vs. other organizations that could not. In high to low order of importance, the "key capabilities" for implementing sustainable change efforts were:

- "Clear organization-wide ownership and commitment to change across all levels of the organization"
- "Ability to focus organization on a prioritized set of changes"
- "Clear accountability for specific actions during implementation"[2]
- "Effective program management and use of standard change processes"
- "Planning from Day 1 for the long-term sustainability of changes"
- "Continuous improvements during implementation and rapid action to devise alternative plans, if needed"
- "Sufficient resources and capabilities to execute changes"

In the report on their global 2013–2014 survey on Communication and Change ROI, Towers Watson (*n.d.*) chimed in with their own (again, different) list of critical factors affecting the sustainability of change:

Most change projects fail to meet their objectives. Only 55% of change projects are initially successful and only one in four are (sic) successful in the long run. **Consistent with our findings over the last 10 years, organizations that are able to sustain change over time are those that focus on the <u>fundamental levers</u> that are known to drive success: Leadership, communication, involvement, training/learning and measurement. The difference between high-effectiveness and low-effectiveness companies on these fundamentals is striking.**

(Emphases added)[3]

I've read half a dozen similar studies. I can summarize the whole lot succinctly: Different consulting companies/different researchers/different experts = different "critical" factors leading to sustaining performance gains.

Positive and Negative Sustainability-Impact Factors Identified via Literature Reviews and Meta-Analyses

Scheirer (2005) synthesized "19 empirical studies of the sustainability of American and Canadian health-related programs." She identified five common characteristics of the change process that are related to the "extent of sustainability achieved." That is, the more of these characteristics that are present, the more likely that the program or innovation will be sustained. The factors are:

- The program or innovation can be modified as experience with it grows
- A "strong champion" is present throughout implementation
- The program or innovation "fits" with its organization's mission and procedures
- Benefits to staff members and/or clients are readily perceived
- Stakeholders in other organizations provide support.

In a review of 125 medical studies Wiltsey Stirman et al. (2012) identified the following predictors of sustained change:

- Innovation characteristics (fit, ability to be modified, effectiveness/benefit)
- Context (climate, culture, leadership, setting characteristics (structure, policies))
- Capacity (champions, funding, workforce quality, stakeholder support)
- Processes/interactions (engagement, relationships, shared decision-making, alignment, feedback, training, partnerships, navigation of on-going demands, on-going support).[4]

Although it preceded all of the studies mentioned thus far in this section, a literature review conducted and reported by the U.K.'s National Health Service (Buchanan et al., 2005, p. 203) provided (in my opinion) the most insightful analysis and the richest—but most complicated and ambiguous—conclusion: "No simple prescription for managing sustainability emerges from this review." Rather, the researchers conclude that "the process of sustaining strategic or large-scale change is influenced by a range of issues, operating at different levels . . . across different time frames."

That "range of issues" is given in Table 11.2.

This particular perspective makes total sense to me and aligns perfectly with my experiences over the last 40+ years. The reality is that **all of these variables are in dynamic interaction**—the pattern of which is different in different organizations and even within an organization (e.g., compare a P&G plant in Cincinnati, Ohio, with one in Egypt). To further complicate things (if this viewpoint isn't already mind-boggling), those patterns of interaction typically change—often dramatically—*during* enterprise-wide change implementations.

This way of framing the factors that impact performance improvement sustainability is not only complicated conceptually, it is vexing in terms of implementation and measurement. I have to admit that I often *don't* share this framework with clients for a variety of situation-specific reasons. I reserve it for those who have extensive, successful experience with enterprise-wide organizational change. Let's compare this complicated view with the much simpler, more frequently taken, often necessary approach.

It's often ignored in organizational *practice*, but **most experts believe that you have to plan how you will sustain any performance improvements** you might be able to achieve by making a large-scale change **at the time that you are planning the change itself** (more likely, *changes* themselves). That is, experts recommend that you plan for sustaining a change *prior* to the implementation of the change. However, because the interaction of the variables in Table 11.2 is dynamic and at least partially unpredictable across time, you can't know on the

TABLE 11.2 Factors Affecting Sustainability in National Health Service study (U.K.)

Substance	Nature and scale of change, fit with organization	Culture	Shared beliefs, perceptions, norms, values, priorities
People	Commitment, competencies, expectations	Emotion	Emotions affecting response to change
Managers	Style, approach, preference, behaviors	Leadership	Setting vision, values, purpose, goals, challenges
Politics	Stakeholder and coalition power and influence	Processes	Implementation, project management structures
Environment	External, conditions, stability, threats	Time	Timing, pacing, flow of events
Organization	Policies, mechanisms, procedures, systems, structures		

front-end of a change *exactly* what you need to do to keep performance improving during and after a large-scale change. I believe that a quote attributed to General Eisenhower during WWII is especially cogent here: "In preparing for battle I have always found that plans are useless, but planning is indispensable."

Let's apply Eisenhower's view of battle plans to sustaining gains achieved via change. From the very beginning of your efforts, you have to design into your plan(s) specific "on-call" tactics that *could be* implemented *during the change process itself* that will maximize the probability that the gains will be increased (not just sustained) over time in the "normal" course of managing your operation or business.[5] **The selection of tactics to be used would be different depending on several core factors including the history, culture, communication climate and structural alignment of the organization** (Aalbers & Dolfsma, 2014; Hansen & Birkinshaw, 2007).

EXPERTS' INSIGHTS: SUPPORTING AND SUSTAINING CHANGE OUTCOMES "ON THE GO"

In this Experts' insights, TiER1 Principal Consultant, Leia McKinnon, provides some examples of the type of "on-call" or ad hoc sustainment-supporting tactics that she's used successfully in diverse circumstances.

Scenario 1.

Situation: A large-scale natural resources company tried to implement a safety oriented culture. The first attempt included a generic safety vision, limited sponsorship and metrics that actually promoted unsafe behaviors. Under this program injury rates actually increased over time.

Tactics undertaken: The program was re-launched using a compelling vision with a clear, stretch target (zero harm). Additionally, safety principles were incorporated into the company's core values and strategy. They were also supported by redesigned metrics that served to promote safe behaviors and were integrated into the company and personal bonus programs. The CEO became a visible sponsor leading by example. He mandated that all employees and contractors were required to watch a safety video prior to entering the corporate or regional locations. He also took the first five minutes of each meeting to share a safety message. Soon thereafter, his direct reports began to follow suit and this practice was cascaded through the organization. The CEO regularly publishes health and safety statistics in his monthly business review which helps to maintain the focus on safety.

Results: As a result, safety is at the forefront of people's minds. Employees and contractors can be seen looking out for the safety of themselves and others (notifying of tripping hazards, helping carry heavy objects, etc.). They understand that there is a zero tolerance policy with regard to unsafe behaviors and **their bonus incentives are tied to meeting corporate and personal safety goals**.

Across-the-company injury rates have steadily declined (down 9 percent in Q1 2015 vs. Q1 2014).

Scenario 2.

Situation: The CIO of a mid-sized natural resources company launched a project to redefine IT services in terms of business value. He was faced with the demand for IT services far exceeding the supply which over time had led to his internal customers getting frustrated with IT's inability to deliver. In an effort to appease their customers, IT began to over commit resources which only made the problem worse by leading to a degradation of service quality. Unhappy with the services they were receiving, the business failed to realize the value of IT. As a result business leaders began to put intense pressure on IT to cut costs.

The CIO implemented a multi-faceted solution that required IT to utilize new, more formalized processes which were highly scalable, easily repeatable and more reliable. It also focused on educating the business about the services IT could deliver and **being transparent about the cost of those services so that business units could make informed decisions when requesting service from IT**.

Employees initially resisted this change due to the increased amount of rigor associated with the new processes, among other reasons. Over time it became apparent that there was a high degree of non-compliance and service quality had not improved.

Tactics undertaken: The CIO engaged every single one of the 150+ employees within the IT department and solicited their help in redesigning the new processes (which accounted for approximately 70 percent of the total number of processes). Future-state process maps were initially created using functional Subject Matter Experts and a team of external process design experts.

The large-scale process maps were printed and hung up in a conference room. The CIO then notified the entire IT department that for a two-week period he would be opening a process improvement room in which a facilitated guide would walk them through the process steps (Visio diagrams). He also communicated his expectation that every person in the department was to question some aspect of the design and/or offer suggestions on how to improve upon it.

Employees were thrilled to have the opportunity to help design the solution. Some even visited the process improvement room multiple times helping to refine one or more process areas.

Results: This level of collaboration resulted in a higher rate of engagement which ultimately supported the adoption and continued adherence to the new processes. With all employees participating in the design, they had a vested interest in ensuring that the new processes were executed successfully. They also were so familiar with the new processes early on and that familiarity decreased the level of training needed upon go-live.

Scenario 3.

Situation: An HR department within a large mining company chose to redesign their performance management process. They placed an increased emphasis on aligning performance goals to company metrics and creating a cascade from manager to employee. They also deployed a new performance management software package to document and manage employee performance goals and annual ratings.

The existing system was not user friendly and had created a great deal of frustration and a pattern of inconsistent use. Some regions/business units had chosen to bypass the system altogether and document performance ratings manually using a spreadsheet.

The new software was much more intuitive and would integrate with their ERP system to enable performance management and succession planning on a global scale. It also allowed HR to reduce the manual effort associated with maintaining multiple spreadsheets which had an added plus of reducing error rates.

Shortly after rolling out the new program it became evident that senior leaders were not using the new system. This precluded the ability to cascade goals and maintain the degree of alignment desired.

Tactics undertaken: We developed an adoption measurement plan to focus on improving the rate of adoption as well as sustaining and continuously improving usage over time. We defined discrete behaviors that we expected to see during performance year 1, year 2 and year 3 (ex: 30 percent of goals are aligned through a manager's down line).

We established a defined measurement process and assigned ownership to the Talent Management lead within HR.

We also defined how we were going to measure employee behavior and documented proposed mitigations to address any gaps uncovered via spot audits and system usage reports.

Results: Employees are consistently using the new system to document and manage personal performance objectives. They're also beginning to use advanced functionality as they become more proficient with the tool. We were able to eliminate the use of manual spreadsheets and improve the alignment of goals across the company.

Thanks for those Expert Insights, Leia!

I'm Retaking the Helm Here to Propose a Re-Framing of the Concept of "Sustainment"

From the time of Kurt Lewin's presentation in 1947 on his change "theory" (Unfreeze[6]—Change—Refreeze) (Lewin, 1947), organizational change has usually been envisioned as a process characterized by three (e.g., Lewin) or four (e.g., Deming's Plan-Do-Study-Act) (The Deming Institute, 2015) phases or stages.

I've seen consulting teams (especially ones that are involved with ERP or other mega-software-platform implementations) strongly reinforce/perpetuate a phases/ stages framework for large-scale change. Often the motive here is to help people in the client organization feel like they're getting somewhere ("Two stages down, only one more to go!") or to create natural milestones for celebrating progress. Many Change Leaders (including TiER1's Senior Change Leadership Consultants) believe a change model that includes stages is the most effective and efficient way to get decision-makers in a focal organization to obtain a realistic conception of what is going to happen—or how changes in emphasis will need to occur across time. **I can see the logic in such approaches and know that many of them have worked quite well in the past.** My own, personal belief, however, is that **the best way to assure continual performance improvement is to conceptualize everything that an organization does as a** *business-as-usual* **managing of stability** *and* **innovation**.[7,8]

For a moment, I'd like to use statistical process control[9] (more specifically, Six Sigma[10]) as a lens through which management of stability (continuity) and innovation (change) can be viewed simultaneously. Today, most people in the process improvement field attribute Six Sigma's origin to Motorola in the mid-1980s. Thanks to the proselytizing of its methods by Motorola, companies such as Allied Signal, General Electric, IBM and Ford Motor Company adopted and adapted Six Sigma and, given the collective, almost incredibly fantastic results these organizations experienced, it wasn't long before Six Sigma was implemented in hundreds of organizations around the world. However, with Six Sigma's primary goal of maximizing stability through the reduction (if not elimination) of variability, it also wasn't long before Six Sigma was scorned for its "smothering" effect on innovation and creativity (Hindo, 2007).

Interestingly, the history of strategy changes at 3M (an effective—and highly profitable—focus on creativity was replaced by an unsuccessful focus on process improvement followed by a return to a focus on creativity—the last of which was accompanied by a return to higher profitability (Hindo, 2007)) is often used as evidence that Six Sigma and innovation are incompatible, so organizations must decide which *one of the two is better for their purposes and needs.*

In my own view, Six Sigma doesn't stifle innovation or creativity, it ignores it.[11] That's why when Six Sigma is implemented, there should be a corresponding, tandem effort invested in and focused on innovation/creativity.[12] **It's only through creative innovation that the business growth can be achieved that will supply the resources needed for sustainment of change effects over the long term** (Smith, 2014).

"Self-Sustaining Sustainment"

I'd like to return to the concept of business-as-usual management of stability and innovation. When I think back on the organizations with which I worked over the years and rate them in terms of success in implementing *and* sustaining large-scale change, I can point to a consistent, critical difference between those that I would put in the top 10–15 percent and in the bottom 10–15 percent. The organizations that were most successful didn't position big changes as distinct or discontinuous. **Rather, they were seen as normal and necessary adaptations that were important parts of those organizations' overall process of renewing themselves frequently.** "It's just how we do *improve* things around here."

At the other end of the success continuum are those organizations that positioned their large-scale changes as discrete projects (what Hamel and Zanini (2014) call "episodic interruption[s] of the status quo") with a beginning, a middle and an end. In the majority of organizations in the lowest success category, the message that was usually given to employees at the outset would be clear, though not necessarily overt, and go something like this:

> The scope of this great project that we are about to undertake is huge. We know that the project will require Herculean efforts, many sacrifices and thousands of contentious meetings. But, first, let's have a pep rally to help ourselves pretend to be excited about getting started![13]

Organizations characterized by business-as-usual management of stability and innovation are always change-ready—though most of them wouldn't use the "change-ready" term, just as they would typically avoid terms such as "project" or "sustainment." That's business-as-*un*usual jargon.

The "Organizational Health" Factor and Sustainable Results

In the book *Beyond performance: How great organizations build ultimate competitive advantage* (Keller & Price, 2011), the authors present the culmination of studies conducted by McKinsey & Company consultants over a ten-year period. The book is based on descriptions of management/organizational practices by hundreds of thousands of executives anchored by objective organizational performance data from Bloomberg and Compustat. In the book's Foreword, Gary Hamel (proclaimed by *The Wall Street Journal* as "the world's most influential business thinker" (Talbott, 2013)) describes the work as "unprecedented in its scope and revolutionary in its conclusions," with its "insights being forged in the crucible of real-world practice." No faint praise, that.

Keller and Price argue powerfully that the nature of our information- and technology-based global marketplace has made the traditional sources of competitive advantage (e.g., strategy, assets, reputation, etc.) obsolete and replaced them with **company culture** and **leadership effectiveness**. This means that sustainable organizational change and renewal can no longer be achieved by a focus on performance alone (that is, concentration on the traditional drivers of business performance). There must be a simultaneous focus on what Keller and Price have termed "organizational health."

In their deep, empirical, practice-based view, **performance** is defined as what "an enterprise delivers to its stakeholders in financial and operational terms, evaluated through such measures as net operating profit, return on capital employed, total returns to shareholders, net operating costs, and stock turn." **Organizational health**, in contrast, is "the ability of organizations to align, execute and renew themselves faster than their competitors so that they can sustain exceptional performance over time." That health component is the "ultimate competitive advantage" of the book's title.

In the research supporting this necessary management of dual systems, Keller and Price (and other McKinsey & Company operatives/practices) have found that **companies that focus on performance and health *simultaneously* consistently outperformed businesses that focused on performance alone by a margin of three-to-one on a wide variety of measures of organizational effectiveness** (including EBITDA margin, growth in enterprise value/book value and growth in net income/sales).

They have also concluded from integrations of several types of their studies that organizational health has nine important dimensions: 1) Direction, 2) leadership, 3) culture/climate, 4) accountability, 5) coordination/control, 6) capabilities, 7) motivation, 8) external orientation and 9) innovation and learning (see Table 11.3). Are there any surprise appearances here? I don't think so. In fact, I can't recall ever reading any study or working on any large-scale organizational change in which there was evidence that even one of these "usual suspects" was unimportant. Table 11.3 also shows Keller and Price's criteria for success on each dimension (i.e., Ailing, Able or Elite).

The nine dimensions of organizational health are further broken down into 37 practices and their descriptions.[14] For example, Table 11.4 shows the Practices and Descriptions for "Innovation and Learning."

The data-supported proposition on which these tables are based is: To sustain excellent performance over the long term, organizations must be classifiable as "able" on all nine dimensions of organizational health and as "elite" on at least six to ten of the 37 practices. Keller and Price argue that this standard is attainable by "almost any organization," but I can't share their optimism. This proposition seems to me to call for performance and alignment that is attainable only by a small percentage of organizations today, ones that are truly "elite." Recall that being excellent on six to ten of the recommended practices will enable overall organizational effectiveness. But, it doesn't lessen the demands of the performance side of the performance/health dual focus.

TABLE 11.3 Relative Performance Levels on Nine Dimensions of Organizational Health

	Ailing	*Able*	*Elite*
Direction	Creates a strategy that fails to resolve the tough issues	Crafts and communicates a compelling strategy reinforced by systems and processes	. . . and provides purpose, engaging people around the vision
Leadership	Provides excessively detailed instructions and monitoring	Shows care for subordinates and sensitivity to their needs	. . . and stretch goals and inspires employees to work at their full potential
Culture and climate	Lacks a coherent sense of values	Creates a baseline of trust within and between organizational units	. . . and creates a strong, adaptable organization-wide performance culture
Accountability	Creates excessive complexity and ambiguous roles	Creates clear roles and responsibilities; performance and consequences are linked	. . . and encourages an ownership mindset at all levels
Coordination and control	Establishes conflicting and unclear control systems and processes	Aligns goals, targets and metrics managed through efficient and effective processes	. . . and measures and captures the value from working collaboratively across organizational boundaries
Capabilities	Fails to manage talent pipeline or deal with poor performers	Builds institutional skills required to execute strategy	. . . and builds distinctive capabilities that create long-term competitive advantage
Motivation	Accepts low engagement as the norm	Motivates through incentives, opportunities and values	. . . and taps into employees' sense of meaning/identity to harness extraordinary effort
External orientation	Directs the energy of the organization inward	Makes creating value for customers the primary objective	. . . and focuses on creating value for all stakeholders
Innovation and learning	Lacks structural approaches to harness employees' ideas	Able to capture ideas and convert them into value	. . . and able to leverage internal and external networks to maintain a leadership position

Source: Adapted with permission from Exhibit 3.1 (Assessing Organizational Health) in Keller and Price (2011; Kindle location 1408).

TABLE 11.4 Key "Practices" in the "Innovation and Learning" Dimension of Organizational Health

Practice	Description
Top down innovation	Driving innovation and learning through high priority initiatives sponsored by senior leaders
Bottom up innovation	Encouraging and rewarding employee participation in the development of new ideas and improvement initiatives
Knowledge sharing	Enabling collaboration and knowledge sharing across the organization
Capturing external ideas	Importing ideas and best practices from outside the organization

Source: Adapted with permission from Exhibit 2.3 (The Practices Underlying Organizational Health) in Keller and Price (2011; Kindle location 951).

I can't argue with Keller and Price's data or logic. But, I do know that **most organizations today struggle mightily with 1) leadership and 2) organizational culture issues/challenges** *alone*—and these are only two of nine dimensions of organizational health that Keller and Price have identified as crucial.

At the same time, I've worked with a number of organizations over the years that were and are admirably healthy (by my standards, anyway) and good enough to foster or achieve "self-sustaining sustainment" on most of their performance gains without truly living up to this daunting, nine-dimensional criterion.

On how many of these elements can a large organization reasonably retain focus? I think that that depends on where a company finds itself when the decision has been made to plan and undertake a large-scale change.[15]

The Best Time to Plant a Tree was 100 Years Ago; the Second Best Time is A.S.A.P.

Organizations that *must* implement large-scale changes have an enormous range of starting points—from the relatively ideal to the extremely, discouragingly problematic. Yet, success can be experienced in organizations in even the worst initial circumstances—as can be seen in the story of the electronic device manufacturer that "healed itself" (cf., the "Winning while unhealthy" box). Unfortunately, those fairy-tales-come-true stories are extremely rare. Remember that the initial success rate (not the much lower long-term, sustained success rate) of large-scale changes is estimated (arguably) to be anywhere from 50 to 80 percent with most in the upper third of that range (Black & Gregersen, 2013) and that represents organizational performance across the full range of starting points. The closer organizations are at the outset to the problematic end of the continuum, the (much) more unlikely they are to make a change successfully and the odds of *sustaining* performance gains are one-in-wishful-thinking.

So, the best time to establish all the elements of a change-supportive culture is "long before now." That is, the "right" culture should exist long before a large-scale change must be undertaken. But, when they both have to be tackled simultaneously, I encourage my clients to focus on processes and practices that bridge or transverse the nine key organizational dimensions identified by Keller and Price, three or four at a time. For example, a focus on recognition and rewards operates at the intersection of leadership, motivation, culture and accountability. Different? A bit. Better? No. It's just the way I skin my cats.

With a tip of my hat to film director, John Sturges, here are my Quasi-Magnificent Seven focal points for building and maintaining a "self-sustaining sustainment" culture (**all of which have been explained and recommended elsewhere in this Guide—as annotated below**). If your organization doesn't meet Keller and Price's criteria for "organizational health," pick two or three of these and get to work!

1. Insist that leaders/managers are truly trustworthy and hold them accountable for being so.

•   Warren Bennis: "Character [integrity, etc.] is the key to leadership . . . Research at Harvard University indicates that 85% of a leader's performance depends on personal character." (Chapter 1, p. 14, n. 1)
•   Train managers how to build trust and how to be perceived as trustworthy; expect every one of them (including executives) to be their "best-selfs" (sic) every day. "Effective Change Leaders: Characteristic

Winning While Unhealthy: The Case of the Extremely Hostile Take-Over

An electronic device manufacturer, for which I eventually consulted, had just completed a six-year long, traumatic planning, installing, testing and fixing/patching of an ERP system. Hostility, umbrage and bitterness were the leftovers; wounds definitely had not healed. Six months later, with no sign of recovery, the company's **health** was dire, its condition possibly fatal. At that point, the company was bought out by a colossal-sized, autocratic mega-organization headquartered in Germany. Among other system-shocking directives, the new parent company ordered its acquisition to immediately begin a conversion to a different ERP system and gave them two years to do it. If there was such a thing as an organizational health life-support system, it was needed right then. And, it was clear that there was not going to be any "massage therapy" (re-team-building, mindfulness training, a negotiated extension of the deadline, etc.) to ease the pain. There'd be no mercy from Munich. It was "Acquisition, heal thyself."

Over the next two or three months, anger dissipated and was replaced a deep fatalism—one that was given a big boost by an extremely tight labor market. Basically, other jobs were not to be had. Then, a very strange thing happened. Anger reared its ugly head once again. But, it was anger toward those (fill in here any inflammatory, pejorative plural noun that comes to mind) in Munich. The presence of an external, Bluto-like enemy was like a six-pack of spinach for Pop-eye. The new ERP system was up and running within the allotted time period and the company's culture—aside from some largely dormant scar tissue—had, in fact, healed itself.

Predispositions and Behaviors" (Chapter 1, p. 2); "Acting with Integrity." (Chapter 1, p. 3)

2. Recognize/reward high performers: This includes recognizing/rewarding high performers by dealing effectively with (or getting rid of) poor performing or toxic employees.

- "Does performance matter?" Consequences for (continued) undesired behaviors are crucial. (Chapter 6, p. 126)
- Always make clear the tie between the recognition/rewards and strategy-supportive, change-embracing, performance-improvement-focused behaviors. "Helping People Understand and Internalize the Organization's Overall Strategy and How the Planned Change(s) Are Necessary for the Strategy's Successful Execution." (Chapter 1, p. 9)
- "Making People Feel Good About their Performances: **Experts' insights**." (Chapter 2, p. 24)
- "If you want your praise to have the intended impact, watch out for 'blanket recognition.'" (Chapter 2, p. 24)
- Sponsorship team members are responsible for "Adapting and monitoring reward systems to assure that change-facilitative high performance is recognized and rewarded." (Chapter 3, p. 65)
- Eliminate all informal or formal recognition/rewards for existing practices or behaviors that don't directly support the changes (much less operate as a obstacle to their successful execution). "Metrics should drive the right behaviors." (Chapter 9, p. 155)
- Develop, support and often recognize formal networks of Change Leaders/Champions. "Driving and Sustaining Change with Formal Networks of Change Leaders/Champions: **Experts' insights**." (Chapter 11, p. 188)

3. Create a brain-friendly, threat-free environment with a strong emphasis on continuous performance improvement.

- "Managing by SCARF." (Chapter 2, p. 50)
- Establish, maintain and protect a "Positive Communication Climate." (Chapter 10, p. 164)
- Overcommunicate, transparently and without distortion. "Ten Brain-Based Communication Principles and Tactics for Change Leaders." (Chapter 12, p. 198)
- Keep people engaged in/talking about what needs to be maintained/sustained/continued and where innovation is needed. "Helping People Understand and Internalize the Organization's Overall Strategy and How the Planned Change(s) Are Necessary for the Strategy's Successful Execution." (Chapter 1, p. 9)

4. Build feedback for performance and alignment into every part of the organizational communication system. Train managers how to coach for accountability and expect all employees and teams to be fully accountable. (Chapter 10)
5. Systematically identify and eliminate barriers to high performance.

- Make the desired behavior as easy as possible; don't let your brain take the easier—but less desirable—option as a default (Chapter 1, p. 14, n. 7); "Internal and External Influences on Behavior" (Chapter 2, p. 18); "Are there obstacles to performing as desired?" (Chapter 6, p. 126)
- Sponsorship team members are responsible for "staying abreast of progress and problems and intervening to remove obstacles." (Chapter 3, p. 65)
- If you want to know the obstacles that are constraining performance and how to overcome them, ask the people who do the work. "Ask employees to be alert for and resolve any obstacles that prohibit or slow down strategic execution." (Chapter 1, p. 10)
- Have budget line-items for implementation, sustainability and surprises. "Dedicated Resources." (Chapter 4)

6. Measure performance accurately, constantly and make the resulting metrics accessible in real time.

- Develop and manage by performance dashboards and scorecards: "Decision Cockpits." (Chapter 9, p. 157)
- "Specific measurement of whether objectives have been attained." (Chapter 5, p. 90)
- "Follow through/assessment of progress." (Chapter 7, p. 132)
- "The most important metrics in any change project are the ones that bear directly upon key business outcomes for the organization as a whole." (Chapter 9, p. 154)
- "Measurement systems that include internal and external customer satisfaction, before, during and after the change, are strongly preferred to those that do not." (Chapter 9, p. 155)
- "Unobtrusive measures: **Experts' insights**." (Chapter 9, p. 157)

7. Keep the focus on strategy and make that focus central to all operational components of the organizaton.

- "Helping People Understand and Internalize the Organization's Overall Strategy and How the Planned Change(s) Are Necessary for the Strategy's Successful Execution." (Chapter 1, p. 9)
- Sponsorship team members are responsible for "making sure that the change plan fits well with and strongly supports the organization's strategic plan." (Chapter 3, p. 65)

- "Effective, Strategic Communication Campaigns: As Seen from the Front Line." (Chapter 5, p. 88)
- "The most important metrics in any change project are the ones that bear directly upon key business outcomes for the organization as a whole." (Chapter 9, p. 154)

EXPERTS' INSIGHTS: DRIVING AND SUSTAINING CHANGE WITH FORMAL NETWORKS OF CHANGE LEADERS/CHAMPIONS

Consider these trending disruptions, distractions and difficulties:

Trend No. 1: According to the 2015 Mergers & Acquisitions (M&As) Survey Report (Nachman, 2014), the 5,843[16] deals completed in the U.S. during 2014 are among the very highest frequencies ever and represent a 33 percent increase in total value over 2013. All indications are that the frequency of deals will continue to rise in the next three years. A decades-long study (e.g., Galpin & Herndon, 2014) concludes that, in the vast majority of cases, both parties in mergers or in acquisitions suffer **major disruptions in performance** often lasting for years.

Trend No. 2: According to a survey by Fortune Magazine (Sonnenfeld, 2015), CEO tenure at Fortune 500 companies currently rests at 4.9 years. So, there have been a lot of new CEOs taking the reins and new CEOs like to make their "mark" or demonstrate their impact early in their tenure, often through re-strategizing and re-structuring or re-organizing (Ashkenas, 2011; C. Raben, personal communication, March 31, 2015) that interferes with major changes underway and results in **employee distractions and demoralization** (Ghislanzoni, Heidari-Robinson & Jermiin, 2010).[17]

Trend No. 3: Large businesses today are very complicated social-technical-financial (STF) systems that, thanks to the often chaotic turbulence in their environments, are becoming ever more complex thereby making crucial alignments: 1) among subsystems (departments, divisions, functions, etc.) and 2) between subsystems and strategy/operations/execution increasingly difficult to attain and even more difficult to maintain. More than ever, STF systems need integration and coordination mechanisms (Bernardo, Simon, Tari & Molina-Azorin, 2015).

Left to their own devices, most organizations rely on existing downward communication channels to inform employees about forthcoming changes and the implementation of those changes once they start being put in place (Dieser & Newton, 2015). Unfortunately, **vertical communication channels (working in either direction) are the ones that are most likely to be knocked for a loop by one or more of the three major trends I just listed above**. In addition, the volume of downward communications in most organizations is huge, so it's hard to make one particular focus stand out.

If vertical communication channels can't do the job alone, something has to take up the slack or fill the holes or whatever. Not a lot of choices for this "something"; horizontal communication has to be it.

In the studies (on sustaining changed behavior) that have been summarized in this chapter, you might have noticed repeated recognition of the importance of **horizontal communication, specifically through formal networks,** for success: "An active network of innovation supporters across units and divisions" (Martin et al., 2012); "Coalition power" (Buchanan et al., 2005); "Captures the value from working collaboratively across organizational boundaries" (Keller & Price, 2011); etc.

Formal networks of Change Leaders/Champions have been found to facilitate implementation of innovations (Mohrman, Tenkasi & Mohrman, 2003; Musiolik & Markard, 2010), **improve lateral communication and knowledge-sharing about innovation** (Aalbers, Dolfsma & Koppius, 2013) **help sustain performance gains** (Martin et al., 2012) **and provide stability and continuity during organizational upheavals or disruptions** (Aalbers & Dolfsma, 2014). The Corporate Executive Board (2014) even argues for a new concept, Network Leadership[18] ("a more 'horizontal' leadership culture which fosters cross-boundary dialogue, participation, and collaboration among internal and external stakeholders") that they suggest should be right up there with Transformational and Transactional Leadership in terms of conceptual-importance.

Over the years, several of my clients have initiated lateral, cross-departmental networks of Change Leaders/Champions to good initial effect. Yet, they either failed to, or were unable to, keep them functional for more than a year or two. However, several companies, including Pitney Bowes (Pitney Bowes, *n.d.*) and Sun Microsystems (Barker, 2008) **have had great success using social media as a vehicle for making such networks "stick."** Recently, McKinsey & Company (Gast & Lansink, 2015) has created a structural center-point for these networks that they call "Digital Hives" that I believe shows great promise.

The bottom line is that planning, implementing and sustaining large-scale organizational changes requires the development and sustainment of effective horizontal communication channels.

Notes

1 A rose by any other name: With amusement, I noted that there has been special creativity devoted to creating names for projects and other large-scale interventions or innovations with outcomes that failed to be sustained. For example, "improvement evaporation effect" (Buchanan & Fitzgerald, 2007), "fade away" (Scheirer & Dearing, 2011), "initiative decay," "project drift" and "voltage drop" (Chambers, Glascow & Stange, 2013) as well as "de-adoption" (Wiltsey Stirman et al., 2011).

2 Note the importance for sustainability of setting up an accountability system *during* the implementation.

3 An interesting shift occurred between the 2011–2012 Towers Watson Communication and Change ROI Study and the one that followed (2013–2014). In the former, companies with highly effective communication and change management practices were twice as likely to surpass their competitors on measures of financial performance. In the latter study, that multiplier jumped to 3.5 times as likely for the 651 participating firms. **I interpret this to mean that change management (and change-related**

communications) is becoming more important for organizational success. Yet, very few organizations today have increased the skills and the capabilities they need to get better at dealing with enterprise-wide organizational changes effectively.

4　I would say that this range of variables pretty much covers the entire waterfront. Upon close examination of the data that were provided, I noticed that some of these variables were mentioned in only a few studies. When I compiled the total appearances for each variable, workforce quality, leadership, stakeholder support and on-going (financial) support were the top four with a big drop-off after them.

5　During planning, you also have to identify and commit resources that will be needed to implement these tactics.

6　As I've indicated in a couple of previous sections, we now know that anything that threatens one's self-image (e.g., "the way you're doing this doesn't work"), which is at the heart of "Unfreeze," is likely to increase rather than decrease resistance.

7　Nasim and Sushil (2011) and others refer to this concept as the "confluence of continuity and change." My view is not so Zen-ish. I see stability (continuity) and innovation (change) as two, independent concerns that each must be managed well if the organization is going to *continuously improve*—which, in today's world, means the same as *stay in business*. Another personal nuance from the majority view, I see the stability (continuity) function as effective management of everything that is not being changed (much) at the moment, not in any way as a tie to the organization's history or values, etc.

8　I've substituted "innovation" for "change" here for reasons that will be explained a bit later.

9　By "statistical process control," I'm referring to any of the established means of quality control designed to reduce variability in performance and then maintain the reduction within "tiny" statistically determined limits.

10　Six Sigma is an extremely sophisticated toolbox of concepts and methods which collectively focus on the effective elimination of any variation in a process, especially a manufacturing process. The goal is to tolerate only 3.4 mistakes (waste, variation in performance, rejects) in each one million products manufactured or services provided.

11　My reference here is to creativity that is outside of the process improvement function itself. It, of course, takes a lot of "creativity" to imagine continually better ways of making a process more efficient.

12　The "tandem effort" I'm suggesting here is not equivalent to the type of "Strategic Innovation" long taught at the IBM Executive Business Institute (2005) and based on the concept of "ambidextrous organization" first proposed by Tushman and O'Reilly in 1996. That concept calls for two distinct cultures and two distinct structures each with their own values, operations and key performance indices. I'm talking about tandem "teams" which fits with the "Champions" proposal I make later in this chapter.

13　Musselwhite and Plouffe (2011) add that organizations re-enforce the idea of large-scale change representing business-as-*unusual* by hiring expensive consultants, giving people additional job titles to reflect their function within the project and "hosting special one-time training and meetings."

14　The "Organizational Health Index," a survey for assessing an organization's current state of health is available as part of McKinsey and Company's consulting services.

15　Long ago, David Nadler (e.g., Nadler & Tushman, 1989) argued that during major organizational changes, it's vital that themes (or what today might be called stories) be created to communicate and frame the changes. It's such themes that enable employees to understand the "whole" (my word choice) of the changes by integrating the themes (representing parts) that are communicated frequently around them. Nadler believed that three (themes) is near the upper limit of what employees can reasonably be expected to integrate conceptually. Through many different types of experiences over the years, I've found the three-to-four "cap" to be right on the mark.

16 According to the same report, two sectors lead the pack in deals: 1) Healthcare-Pharmaceuticals-Life Sciences and 2) Technology-Media-Telecom.

17 Trends 1 and 2 are each major enterprise-wide changes in themselves. Yet, each occurs with great frequency when other large-scale changes are being implemented.

18 The Corporate Executive Board (2014) provides a list of competencies required of network leaders; meanwhile, The University of Colorado–Denver, School of Public Affairs, is teaching a somewhat different set of competencies in its annual "Network Leadership Training Academy." The web site for this Academy can be found in the references (University of Colorado–Denver, 2015).

References

All web site URLs accessed on December 12, 2015.

Aalbers, R. & Dolfsma, W. (2014). Innovation despite reorganization. *Journal of Business Strategy, 35(3)*, 18–25. DOI: 10.1108/JBS-06-2013-0046.

Aalbers, R., Dolfsma, W. & Koppius, O. (2013). Rich ties and innovative knowledge transfer within a firm. *British Journal of Management, 25*, 833–848. DOI: 10.1111/1467-8551. 12040.

Ashkenas, R. (2011). Solving the Rubik's Cube of organizational structure. *Harvard Business Review Online*, March 15. Retrieved from https://hbr.org/2011/03/solving-the-rubiks-cube-of-org.html.

Atkinson, T. (2012). Sustaining behavior change and business results: Lessons from the leaders. Forum Corporation White Paper. Retrieved from www.forum.com/2012/05/25/sustaining-behavior-change-benchmark-against-your-peers/#.

Barker, P. (2008). How social media is transforming employee communications at Sun Microsystems. *Global Business and Organizational Excellence, 22(4)*, 6–14. DOI: 10.1002/joe.20209

Bennis, W. (2000). *Managing the dream: Reflections on leadership and change.* Cambridge, MA: Basic Books.

Bernardo, M., Simon, A., Tari, J. & Molina-Azorin, J. (2015). Benefits of management systems integration: A literature review. *Journal of Cleaner Production, 94*, 260–267.

Black, J. & Gregersen, H. (2013). The challenge of leading organizational change. *Financial Times Press*, December 6. Retrieved from www.ftpress.com/articles/article.aspx?p=2160899& seqNum=8.

Buchanan, D. & Fitzgerald, L. (2007). Improvement evaporation: Why do successful changes decay? In D. Buchanan, L. Fitzgerald & D. Ketley (Eds.), *The sustainability and spread of organizational change* (pp. 22–40). New York, NY: Routledge.

Buchanan, D., Fitzgerald, L., Ketley, D., Gollop, R., Jones, J., Saint Lamont, S., Neath, A. & Whitby, E. (2005). No going back: A review of the literature on sustaining strategic change. *International Journal of Management Reviews, 7(3)*, 189–205. DOI: 10.1111/j.1468-2370.2005. 00111.x.

Chambers, D., Glascow, R. & Stange, K. (2013). The dynamic sustainability framework: Addressing the paradox of sustainment amid ongoing change. *Implementation Science, 8(117)*. DOI: 10.1186/1748-5908-8-117.

Dieser, R. & Newton, S. (2015). *Social technology and the changing context of leadership.* The Wharton School of the University of Pennsylvania White Paper. Retrieved from http://wlp.wharton.upenn.edu/research/social-technology-changing-context-leadership/.

Galpin, T. & Herndon, M. (2014). *The complete guide to mergers and acquisitions: Process tools to support M&A integration at every level.* San Francisco, CA: Jossey-Bass Professional Management.

Gast, A. & Lansink, R. (2015). Digital hives: Creating a surge around change. *McKinsey Quarterly,* April. Retrieved from www.mckinsey.com/insights/organization/digital_hives_creating_a_surge_around_change.

Ghislanzoni G., Heidari-Robinson, S. & Jermiin, M. (2010). Taking organizational redesigns from plan to practice: McKinsey global survey results. *McKinsey and Company.* Retrieved from www.mckinsey.com/insights/organization/taking_organizational_redesigns_from_plan_to_practice_mckinsey_global_survey_results.

Hamel, G. & Zanini, M. (2014). Build a change platform, not a change project. *McKinsey & Company Insights and Publications,* October. Retrieved from www.mckinsey.com/insights/organization/build_a_change_platform_not_a_change_program.

Hansen, M. T. & Birkinshaw, J. (2007). The innovation value chain. *Harvard Business Review, 85(6),* 121–130.

Hindo, B. (2007). At 3M, a struggle between efficiency and creativity. *Business Week, Issue 4038,* June 11. Retrieved from www.bloomberg.com/bw/stories/2007-06-10/at-3m-a-struggle-between-efficiency-and-creativity.

IBM Executive Business Institute. (2005). *Strategic innovation.* IBM. Retrieved from www-935.ibm.com/services/sg/igs/pdf/vn-asymmetries.pdf.

Keller, S. & Price, C. (2011). *Beyond performance: How great organizations build ultimate competitive advantage.* Hoboken, NJ: Wiley.

Lewin, K. (1947). Frontiers in group dynamics. *Human Relations, 1(1),* 5–41.

Martin, G., Weaver, S., Currie, G., Finn, R. & McDonald, R. (2012). Innovation sustainability in challenging health-care contexts: Embedding clinically led change in routine practice. *Health Services Management Research, 25(4),* 190–199.

Mohrman, S., Tenkasi, R. & Mohrman, A. (2003). The role of networks in fundamental organizational change: A grounded analysis. *The Journal of Applied Behavioral Science, 39(3),* 301–323. DOI: 10.1177/0021886303258072.

Musiolik, J. & Markard, J. (2010). Creating and shaping innovation systems: Formal networks in the innovation system for stationary fuel cells in Germany. *Energy Policy, 39(4),* 1909–1922.

Musselwhite, C. & Plouffe, T. (2011). Communicating changes as business as usual. *Harvard Business Review Blog Network,* July 19. Retrieved from http:///blogs.hbr.org/2011/07/communicating-change-as-busine/.

Nachman, S. (2014). The 2015 M&A Outlook Survey Report. KPMG International. Retrieved from www.kpmgsurvey-ma.com/.

Nadler, D. & Tushman, M. (1989). Organizational frame-bending: Principles for managing reorientation. *Academy of Management Executive Magazine, 3(3),* 194–204.

Nasim, S. & Sushil. (2011). Revisiting organizational change: Exploring the paradox of managing continuity and change. *Journal of Change Management, 11(2),* 185–206. DOI: 10.1080/146970.2010.538854.

Pitney Bowes. (*n.d.*) *Pitney Bowes achieves strategic transformation through innovation.* Pitney Bowes, On-Line Case Study. Retrieved from http://imaginatik.com/resources/case-study-pitney-bowes-achieves-strategic-transformation-through-innovation-0.

Pustkowski, R., Scott, J. & Tesvic, J. (2014). Why implementation matters. *McKinsey & Company Insights & Publications,* August. Retrieved from www.mckinsey.com/insights/operations/why_implementation_matters.

Scheirer, M. (2005). Is sustainability possible? A review and commentary on empirical studies of program sustainability. *American Journal of Evaluation, 26(3)*, 320–347.

Scheirer, M. & Dearing, J. (2011). An agenda for research on the sustainability of public health programs. *American Journal of Public Health, 101(11)*, 2059–2067.

Smith, W. (2014). Dynamic decision making: A model of senior leaders managing strategic paradoxes. *Academy of Management Journal, 57*, 1592–1623.

Sonnenfeld, J. (2015). CEO exit schedules: A season to stay, a season to go. *Fortune*, May 6. Retrieved from http://fortune.com/2015/05/06/ceo-tenure-cisco/.

Talbott, C. (2013). *Essential career transition skills*. New York, NY: Routledge.

The Corporate Executive Board. (2014). *The rise of the network leader.* The Corporate Executive Board White Paper. Retrieved from http://ceb.uberflip.com/i/199263-the-rise-of-the-network-leader/1.

The Deming Institute. (2015). The PDSA Cycle. The Deming Institute Web Site. Retrieved from www.deming.org/theman/theories/pdsacycle.

Towers Watson. (*n.d.*). Change and communication ROI study report. Towers Watson White Paper. Retrieved from www.towerswatson.com/DownloadMedia.aspx?

Tushman, M. L. & O'Reilly, C. A. (1996). The ambidextrous organization: Managing evolutionary and revolutionary change. *California Management Review, 38*, 1–23.

University of Colorado–Denver. (2015). *Network Leadership Training Academy.* Online program flier. Retrieved from www.ucdenver.edu/academics/colleges/SPA/research andoutreach/Buechner%20Institute%20for%20Governance/profdev/NLTA/Pages/default.aspx.

Wiltsey Stirman, S., Kimberly, J., Cook, N., Calloway, A., Castro, F. & Charns, M. (2012). The sustainability of new programs and innovations: A review of the empirical literature and recommendations for future research. *Implementation Science, 7(17)*, 1–19.

PART III

Application and Anticipation

12

THE TIER1 PERFORMANCE SOLUTIONS' CHANGE LEADERSHIP MODEL AND METHODOLOGY (CLM&M)

An Example of the Execution of the CLM&M at PPG Architectural Coatings

PART 1: THE TIER1 PERFORMANCE SOLUTIONS' CHANGE LEADERSHIP MODEL AND METHODOLOGY

Contributed by:[1]

Model and Methodology: John Perkins, Managing Director, Leia McKinnon, Principal Consultant, Brandee Abel, Principal Consultant, and Danyele Harris-Thompson, Principal Consultant

Graphics: Mark Hilvert, Senior Solutions Consultant, and Katie Frey, Senior Solutions Consultant

The TiER1 CLM&M and How it is Informed by Social Cognitive Neuroscience

model (MOD/-ul), n. A standard or example for imitation; v.t. To give *shape* or *form* to. (*Random House Collegiate Dictionary*; emphases added)

Most successful enterprise-wide organizational changes are given shape and form by a change management model of some sort. The characteristics of the models that are well-regarded and widely used vary greatly. Some are academic in origin (e.g., John Kotter's Eight-Step Process for Leading Organizational Change, developed initially while he was a Harvard professor; Kotter, 1996). Others have been cultivated in the course of consulting practice (e.g., McKinsey & Company's "Integrated Transformation Approach"; Dichter, Gagnon & Alexander, 1993). Some are quite complicated (e.g., Nadler's "Organizational Architecture"; Nadler, Gerstein & Shaw, 1992) while many are relatively simplistic (e.g., Prosci's ADKAR;

Hiatt, 2006). **However, ours is one of only an exclusive few that have been fully informed by the latest insights garnered through SCN.**

Let's consider communication. You know from previous chapters in this Guide that: 1) communication is a critical component of every large-scale organizational change and that 2) SCN has provided insight into the brain's processing of communication that simply wasn't available prior to ten years ago when most change management models were conceived. Furthermore, you know that: a) throughout the long periods of uncertainty that inevitably occur during major changes, the brain's perceptual filters are on high alert and might distort the meaning or intent of messages, b) we learn through metaphors and remember via stories, c) messages that provide a threat to an employee's self-images might be "dismissed" by their brain's spam filters and d) people are more likely to commit to a new course of action if they reach the conclusion on their own that the newly expected action(s) should be taken.

At TiER1, we've turned these and other communication-based SCN findings into principles and tactics that we have adopted. Here are some illustrations of those.

TIER1 PERFORMANCE SOLUTIONS: TEN BRAIN-BASED COMMUNICATION PRINCIPLES AND TACTICS FOR CHANGE LEADERS[2]

1. You cannot over-communicate.

   - Allow experts to come up with an overall communication campaign or plan and then double- or triple-down on the frequency of messages they recommend.

2. Communicate the same ideas many times, in varied means, via multiple channels—but the core/nutshell of the message must be repeated in each communication and be easily recognized and remembered.

   - Use metaphors ("Best Buy has become a showroom for people who purchase electronics on the Internet") to increase understanding and stories to increase retention.
   - Maximize the use of visuals/graphics/images in telling stories.

3. Use personal and organizational values to guide the change and enable course corrections or to challenge undesirable behaviors.

   - Example: "Please help me understand how that would fit with our commitment to assume good intentions, at all times, by people in other units and departments."

4. You have to test whether messages are being received clearly.

   - In an organizational change communication campaign, getting information back from people (and checking it) is every bit as important as getting information to people.
   - Anonymous upward feedback (on how the change is being perceived, problems that have arisen and unanticipated outcomes) is critical.

5. You must communicate via rewards and recognition.

   - People who support the change and help to lead/execute it must be widely seen as obtaining greater rewards and more recognition.
   - Avoid "blanket recognition"—e.g., thanking or expressing gratitude at a team level when it is obvious (even if only to a few) that some team members didn't contribute or even made goal accomplishment more difficult.
   - Diversity of thinking/behavior and principled dissent should be encouraged; at the same time, intentional sabotage should never be ignored or allowed. What you ignore, you condone.

6. You should communicate the importance of the change by being noticeably more visible and interactive than usual.

   - Persistently engage people at all levels in two-way communication.
   - Involve yourself in "planned, casual conversations."

7. Communicate progress often, but use simple, real-time measures to communicate daily.

   - Use "right measures" (or messages) rather than "wrong measures" (or messages) (e.g., "High quality production has climbed to 97 percent," not "Poor quality production has been reduced to 3 percent").

8. Neither exaggerate progress nor hide a lack thereof.

   - Don't use one-offs to make a point; that's an exaggeration in itself.

9. Communicate priorities repeatedly and show support for thoughtful decisions and behaviors that are based on those priorities.

10. Without exception and at all times, model *exactly* the behavior expected
    of others (e.g., the implementers, the recipients of the change, employ-
    ees who come on board or become involved during the change).

**We create the same sorts of SCN-based principles and tactics for the
other main or crucial components of Change Leadership—whether it be
reducing resistance, accelerating learning, making meetings more effective—or whatever the case or focus may need to be**. For example, let's look
at the concept of making sure that people have the time and support they need to
adjust to a major change and how we *visually* help people to understand this need.

Helping People View Change as an Adaptation Process

As you read earlier in the Guide: 1) managers tend to see even very large-scale
changes as discrete events or experiences (e.g., a physical change-over from one
way of doing things to another), but 2) that's not how employees experience such
changes. **Major changes are** *experienced* **as a psychological adaptation process** that occurs in phases or waves. Very few managers in charge of planning and
implementing major changes understand the true nature of that process and the
variety of ways in which it can unfold. And, when that understanding is absent,
managers typically expect employees to "just get over it," that is, adjust more
quickly than they are able. Unfortunately, many of those managers unwittingly dis-
play their frustration (and sometimes anger) with the pace of adaptation. And that,
of course, can cause the adaptation process for non-managers to last even longer.

To be effective as leaders of change, managers must understand that: 1) people
usually need more time to adapt to large-scale changes than they are given by
the organization and 2) **the adaptation process is an individual-level phenomenon**. The journey to emotional acceptance can look and feel very different
depending upon the individual, the type of change that is being experienced, the
organization's culture and its performance history with change, as well as many
other variables.

Figure 12.1 provides a visual illustration of how a given person might respond to
change and how that response can result in periods of decreased performance. The
wavy line represents three common performance "dips" that occur for many individuals who are at the user- or execution-end of a large-scale change. The first dip
in individual performance is likely to occur shortly after the change is announced
and as employees gain an increased level of awareness for the change. Regardless
of how people view a major change in the abstract (i.e., at the outset), they will
very quickly focus on[3] what the change will mean for them personally. These
focus changes and other adaptations are usually followed by a period of (eventually declining) uncertainty as more details about the change are communicated.

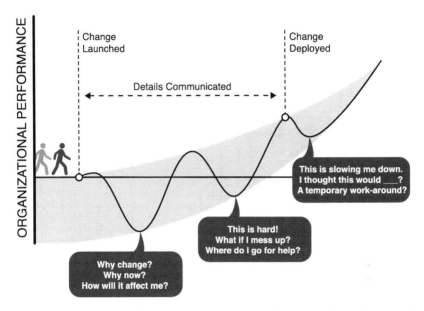

FIGURE 12.1 Depiction of How a Given Person might Respond to Change and How That Response Can Result in Periods of Decreased Performance ("Performance Dips")

A second performance dip often occurs at the point in time when people are adapting to changes in their roles, the technology they use to perform their jobs, or any new processes they must use to complete a task. It's normal to see people working less efficiently or effectively as they learn and attempt to gain proficiency with a new skill. Some people might also experience a third productivity dip as they discover technology constraints, process limitations or as they confront outcomes that don't meet their personal expectations.

This type of visual example (Figure 12.1) is usually very helpful in bringing people around to the view of change as a process—and a complicated one. However, there is more to be gained with such examples than that single benefit. **We also use discussions around these types of examples to help us anticipate potential variations in the change journey for different individuals or groups of employees.** That enables us to be prepared in advance to deal with the challenges that people are likely to face and have the right people and the right kind of support at the ready so that the impact of potential performance dips can be minimized (as depicted in Figure 12.2) if not avoided altogether.

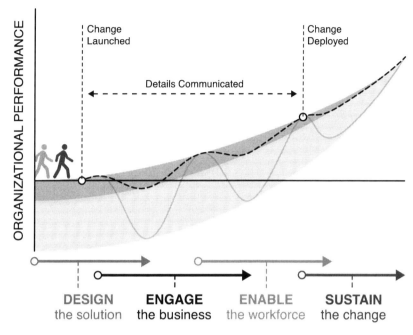

FIGURE 12.2 Depiction of How Performance Dips can Be Attenuated with the Application of TiER1 Performance Solutions' Change Leadership Model and Methodology

A Structured, Strong-Science Approach to Change Leadership

As indicated previously, at TiER1 Performance Solutions, we use many of the neuroscience insights presented in this Guide to design customized, dynamic and resilient Change Leadership solutions for our clients. This solid foundation in ultra-strong science provides the basic structure of our approach to Change Leadership. Beyond SCN, our approach is highly effective because it is very "personal." That is, we focus directly on the "performers" themselves (i.e., the people who perform the work or processes that are being changed). By engaging them *personally* and in a *variety of ways* (including, where possible, allowing them to influence some aspect of the design or implementation of the changes), we help performers develop a shared, deep understanding of the need for the changes and how those changes should best be implemented—as well as a shared sense of ownership in the entire change process. This personal approach and the shared perspectives that are created, result in higher levels of employee motivation to implement change and the knowledge that is necessary to sustain it.

In our presentations to clients, we break the large-scale change process into four distinct, but highly interactive and interdependent phases:

Design the Solution, Engage the Business, Enable the Workforce and Sustain the Change. Table 12.1 delineates the focus or substance of each of these phases and provides examples of some of the key activities we typically undertake

TABLE 12.1 Focus and Key Actions for Each Phase of TiER1 Performance Solutions' Change Leadership Model and Methodology

	Focus	Key actions
Design the Solution	Establish the change process by strategically assessing key aspects of the organization, understanding the impact of the changes and developing a strategy designed to support and accelerate the change adoption.	• Partner with client teams to uncover the underlying business drivers and objectives for implementing the organizational change; • Engage with key stakeholders to establish a foundational understanding of the business case and how it aligns with strategic business objectives; • Assess the organizational culture, leadership styles, experience with change as well as current perceptions and expectations to better understand potential opportunities or barriers affecting the change; • Identify key stakeholders and develop a plan for how to engage them in relevant aspects of the process to build awareness and ownership of the changes; • Assess the people, process and technology impacts across functional roles and share the findings with relevant stakeholders to establish alignment and buy-in; • Create a change strategy that outlines the scope, schedule and complexity of the change program and defines the roles/responsibilities and governance structure for managing the change; and • Develop a change plan to document the learning and communications needs of each impacted audience group as well as the actions, timelines and resources needed to support the adoption of the change.
Engage the Business	Execute change plan to build awareness and ownership of the change and to create accountability for the successful adoption of the changes.	• Mobilize the change teams and equip them with the tools/resources they need to execute the activities outlined within the change plan; • Equip and empower leaders to promote the change and support their team; • Tell the "story"—the rationale for change, why an individual should care, paint the big picture; • Establish key performance metrics to measure the efficacy of the change process; • Implement feedback loop to gather and respond to stakeholder comments, concerns or recommendations; and • Validate stakeholder information needs and begin building the communication materials and training resources.

TABLE 12.1 continued

Focus	Key actions
Enable the Workforce Ensure that individuals have: 1) the knowledge, skills and capabilities to adopt new processes and procedures, 2) the motivation to take ownership of them and 3) the tools, technology and support they need to rapidly achieve high performance.	• Deploy learning activities to ensure employees are prepared to use the new technology, processes or procedures; • Implement process and organizational design policies and procedures to reinforce the behaviors associated with the change; • Evaluate readiness of individuals; and • Deploy and evaluate the effectiveness of application-based training.
Sustain the Change Confirm that appropriate steps have been taken to reinforce the behavioral shifts necessary for maintaining and continuously improving upon the change.	• Transition organizational change management activities/tactics to internal teams (e.g., converting select Sponsorship Team and Implementation Team members to Change Champions and networked coaches) to build institutional knowledge/capacity for managing the changes; • Integrate new behaviors and organizational goals into performance appraisals and other incentive/recognition programs to motivate employees to fully adopt the new ways of working; • Establish measurement techniques and KPIs (Key Performance Indicators) to monitor performance and adherence to the new processes/procedures; • Establish ownership of KPIs and recognize employees for meeting or exceeding performance thresholds; and • Celebrate milestones to build and maintain momentum for the change program.

within each phase. While the printed page limits us to presenting these phases as linear or step-wise, *our clients know that our approach, while structured and guided by SCN, is agile, dynamic and creatively opportunistic.*

In Part 2 of this chapter, we provide concrete examples of the type of outcomes our clients have come to expect when we implement our Change Leadership Model and Methodology across an enterprise.

PART 2: AN EXAMPLE OF THE CLM&M'S EXECUTION FOR PPG ARCHITECTURAL COATINGS

Contributed by:

Abby Bolton, Senior Consultant, and Brandee Abel, Principal Consultant

The Client

TiER1 Performance Solutions assisted PPG Industries' Architectural Coatings (PPG AC) business with a large-scale Enterprise Resource Planning system implementation. PPG Industries is a Fortune 500 company with more than $15 billion in annual sales and more than 46,000 employees working all over the globe. PPG AC acquired the North American branch of AkzoNobel, more than doubling its number of employees, products and supply chain sites in its business in the region. Along with significant growth, this landmark acquisition resulted in two "sides" of the business (one acquired, one existing) with different systems and ways of working. Furthermore, processes and practices even within each group varied significantly across locations and regions. The challenge was to bring them all together onto one central technology platform with harmonized business processes.

The Need

PPG AC set out to streamline its systems, processes and information by implementing a centralized technology platform (ERP system) to create the greater consistency, efficiency and speed needed to enable enhanced customer service and overall business growth. SAP, the ERP system already in use by PPG's European Architectural Coatings business, was selected as that system.

While the efficiencies and benefits of standardized processes and integrated, real-time data were clear, the process of reaching that destination involved a huge amount of complexity, change and risk. Implementing a new ERP system is never easy. However, in addition to typical factors—including the stress of an acquisition itself, the sheer system/process scope of the implementation, the obstacles of learning a new system and the challenge of changing deeply ingrained work habits in thousands of people—this initiative was further complicated by a headquarters relocation that increased turnover and affected the broader effort to reconcile organizational structures following the acquisition.

"The integration of the AkzoNobel North American Architectural Coatings business was unlike any other acquisition in the recent history of PPG Industries," said PPG Architectural Coatings Global Business IT Director, Chris Caruso:

> The scope of the IT integration spanned every aspect of technology, including desktop computers, point-of-sale systems, websites and ERP sub-systems. We recognized that an acquisition of this size and complexity required a unique approach and set of skills that weren't available within PPG, and therefore, we chose to engage TiER1 to assist in our ERP initiative.

The Solution

PPG was well aware of the mighty challenges involved with ERP implementations. They wanted to be sure that they would avoid having upset customers, negatively impacted revenue and disgruntled employees. So, they engaged TiER1 Performance Solutions to lead and manage the *people side* of the changes required for a successful implementation.

Based on a collaborative partnership and blended working teams, the PPG/TiER1 solution included two years of change management, communication and learning support. Highlights of the solution include launching a Power User/Change Champion network, documenting role-specific changes, creating change communication to meet the needs of multiple audiences with varied SAP familiarity and designing/executing a full-scale instructor-led and eLearning program.

Below is a snapshot of the deliverables created as part of this solution:

- 70 training courses spanning multiple business functions—finance, logistics, manufacturing, purchasing, planning, business intelligence and order management (sales and distribution, including customer service, sales admin, credit, etc.)
- 3,000 hours of training delivery
- 350+ change impacts identified and mitigated
- 25+ Role Discussion Guides, to help managers review upcoming role-specific changes with team members
- one project web site, featuring:

  - 130+ FAQs
  - 200+ glossary terms
  - 35 web site articles

- 50+ employee email communications, segmented by audience as relevant
- 12-part poster/table tent/site TV screen series
- one suite of branded project communication templates (email, Word, PowerPoint)
- 32 individual road show sessions
- 212 engaged Power Users
- 150 engaged stakeholders.

"One tangible example of a change campaign that was particularly effective was our STOP campaign," explained PPG's SAP Program Director Amy Mercante:

> Inputting data incorrectly or working around system issues when they arise can create large-scale problems in an integrated system. So this campaign empowered end users to STOP and ask for assistance when something was

not working as it should. This enabled us to identify and address problems immediately, which is a key to success when implementing an ERP system. Understanding how people feel when faced with change, TiER1 created a meaningful campaign that articulated specific examples of common problem situations. Together, we delivered the message in several ways over a period of time to effectively reinforce the STOP concept, and therefore protect the health of our system and our business.

The Results

PPG went live with the initial phase of their SAP implementation in August 2014. On the first day, they took orders, made product, shipped product, invoiced customers and processed payments. The supply chain was operating at standard levels within six days of Go Live. Customers got the right products on time and revenues remained stable. But, how about PPG employees?

Employees knew what was changing and how it would impact them prior to training. Communication and preparedness repeatedly scored top marks in surveys, and TiER1 met each and every change readiness metric between project kickoff and Go Live.

Efforts leading up to the August Go Live had a significant impact on PPG AC's ability to implement SAP successfully. A tremendous amount of training was developed and delivered on time. And while most people don't particularly enjoy systems training, the feedback PPG received was startlingly positive: more than 80 percent of trainees were satisfied with the training and 100 percent felt that the training would make their jobs easier.

"From PPG's perspective, we took an unprecedented approach to change management for this initiative," said Mercante:

> We knew this would be one of the most significant changes we experienced as a business, and we needed to do it right. Having a structured yet constantly adaptive approach to helping our people successfully navigate this change – *and having a team dedicated to preparing our people* – were some of the key success factors of this project.

Notes

1 Note from contributors: All members of the TiER1 Change Team have had input to and an impact on the Model and the Methodology; those listed here produced the specific description below.
2 These particular principles and tactics were initially developed by the author (Snyder) for a TiER1 health care client.
3 If people have reason to believe that the forthcoming change will negatively impact them in a big way, we could substitute the phrase "focus on" with "obsess about" those negative outcomes.

References

Dichter, S., Gagnon, C. & Alexander, A. (1993). Leading organizational transformations. McKinsey & Company, White Paper, February. Retrieved December 12, 2015 from www.mckinsey.com/insights/organization/leading_organizational_transformations.

Hiatt, J. (2006). *ADKAR: A model for change in business, government and our community.* Loveland, CO: Prosci Research.

Kotter, J. (1996). *Leading change.* Cambridge, MA: Harvard Business Review Press.

Nadler, D., Gerstein, M. & Shaw, R. (1992). *Organizational architecture: Designs for changing organizations.* San Francisco, CA: Jossey-Bass.

EPILOGUE: THE FUTURE OF ORGANIZATIONAL CHANGE LEADERSHIP

Social Cognitive Neuroscience.

That's the future of Change Leadership. It's also the future of personal, managerial and organizational effectiveness.

What we've learned about human thinking and behavior (and how to change it) in the last five years has been truly wondrous. So, can you imagine what we're going to learn about human dynamics in the next five years?

No. No, you can't. And, that's the beauty of it.

INDEX

Abel, B. 197, 204
accountability 66, 144–145, 174, 182–187,
    203
affective forecasting 123–124
affect-labeling 18
alignment 9–10, 87
Ariely, D. 14–15
automatic behaviors 14 (n.1), 28, 30, 45,
    110

ballparking 73
basal ganglia xx
behavior: internal vs. external influences
    18; neuro-emotional causes 33–37;
    rational vs. irrational 33–34, 36, 99
belief system 31–32, 47, 81; *see also*
    cognitive map; mental model; schema
best practices xix, 184
best self 5, 6
bias xvii, xx, 31–33, 154, 157–158
blanket recognition 24, 199
Bolton, A. 204
Branden, N. 164; positive communication
    climate 164
Bridges, W. 113
brain circuitry 28, 30, 35–36, 44, 110,
    119, 123, 146–147; hard-wiring 26,
    28, 36, 43–44, 123; passively learned
    connections 33, 147; pruning 26–27,
    141; strong circuit 27, 30, 34
brain-based communication principles
    and tactics 198

Campbell, D. 157
Caruso, C. 205
Center for Creative Leadership 2
change: adjustment to 72, 91, 113–114,
    116, 200–201; champions of 65, 73,
    115, 175, 188–189, 204, 206; change
    facilitative values 3, 6, 65–67; factors
    that inhibit or facilitate 45–46, 95, 108,
    110–112, 123–128; sustaining change
    xix, 7, 15, 93–96, 120, 164, 173–189;
    TiER1 Performance Solutions' Change
    Leadership Model and Methodology
    197–204
Change Enforcers 108–109
change fatigue 110, 117
change leadership vs. change management
    2
change management skills 2
coaching 68, 128, 145–146, 161–162, 204
cognitive map 31, 79, 81, 119–120, 154;
    see also belief system; mental model;
    schema
conscious awareness xv, 32, 34, 50, 150,
    168–169
conservation of energy 28–29, 33, 35, 41,
    45, 49, 81, 170
continuous process 126, 174, 179, 181,
    204
cortex: neocortex 46–47; prefrontal cortex
    xviii, 48
cortisol xviii, 47–48
culture *see* organizational culture

Printed in Great Britain
by Amazon